AMERICAN DIPLOMATIC HISTORY SERIES

GENERAL EDITOR: *Armin Rappaport*

Prelude to World Power: 1860–1900
FOSTER RHEA DULLES

The Uncertain Giant: 1921–1941
SELIG ADLER

Challenge and Rejection: 1900–1921
JULIUS W. PRATT

The Origins of American Diplomacy: The International History of Angloamerica, 1492–1763
MAX SAVELLE

Colonies into Nation: 1763–1801
LAWRENCE S. KAPLAN

Colonies into Nation:

AMERICAN DIPLOMACY

1763-1801

Colonies into Nation:

AMERICAN DIPLOMACY

1763-1801

☆ ☆

☆

Lawrence S. Kaplan

The Macmillan Company, New York, New York

Collier-Macmillan Limited, London

The Macmillan Company
866 Third Avenue, New York, N.Y. 10022
Collier-Macmillan Canada Ltd., Toronto, Ontario

Library of Congress Catalog Card Number: 71-171989

FIRST PRINTING

Printed in the United States of America

TO

Debbie and Josh

Contents

Preface

THIS VOLUME is intended to be an interpretive history of American diplomacy from the Treaty of Paris in 1763 to the inauguration of President Jefferson in 1801. These two important generations are critical years in the emergence of the new nation and represent a reasonable division in the periodization of American history. Both Arthur B. Darling and Esmond Wright have used roughly the same time span in their contributions to American historiography. Where the diplomatic historian encounters difficulty is in the natural disjunction between the pre-Revolutionary and post-Revolutionary segments of this period, when the Angloamerica of the British Empire—to use Max Savelle's term—becomes Anglo-American relations during the Confederation and Federalist eras. The term "diplomacy" must be applied loosely to the activities of colonial agents and colonial governors. The proto-State Department is even more elusive as it moves from colonial legislatures to continental congresses. The diplomatic history of colonial America reflects this problem; leading scholars, such as L. H. Gipson and Michael G. Kammen, do not usually look upon themselves as diplomatic historians.

American history viewed from the angle of foreign relations reinforces the image of *e pluribus unum.* There was no clearly perceived common stance among the colonies toward the mother country in 1763. This had to be worked out painfully over the next dozen years when the issues that aroused the Empire forged a national position toward the outside world. Diplomacy played a major role in the successful detachment of the colonies from Great Britain, uniting during the Confederation such differing views of the nation's future as Jefferson's and Adams', Madison's and Hamilton's. The conduct of diplomacy in the early years of the Republic became a vital function of the young nation struggling for survival and expansion in a hostile environment. It is not surprising that arguments over the direction of foreign policy would become one of the great divisions between Federalists and Jeffersonians in the 1790s. This volume ends with the Convention of Mortefontaine, which terminated the French alliance and presented Jefferson with an opportunity to assert that differences among Americans were less important than similarities over foreign relations. The path of independence led not to Anglophilism or Francophilism, but to a political isolationism that the next generation was to complete.

The literature of American diplomatic history is rich and voluminous. While primary materials—particularly those related to my own researches in the period—have been consulted, major attention has been given to the evaluation and correlation of monographs which have accumulated over the last generation. Some of the more significant works are identified in the text. In almost every case the studies listed in the bibliographical note have been useful in the writing of this book. The results represent less a new personal interpretation of American diplomacy and foreign policy than a synoptic account of the historiography of these years. I have frequently pronounced my own judgments on conflicting views, but hopefully with recognition that the infrastructure built by the scholarship of my predecessors has undergirded my own evaluations.

I am pleased to have this space to acknowledge the assistance of individuals and institutions that have facilitated my work over the past few years. The most pervasive of them has been Kent State University whose sabbatical program in 1969–1970 granted me the time to spend on this project, whose Research Committee provided me with funds for travel and typing, and whose librarians have accepted patiently my sometimes unreasonable demands upon their time. The Institute of United States Studies, under its former Director, H. C. Allen, offered me a headquarters in London during my sabbatical year which not only served to quicken the pace of my labors but made them particularly pleasant. Officials of the Institute of Historical Research of the University of London, of the Public Record Office, and of the Archives du ministère des affaires étrangères in Paris extended the courtesies of their libraries for which I am grateful. Many of my travel expenses were assisted by the Penrose Fund of the American Philosophical Society.

The manuscript has been examined by a number of skilled readers whose comments I have always appreciated even when I have not always incorporated them. Armin Rappaport, the General Editor of this series, has been a source of support throughout my involvement with this project, and his brief notes regularly contained advice that kept me from wandering off my path. Albert H. Bowman of the University of Tennessee at Chattanooga has drawn from his specialist's knowledge of Franco-American relations to give me the benefit of his views. James B. Gidney, my colleague in American diplomatic history at Kent, has read the entire manuscript with considerable profit to me. Mrs. S. J. Rice, Mrs. Genevieve R. Walter, and Miss Karen Young have provided typing services for portions of the manuscript. The copyediting department of Macmillan, headed by Mrs. Miriam Hurewitz, has smoothed out some of the angularities of my prose. Such errors of fact or of judgment that are found in the text remain my responsibility, despite my ungracious attempts to transfer it to scholars, editors, typists—and to my wife.

Colonies into Nation:

AMERICAN DIPLOMACY

1763-1801

CHAPTER I

Diplomats in Search of a Nation

☆ 1763 ☆

THERE IS NO satisfactory measuring instrument that can identify precisely when a people becomes a nation. Nor is there an accepted means of determining the components of nationhood. Common language, common racial descent, common laws, common territory are all familiar attributes of a nation, according to Hans Kohn. But he confessed that the American experience did not fit the conventional pattern. Instead, he attributed the origins of the American nation to the transplantation of British liberties to the western shores of the Atlantic. If this explanation is unsatisfactory there are many others to replace it—from Ralph Barton Perry's flowering of a secularized Calvinism to Frederick Jackson Turner's metaphysical frontier experiences.[1]

Most American historians do not disturb themselves with any conscious conceptualization of nationalism, preferring with Daniel Boorstin to accept the "givenness" of the American scene, and to assume that in the generation before the Revolution a nation was in the making. When it seems useful to locate a particular date at which the nation could be distinguished from colonies, the historian has many choices. As early as 1740,

[1] Hans Kohn, *American Nationalism* (New York, 1957); Ralph Barton Perry, *Puritanism and Democracy* (New York, 1944); Frederick Jackson Turner, *The Frontier in American History* (New York, 1921).

during King George's War, Boyd Shafer perceived "an incipient national loyalty" that took a century to mature. Paul Varg cited 1759 as the year in which "the name 'Americans' became more than a geographical expression." Robert K. Lamb pointed to 1760 as the dividing line between the provincial city states and the new community that became aware of a common position toward England.[2]

Perhaps the most ambitious effort to isolate the beginning of an American nation was that of Richard Merritt, who used the techniques of quantitative analysis to determine when a nation had come into being. Nationalism, he found, was intimately linked to the growth of communications in the colonies. Therefore it is important to observe that a letter sent from New York to Philadelphia required three days for delivery in 1720, but only one day in 1764. The vital question of course would be the contents of these communications, and in the latter year, unlike the former, they were grievances against the behavior of the British colonial system which produced both a nation and a Revolution. Merritt's major instrument in studying this phenomenon was the colonial newspaper in five large colonial centers. By examining the substance of these newspapers over a generation's time he was able to endow with a symbolic meaning the terms "America" and "American," as opposed to "British colonies" and "colonial." The year of his decision was 1770, at which time the American symbols surpassed in number the British. A national consciousness was then evident.[3]

Whatever the merits of the above approach—or of any other approach to the problem—the year 1763 had long been a staple of textbooks before scholars employed content analysis to find it. The year in which the Treaty of Paris granted all of Canada to Great Britain also saw America granted a freedom from fear of French and Indians and freedom from the need of future

[2] Daniel Boorstin, *The Genius of American Politics* (Chicago, 1953); Boyd C. Shafer, *Nationalism: Myth and Reality* (New York, 1955), p. 107; Paul Varg, "The Advent of American Nationalism, 1758–1776," *American Quarterly*, XVI (Summer, 1964): 168–169; Robert K. Lamb, "The Entrepreneur and the Community," in William Miller, *Men in Business* (Cambridge, Mass., 1952).

[3] Richard L. Merritt, "The Emergence of American Nationalism: A Quantitative Approach," *American Quarterly*, XVII (Summer, 1965): 333.

British protection. While victory in war intensified colonial pride in their membership in an Angloamerican community, it permitted them to reflect on the power of the American economy upon which rested the prosperity of the British Empire. Just as the colonies could help the mother country to defeat her enemies, so they could call her to account should she fail to value their contributions sufficiently. In the new world that would emerge from the wreckage of the French empire in America, Angloamerican differences which had been obscured by the French menace would have an opportunity to flourish. France's cession of Canada, as her foreign minister Choiseul observed with frightening clairvoyance during the peace negotiations, could lead to the removal of Britain herself from the continent. Americans no longer needed British protection, and were convinced that the balance of dependence had shifted to the favor of the colonies. Herein lay danger for their future relations.

Whether British colonials, even the bellwethers among them, were really able to recognize 1763 as a political watershed is still open to question. The impressive combination of internal and external forces coming to bear against the past in that decade suggests that all the nation needed was someone to call it by name. Thus Christopher Gadsden may have been speaking for all Americans when he pronounced at the Stamp Act Congress of 1765 that "There ought to be no New England men, no New Yorker, known on the Continent, but all of us Americans." But while Patrick Henry might say that he was "not a Virginian, but an American" at the First Continental Congress, Jefferson could still call his "country" Virginia; and Massachusetts, not America, was still John Adams' country during the Revolution. Their loyalties may not have been to Great Britain any longer, but was the old country replaced by America or by their separate colonies?

Beneath the surface of a formal hierarchy that united the colony to the mother country lay a hidden, or at least unacknowledged, government—quasi-legal, pragmatic, and eminently successful—by which the colonies managed their own affairs without excessive British interference. It provided a school for the training of confident negotiators able to meet statesmen of other colonies or of the parent country on equal terms. And their talents were essentially those of diplomatists. There was a premium placed on the art of persuasion and compromise, on the subtleties of blandishments and intimidation by men whose political status lacked the approval of the formal government. While these qualities should be the property of every politician, they are particularly important to an assemblyman wielding executive authority on a legislative committee in a colonial capital or to a colonial lobbyist in London, each representing a different constituency from that of the governor. In effect they were diplomatists serving distinctly separate sovereigns rather than politicians serving a particular faction in the disarray of the British body politic of the eighteenth century. It is not surprising, then, to find colonial agents in London among the first Americans to discover that their patron was not the royal governor or even the legislature, but an American nation.

The men who came to accumulate political power at the expense of royal authority were also leaders of social and economic life of the colonies, an elite group linked in many cases by ties of kinship, religion, economic interest, or political prejudice. Although frequently members of the governors' councils, they found the lower houses of the legislatures to be a better vehicle than the court atmosphere of the councils in their quest for power. The latter were bound to be dominated by men whose allegiances belonged to the governor by virtue of special favors or of family connections. The lower houses, with somewhat lower social standing, were nonetheless parts of the ruling class, and independent entities. Jack P. Greene notes "a marked correlation between the appearance of economic and social elites produced by the growth of colonial wealth on the one hand and the lower houses' demand for increased authority, dignity, and prestige on the other."[4] Even if one admits that they did not consciously seek to displace king and Parliament by means of a concerted plan, the end product of their actions was not only

[4] Jack P. Greene, *The Quest for Power: The Lower Houses of Assembly in the Southern Royal Colonies* (Chapel Hill, 1963), p. 11.

skill in the art of governance but a spirit of independence of the mother country.

Rarely did the members of the lower houses concern themselves with problems beyond the borders of their own colonies, and when they did it was often with unfriendly glances at neighbors whose common interests were difficult to identify. But all of them recognized that the opponent was not merely a particular royal governor, but Parliament and England. The colonial agents, particularly those of Massachusetts and South Carolina, were among the first to realize the nature of the differences between mother country and colonies and to recognize from their base in London the common cause of all the colonies.

The colonial agents of the eighteenth century, the diplomats who helped to link colonial interests, were either well-disposed—and well-placed—Englishmen or Americans of the governing classes. They were not a new phenomenon in Angloamerican history. From the beginnings of colonial life special agents had been necessary for particular missions. They were all the more necessary because of the irregular or confused relations between crown and colony in the seventeenth century. While many of the special agents were also special pleaders—a Nathaniel Morton complaining of his treatment in Plymouth or a Governor Yeardley petitioning the king to continue the liberties of the House of Burgesses under royal charter—the major impetus for colonial agencies came from England herself, as expressed in the Charter of Pennsylvania of 1681. The provision in the charter requiring the colony's maintenance of an agent in London was one of the elements that induced Andrews to call Penn's colony "half-royal" rather than simply proprietary.[5] The agent was to be an instrument of the crown to answer for any offenses the colony might commit against British authority.

The agents in England had many functions to perform—political, economic, even judicial—and all concerned with constructing an image of colonial behavior as favorable as possible to the exercise of colonial influence on Parliament. The political exigency was usually the most pressing, and the establishment of a colonial agency in the first place in many colonies was

[5] Charles M. Andrews, *The Colonial Period of American History*, 4 vols. (New Haven, 1934–1938), III. p. 285.

forced by a political or constitutional problem that only a personal emissary could solve. Thus Virginia employed Yeardley at a critical moment in 1624 when the Virginia Company's charter had been revoked; and Massachusetts and Connecticut in the years immediately following the Glorious Revolution valued their agents primarily for their putative abilities to secure a new charter or to protect an old charter under attack.

Strained intercolonial relations also made agents valuable, and New York's difficulties with New Jersey over land claims first occasioned the appointment of her agent. In fact, much of an agent's time was devoted to ironing out these strained relations, for of all the problems confronting him none dragged on longer than boundary disputes. New York's boundary quarrel with New Jersey, which had begun in 1740 over the exact location of their border, flared up in 1748 when the Jersey proprietors induced the legislature to pass a Boundary Act which would have infringed on the land patents of New Yorkers, most notably those of the powerful De Lancey family. Understandably, much of the pressure for the colonial agent to undo this damage came from property owners in Orange County, the disputed area; its representative in the New York Assembly urged the agent to petition the crown to suspend action on New Jersey's action until New York could marshal its objections. Shrewd delaying tactics on the part of New York's agent, Robert Charles, won for New York a royal disallowance of the New Jersey Act in 1753.

Time-consuming as boundary problems were, the agents' main concerns did not stem from the behavior of rival colonies. They centered on Parliament's legislation and its effects on the colonies' economy. The Molasses Act of 1733, which was intended to force American traders to buy their sugar from the British West Indies, was the occasion of major concerted effort by agents of a number of affected colonies to counter the influence of West Indian sugar planters in Parliament. The latter had demanded the cessation of the colonial trade with the Dutch, French, and Spanish colonies which had flourished illicitly for two generations between New England and the West Indies. At stake was the valuable triangular trade involving slaves, rum, and molasses as well as a vital source of hard currency unavailable in the British imperial trade alone. For the West Indian planters no lobbyists were necessary; most of them resided in England and frequently served in Parliament where they could exert their considerable influence against the interests of the mainland colonies. The result was the passage of the Molasses Act of 1733.

Aside from the fact that the law was unenforced—and probably unenforceable as well—the concerned colonies through their agents in London had made their displeasure felt before the bill became law. Their agitation delayed passage of the act for two years and caused important modifications in the final version. The Board of Trade and Parliament alike were flooded with pamphlets and broadsides warning of the damage the proposed legislation would do to American prosperity. Rhode Island's agent, Richard Partridge, assumed the leadership in London of the colonial position. He framed a protest on behalf of the northern colonies, including the traditional rivals, New York and New Jersey. Although Partridge and his colleagues failed to defeat the measure, their combined pressure against their West Indian rivals showed that an emergency not only can produce effective diplomacy, reflected in the success of their delaying tactics, but also can unite colonies in a common cause.

Despite the natural identification of the agents with colonial interests, even to the neglect of imperial interests, the British government favored the system of colonial agencies down to the eve of Revolution. They provided Parliament presumably with a ready means of checking colonial misbehavior, as if the agents were hostages of sorts for the good behavior of the colonies. And they were deemed a channel of communication more sensitive and more useful than the royal governors, who were not present in all colonies. Disregarding the merits of these essentially unexamined assumptions about the agencies, the Board of Trade (members of which were also members of the House of Lords) even coerced reluctant colonies into appointing resident agents by refusing to act on legislation before them—either to recommend approval or disallowance—until agents appeared before their body.

Because of the agent's critical importance as the man on the scene, control over the appointment of agents early became a major area of conflict between Assembly and governor. With the rise of the lower houses in the eighteenth century the quarrel was usually resolved in favor of the legislature, although in many cases it led to appointment of two and sometimes three agents speaking for different constituencies—General Court, council, and governor. The long-run dangers of such independence were obvious to the Board of Trade and to Parliament, even if they rarely chose to do anything about it. Occasionally, the Board of Trade would give voice to their misgivings. In New Jersey in 1761, the struggle between the governor and the lower house induced the board to challenge the legislature's appointment of Joseph Sherwood as colonial agent by means of a rider to an appropriations bill. The Lords then observed that such an appointment against the will of the governor smacked of powers "that belong only to a Minister of a Foreign Prince." Yet when thirteen years earlier the New York Assembly appointed Robert Charles in the course of a general bill that included the governor's salary, the board had not acted. They then agreed that the governor's objections had much validity, since the appointment removed the agent from his authority; but since the governor had signed the offensive bill—and accepted the salary contained in it—he had disarmed himself in his dispute with the legislature.

What may explain the discrepancy in the reactions of the Lords to two apparently identical cases was the time gap in their occurrences. In 1761 an Assembly's challenge to a governor was part of a pattern of insubordination against the imperial regimen, evidenced so often in the French and Indian War, whereas in 1748 such behavior could be considered with more tolerance, with a touch of condescension for both parties. It was simply a domestic fight between two adversaries in the game of New York politics.

Where the Assembly gained the upper hand in the management of colonial agencies, it was customary for legislative Committees of Correspondence dealing exclusively and directly with the agents to assume many of the powers of an executive. In receiving reports from the agents and in providing instructions to them, their role was much like that of a Ministry of Foreign Affairs instructing an ambassador abroad. In the case of Robert Charles of New York, the transfer of power from governor to Assembly was first managed by the Speaker of the lower house personally in charge of correspondence. His exercise of authority was usually to the disadvantage of interests and factions that did not accord with his own views. As long as Speaker David Jones was in a loose alliance with the dominant DeLancey group against Governor Clinton, the arrangement was satisfactory to the Assembly. When Clinton departed the alliance fell apart, and New York dispensed with this particular power of the Speaker, turning it over to a Committee of Correspondence more responsive to the will of the majority faction.

But even when the British conception of an agency—governor, council, and Assembly in heirarchical harmony—did obtain, the results were rarely what they had had in mind. Too often a conflict of interest would arise with governors who took up the colonial cause less from intimidation than from opportunities for personal enrichment offered by collaboration with Assembly interests. Thus Governor Horatio Sharpe of Maryland and Lieutenant Governor Cadwallader Colden of New York subverted the Molasses Act while giving lip service to instructions requiring their colonies to respect the British West Indian monopoly of the sugar trade. They went so far as to abet colonial violations and justified their course by asserting that Britain's best interests would be advanced by free trade with the Caribbean islands. During the French and Indian War they could call their defiance patriotism, since a benevolent policy toward Spanish colonies conceivably would keep Spain neutral in the Anglo-French war. In taking this stand on the sugar trade these governors were working for patrons closer to the colonial capitals than king or country—or the Board of Trade. The motive of Lieutenant Governor Robert Dinwiddie of Virginia for pushing England into a war with France a few years before was even clearer; he held a financial interest in a land company controlled by prominent Virginians which would benefit from the removal of the French from the Ohio valley.

"The colonial governor was a sort of advance diplomatic agent for the empire," Max Savelle suggests, "and it was his reports and his recommendations relative to specific intercolonial situations that furnished the basic materials for British correspondence with other powers."[6]

Where the governors' interests accorded with those of the mother country, they were indeed spokesmen of empire, but when personal interests conflicted with national interests, as they did on the matter of the West Indian trade or over cession of lands along the Ohio, they were as much diplomatic agents of the colonies—or at least the dominant class in the colonies—as were the Assembly-controlled agents in London.

There seems to be sufficient evidence to conclude that the colonial experience permitted both a growth of a sense of sovereignty and its articulation through the statecraft of a nascent diplomatic corps. Whether it be through governors, assemblymen, or agents, the connections between colonies and Parliament were a species of international relations. While British statesmen had some understanding of this phenomenon they rarely raised a cry of alarm, and still less did they consider acting against the threat potentially posed in the relationship. For one thing, most of the colonial concerns were also the concerns of the empire, especially in the matters of boundaries or fisheries or the Indian problem. The colonies after all were outposts of empire, and expansion of Virginia into the Ohio valley could be rationalized as a service to Great Britain as well as to Virginian land speculators. For another, the high costs of reorganizing colonial administration inhibited the government from action, even where conflicts in policies were blatant. Change would have incurred the expenditure of monies and energies incommensurate with such benefits that the Navigation System might secure.

Was Britain's complacency misplaced in 1763? It is simple enough to assert and even to document the facts of colonial autonomy and colonial diplomacy. They existed; they flour-

[6] Max Savelle, *The Origins of American Diplomacy: The International History of Angloamerica, 1492–1763* (New York, 1967), pp. 305–306.

ished. It is much less simple to infer from this record that the colonies had evolved into a national union and were on the brink of independence in 1763. Not until revolutionary passions had developed in the next dozen years would colonial agents consciously and willingly serve an American nation or regard themselves as aliens to the British Empire. It was rare to find a situation as in the Molasses Act crisis, where agents spoke for more than one colony. The image of Benjamin Franklin with almost a continent for his client was not accurate until 1774. When colonies and their agents joined forces, the issues were specific in content and limited in time. And where the vital interest of one colony seemed remote to others, unified measures were impossible to achieve, as Robert Charles discovered when he tried to mobilize other agents for an attack on the monopoly of the Hudson's Bay Company. The other colonies were unable to see a community of interest that would justify joint action.

Additionally, the majority of agents were themselves Englishmen, and remained Englishmen no matter how sympathetic they may have been to their client's cause. It made sense for the colonies to choose for their representatives men of influence in Parliament, not excluding members of Parliament themselves. In the early part of the eighteenth century Massachusetts would generally select a sympathetic Puritan, and Pennsylvania a wealthy English Quaker. Later in the century the religious affinities of the agents became less important, but to the end of the agencies they were composed of men of liberal outlook and a mercantile background linked to that of the colony. Even the best disposed among them were not the raw material for the making of radical American nationalists.

A useful example of an enlightened agent's view of the colonial relationship may be found in Robert Charles' revulsion from New York's specific defiance of Parliamentary authority. New York's anger over Parliament's prohibition against the colony's issuance of paper money found no echo in the agent. He refused to present a memorial against the Currency Act of 1764, and instead reprimanded the Assembly for its behavior.

Similarly, he could not become exercised about the Stamp Act of 1765. The right of taxation belonged to Parliament.

If agents were unable to accept the constitutional claims of colonies, the governors were even less prepared to accept the implications of the challenge. Their bargaining on behalf of the colonies, either for personal gain or for the Assembly's good will, always had its limits. They never envisioned themselves governors of new nations. Indeed, the royal governors and their official families were the first refugees from the Revolution. But, as Louise Dunbar showed, they departed in peace, not as hated tyrants of the crown.[7]

Great Britain need not have had a revolution on her hands. There was no star guiding the colonies inexorably toward independence, nor even a charismatic leader playing upon a malleable populace. British changes in the Navigation laws after 1763 matched by American reaction to those changes accounted for revolutionary sentiment. The existence of a framework for nationalism, invisible to most Angloamericans at the time, accounted for the success of the revolutionary impulses. Yet an astute British policy might have played upon the genuine loyalties of colonists, upon their pride in being a part of a great empire as well as upon their internal rivalries, to revise the Navigation laws without violating the sensibilities of the colonial governments. When the British ministries failed to meet this challenge, the experience of self-government, including a diplomatic service, gave the new nation an advantage in the securing of its sovereignty that few new nations have enjoyed at any time in history. Michael Kammen has phrased a part of this phenomenon in the following way: "Just as Samuel was simultaneously the last of the biblical judges and first of the prophets, so Arthur Lee was the last of the colonial agents and the first national diplomat."[8] Although the analogy may be a little strained, its idiom and tone fitted the mood of America in 1775.

[7] Louise B. Dunbar, "Royal Governors in the Middle and Southern Colonies on the Eve of the Revolution: a Study in Imperial Personnel," in Richard B. Morris (ed.), *The Era of the American Revolution* (New York, 1939), pp. 267–268.

[8] Michael Kammen, *A Rope of Sand: The Colonial Agents, British Politics, and the American Revolution* (Ithaca, 1968), p. 318.

In 1763, however, there would have been no point in speculating on the chances of separating from the mother country. For the backcountrymen, relations with government were confined primarily to the colonial capital, or to the county seat, where most of their grievances would be redressed or worsened. England's face was more benevolent as the authority which had dispatched troops to rid the west of the Indian menace and to clear the French out of desirable lands in Canada and trans-Appalachia. If the idea of revolution were even an academic matter, it would have been in the east and in the capitals, where the elites' relations with London were governed by complicated and ambivalent attitudes. But for the ruling classes 1763 was hardly the year to express the aggressive side of their feelings toward Great Britain. They shared with the westerner an exhilaration over the future within a greater British Empire, which victory of British arms had opened to them.

Americans regarded the diplomatic, if not the military, achievement of winning Canada from France as the product of their own efforts. While Canada may have been an obvious objective of the imperialist Pitt, it was not so obvious to the Duc de Choiseul, France's foreign minister, after Pitt's ministry was replaced by that of the Earl of Bute. In 1762 the French proposed the restoration of their West Indian islands to compensate for the loss of Canada, a proposition which raised doubts in the ministry about the comparative values of the rich sugar islands and vast territories of Canada. Guadeloupe alone yielded far more revenue than the whole of Canada.

The colonies intruded themselves into this debate. Earlier in the war Israel Mauduit, colonial agent of Massachusetts Bay, criticized Pitt for his emphasis on the war on the Continent at the expense of the war in America. In *Considerations on the Present German War*, published in 1760, he accused England of meddling in the affairs of the Holy Roman Empire to the disadvantage of the nation's true interests. Convinced that the decision to defend Hanover was a French trap to divert British energies from America, Mauduit denied the prime minister's contention that victory in the New World would be won on the plains of the Old World. Britain should direct its attention toward America, using the exposed French West Indies as a hostage for the ultimate cession of Canada.[9]

Benjamin Franklin, representing Pennsylvania in London in 1760, was even more explicit than Mauduit had been, in inserting an American voice into British peace negotiations. He assured doubting Britons in *The Interest of Great Britain Considered with regard to Her Colonies and the Acquisition of Canada and Guadeloupe* that the acquisition of Canada would serve an imperial purpose in which Americans and British shared equally. The securing of Canada would promote the prosperity of the colonies, with a resulting dramatic increase in population that could only be satisfied by increased consumption of British products. Franklin deprecated British fears of commercial rivalry or industrial competition by demonstrating that the availability of new lands would channel the American economy along agrarian lines.

How much influence these pamphlets had upon policymakers is difficult to assess. Certainly they encouraged the work of lobbyists in London seeking the annexation of Canada. From another perspective they reflected an American pride in membership in an expanding empire. As Franklin made clear in his pamphlet, they were all engaged in a common enterprise "in which the interest of the whole nation is directly and fundamentally concerned." In writing these words he was expressing, to use Savelle's term, a British imperial nationalism, which embraced the American as well as the English parts of the "nation."[10]

Concurrent with this sense of imperial harmony evoked by the prospect of a British Canada the old seeds of discord remained firmly embedded in the mind of one great American. In the same pamphlet in which he rhapsodized about Anglo-

[9] Lawrence H. Gipson, *The Great War for Empire: the Culmination, 1760–1763*, in *The British Empire Before the American Revolution*, 14 vols. (New York, 1936–1968), VIII: 289. Gipson strongly endorses the Mauduit argument that success in America was not the result of Britain's participation in the German war. The reason France lost Canada was "not lack of supplies and soldiers, but her inability . . . to obtain command of the seas."

[10] Savelle, *Origins of American Diplomacy*, p. 552.

american solidarity and scoffed at possibilities of future colonial union against England, Franklin could add gratuitously:

> When I say such a union is impossible, I mean without the most grievous tyranny and oppression. People who have property in a country which they may lose, and privileges which they may endanger are generally disposed to be quiet and even to bear much rather than to hazard all. While the government is mild and just, while important civil and religious rights are secure, such subjects will be dutiful and obedient. The waves do not rise but when the winds blow.

The future therefore of Angloamerica was secure as long as the winds did not blow. And whether they would blow or not was a decision that rested with Parliament.

CHAPTER II

Colonial Agents vs. the Grenville Laws

☆ 1763-1766 ☆

GIVEN THE NEW EMPIRE of 1763, Great Britain was forced to reconsider her imperial functions. It could not have been otherwise. The pattern of absentminded growth of colonial policy had already been challenged by the stresses of war. The struggle with France over Canada and the Ohio valley had produced a more articulate America whose aspirations not only invited new ideas about the relationship with the mother country but demanded their acceptance. A territory that now stretched from Hudson Bay in the north to the Gulf of Mexico in the south, from Cape Breton in the east to the Mississippi in the west, alone would have been enough to upset the balance of the past. Who was to govern the new acquisitions? How were they to be governed? The colonists would answer these questions in one way, Parliament in quite another. Once raised, questions of this kind inevitably led to other questions concerning the extent of colonial contributions to the war and the justification of colonial expectations from the war. Parliament also had different responses to these questions from those of the colonies.

An important consequence of this ferment was an intensified awareness on both sides of the distinctive angle of observation from which the colonies looked at the world. It centered on the idea that America possessed an innocence and a superiority that must remain isolated from the corrupting influences of Europe. This theme did not develop solely from the experience of colonial life; it was implied in the thinking of the European philosophies, the men of the Enlightenment seeking to rebuild the Old World on a more rational base. They found their model in the simpler and more equitable society of America. England herself provided rationalizations for this position in the form of the old Tory argument over the value of Continental connections. The latter, with opposition to Hanoverians in mind, had propagated the notion that England needed no entanglement with the Continent and should repudiate its two-century-old balance-of-power role. It was a short step for Americans to adapt English isolationism to their own use, to assert that the colonial stake in England's European policy damaged America's interests. The war with France provided a special opportunity to campaign against the Prussian alliance and Pitt's insistence upon honoring it. It was no coincidence that Israel Mauduit and his brother Jasper, as Felix Gilbert observes, won the colonial agency of Massachusetts as a result of their influential pamphlet against Pitt's German war.[1]

It may be argued that there were logical flaws in Mauduit's assault against a Continental involvement, and by extension, against Britain's maintenance of the balance of power. The classic case of a weak and divided Europe offering Great Britain freedom of movement in other parts of the world had considerable merit. But logic had little concern for colonials, no more than did the Tory passion against the German Georges. Colonial America was simply underlining the difference in the respective characters of America and Europe. Britain was part of Europe, devoted along with other European states to interminable wars and petty dynastic ambitions irrelevant to the welfare of Americans, but which were thrust upon them by the imperial connection. Eventually this line of reasoning led to the assumption that the American way of life could not be reconciled to Europe's and to the predispositions that made Thomas Paine's *Common Sense* so acceptable a dozen years later.

Colonial understanding of the British constitution in 1763

[1] Felix Gilbert, *To the Farewell Address: Ideas of Early American History* (Princeton, 1961), p. 35.

and their place in the system was as ambiguous as their appreciation of Great Britain's European strategy. Benjamin Franklin indicated the distance between the American and the British outlooks shortly after he arrived in London in 1757, when he referred to the subject in conversation with Lord Granville, president of the Privy Council. Responding to Granville's claim that Americans have "wrong ideas of the nature of the constitution," Franklin contended that royal instructions to a British official in the colonies were merely "some trifling point of ceremony." He professed surprise over the idea that the acts of king and council could be considered the law of the colony. "I told his Lordship this was new doctrine to me. I had always understood from our charters that our laws were to be made by our Assemblies, to be presented indeed to the king for his royal assent, but that being once given, the king could not repeal or alter them. And as the Assemblies could not make permanent laws without his assent, so neither could he make a law for them without theirs."

It was difficult to tell who was the more shocked upon discovering the other's point of view, the Englishman or the American. What is surprising about the above colloquy was not the division over the interpretation of the constitution; this could be papered over by conciliatory glosses or by appeals of loyalty to other British institutions. After all, there was no hint at revolution in Franklin's language. What is disturbing was the fact that neither had been aware of the other's conceptions, and neither had been touched by the other's arguments. Their reactions portended trouble for the empire, which could be averted only by statecraft of a high order on the British side, along with tolerance and good will.

Many of the elements vital to stable relations with the colonies were present in the Grenville ministry in 1763. The British attempt to reconstruct the empire self-consciously included the interests of the colonies affected, even if it subconsciously included also resentment of American conduct in the recent war. That it contained special benefits for Britain as well was hardly exceptional in light of traditional understanding of the mercantile system. The motive force for all change was financial in origin. From 1755 the national debt of 75 million pounds rose in eleven years to 133 million pounds despite an unprecedented scale of taxation at home and despite attempts to unload some of the burden on the American colonies. Yet neither Grenville as Chancellor of the Exchequer nor any of his advisers proposed that the debt itself be transferred to America for collection. They wanted Americans to share burdens relating directly to benefits derived from such services as the policing of newly acquired areas in which the Indian menace required heavy military expenditures. Pontiac's uprising, stimulated partly by France's departure, partly by fears of colonial movement into Indian lands, illustrated the reality of the Indian problem. Even if one acknowledges British cupidity in restraining colonial activity west of the mountains and British annoyance over an America which initiated a war she refused either to fight or to pay for, the role of Grenville was not that of a vindictive or heartless administrator punishing Americans for their behavior or denying them either political or economic benefits for the sake of imperial advantage.

Whether Grenville was "one of the ablest men in Great Britain," as Reverend Francis Thackeray characterized him, is open to ridicule as well as debate. Even those scholars who have denigrated his abilities rarely impugned his motives. Conventional characterizations write him off: in Beard's language, "a lawyer who took the parchment view of official duties"; in Becker's, "a dry precise man of great knowledge and industry, almost always right in little matters"; in Channing's, "unable to see beyond the letter of the law books."[2] If he is damned with faint praise, the damns are equally faint. This characterization of Grenville is important, not because a man of good will cannot do irreparable damage if he lacks other qualities, but because the colonial image of Grenville was that of a man of guile, conspiring against their liberties and their prosperity. The conspiracy did not exist; yet Grenville's method of operation gave credence to colonial suspicions.

[2] Charles A. and Mary R. Beard, *The Rise of American Civilization* (New York, 1937); Carl L. Becker, *The Eve of the Revolution: A Chronicle of the Breach with England* (New Haven, 1921), p. 15; Edward Channing, *A History of the United States*, 6 vols. (New York, 1905–1925), III: 138.

From Grenville's point of view the revision of the Navigation laws, his major contribution, was eminently suited to the mutual ends of both parties. Funds raised from the imposition of new duties and the stricter enforcement of old duties were intended to be relatively painless and to be used for the payment of troops guarding the new territories of the west. And since the French and Indian War had exposed a vast amount of smuggling between the British colonies and those of the enemies, abetted by the corruption of royal officials, it was only reasonable to make these changes an opportunity to expunge venality from the British civil service. If such reform would also yield additional revenues, so much the better.

What Grenville had not foreseen was the reaction of the colonies to his new measures, and one of the reasons for failure to anticipate an unfavorable response was his inability to relate his new revenue bills to other new actions affecting Angloamerica at the end of the war. Interspersed with the colonial cheers for Britain's victories were twinges of anxiety over a host of British moves, most of them connected with the war in one way or another, involving writs of assistance, currency restrictions, quartering regulations, and migration barriers. Taken separately each was explicable in the context of a specific problem that needed solving; but once linked to the Grenville program they all seemed to be pieces in a master British scheme against the welfare of the colonies.

The colonies were not without resources in coping with the new challenges that appeared to descend so precipitately upon them. In the person of colonial agents there was a channel of communication and of influence open to them which was not used as well as it might have been. One may almost claim that the agents operated as a quasi-diplomatic corps representing an American interest before the respective colonial superiors of the agents were themselves aware of the common welfare the corps could serve. In many cases in the 1760s the agents were prepared to work in close cooperation only to find themselves hobbled by the narrow vision of a colonial Assembly slow to understand issues at stake. Sometimes the agent himself might take a stand when the committee at home failed to communicate its position, and then found himself repudiated and reprimanded for ignoring or perverting the will of the Assembly. Even more frequently, colonial response to agents' advice was sluggish and ineffective. For example, Massachusetts knew of plans for a new molasses act as early as the spring of 1763, but the House of Representatives did not address itself to the question until December of that year. Other colonies were even slower to react. Governor Stephen Hopkins of Rhode Island did not summon the Assembly until January, 1764; and neither Connecticut nor New York sent protests until March, 1764. Since Parliament acted on the tax rate in the latter month, the net effect of separate protests by affected colonies was slight.

Insufficient as it was, pressure for concerted action was present nonetheless and had some positive results. Although a molasses act would not have direct application to the economics of Virginia and North Carolina, both colonies expressed their dismay over the legislation and urged a working relationship between their agents and those of the northern colonies. Rhode Island specifically instructed its agent, Joseph Sherwood, to seek out and coordinate action against the Sugar Act "in connection with agents of other northern colonies." Massachusetts urged the Mauduit brothers to "join with the other agents," although the year was 1765 and the quarrel then more over the Stamp Act than the Sugar Act. Assembly preoccupation with intercolonial cooperation among agencies in 1764 and 1765 seemed to be in direct proportion to their recognition of danger to their societies.

Actually these instructions to agents were gratuitous, since consultation among agents in London antedated similar action among the Assemblies in America. When Parliament complained of the illicit rum trade between the New England colonies and the West Indies before the French and Indian War, the agents closed ranks in testifying before the Board of Trade against the West Indian lobbyists. Three times a week between October, 1750, and January, 1751, they presented data showing the potential damage to American prosperity in the West Indian monopoly of sugar. Joseph Charles claimed that the Molasses Act of 1733 if enforced would subvert the birthright of the peoples of North America. Their activity in 1764, then, was built on the labors of 1751, which in turn had its foundation in the successful colonial delaying tactics of 1731.

The colonies were fortunate in having in London a few outstanding men among their agents who were able to offer leadership of such a quality that they can be credited with mitigating the effects of the Sugar Act of 1764 and, in the short run at least, with contributing to the repeal of the Stamp Act in 1766. Joseph Sherwood of Rhode Island, Edward Montague of Virginia and Jared Ingersoll of Connecticut, Richard Jackson of Massachusetts, Charles Garth of South Carolina, and the ubiquitous Benjamin Franklin of Pennsylvania presented a formidable colonial front to the ministry and Parliament which acted with greater effectiveness and represented greater distinction than any comparable group chosen from the best of the assemblymen in any given colony. Most of them were Englishmen, either members of Parliament or closely tied to them—in Jackson's case, even serving as secretary to the chancellor of the exchequer—and all knowledgeable in affairs of the business world as well as the political and social worlds. Franklin the American was somewhat apart from the others in background, but then he would be *sui generis* in any circle, and all the more effective because of it. All knew where the seats of power were and how to reach them.

The proposed revenue laws of 1764 proved to be the occasion for revealing their merits, despite their inability to mobilize colonial opposition in the initial stages of the legislation. As Ingersoll admitted with becoming modesty, he would "always have the satisfaction of knowing that I have been able to do a little to alleviate the Act, though I don't think it was in my power, or the power of the colonies together . . . to have prevented it." His friend Thomas Whately, influential secretary to the treasury, confirmed Ingorsoll's role, saying that he "may fairly claim the honour of having occasioned the duty's being much lower than was intended."

How the colonial agents came to influence legislation or its implementation was no mystery. Theirs was not really an arcane art. Private parties and discreet dinners had always been mutually pleasant paths to the confidence of the important middle echelon in the ministries, the more or less permanent secretaries and undersecretaries who bore the brunt of the responsibility for carrying out as well as presenting cabinet programs.[3] Where faction and connection rather than ideology reigned supreme, the man who succeeded in making his ideas felt was usually the Englishman from a similar background who knew the rules of the game. This was particularly true of the period from 1763 to 1768 when there was confusion in the government as the king exercised his powers in factional politics at the expense of stability at the highest ranks. In the Board of Trade alone, four men—Sandys, Townshend, Shelburne, and Hillsborough—occupied the president's chair in the critical year of 1763.

The subministers became all the more important to cultivate in this fluid situation. Even Grenville, considered a master of financial detail by his enemies as well as by his supporters, never gave serious study to American matters and relied heavily upon his subordinates for information. Whately was instrumental in drawing up the Sugar and Stamp acts; John Pownall, secretary of the Board of Trade, and Maurice Morgann, undersecretary of the Southern Department, were largely responsible for the execution of those acts. Pownall was both planner and middleman in the negotiations between the Southern Department and the Board of Trade which culminated in the Proclamation Line of 1763. The details of the military forces distribution needed to placate Indians and man the barrier against colonial immigration were his specific contribution to the program. Morgann, on the other hand, concentrated on the political divisions of Florida and Canada.

Similarly, Whately and Charles Jenkinson, also a secretary to the treasury, not only drew up plans for raising revenue to cover the costs of a new empire, but dealt closely with colonial representatives in the implementation of their program. The subministers, far more than the ministers, were aware of the wishes of colonial and anticolonial lobbyists, most notably men of business—the British merchants and manufacturers, suppliers and brokers, who made their fortunes from the colonial trade.

[3] Francis Wickwire, *British Subministers and Colonial America* (Princeton, 1966), makes a persuasive case for the importance of subministers in the making of colonial policy after 1763.

When a merchant was aroused to the danger a potential law would have to his business, and when he shared a common interest with the colonies affected, he might exert himself more effectively on behalf of American interests than any number of formal memorials to the various boards or to the crown itself might have done. His avenue to influence led directly to the offices of the subministers. And his partner would be the official agent of a colony.

Hence colonial agents in London had considerable advance knowledge of actions in the making in 1763. Unlike the Assemblies they recognized early the interlocking nature of the questions asked of the colonies. If monies could be raised to pay royal troops in the west, they could also be applied to royal officials in the east. Lord Egremont, secretary of state for the Southern Department, had both objectives in mind in May, 1763, when he asked the Board of Trade which would be the most palatable and least burdensome means of taxing the colonies. By resorting to a revision of the Molasses Act of 1733 Parliament would do more than just have a reasonable vehicle for collecting revenue; the process of collection itself could reinvigorate the neglected art of governance in America, since the act would be accompanied by measures requiring nonresident collectors of customs to be at their posts and inhibiting collectors from accepting fees by substituting "a poundage of their respective remittances." Such was the advice relayed through the commissioner of customs.

The critical issue, of course, was the bridging of the gap between theory and practice. Because the old sixpence per gallon had been prohibitive as well as unenforceable for a generation, all the planners agreed on the importance of lowering the amount of duties on foreign products. The act must be practical. It must also be acceptable, which explains the care taken by the authors to discriminate in their final version presumably in favor of colonial sensibilities. The duty on refined sugar was raised, but it was lowered on molasses. The complete ban on the importation of foreign rum was hardly calculated to displease American rivals in the production of rum. While Spanish and Portuguese wines were included in the new duties, and various fabrics—European and Oriental—lost the benefits of the drawback, such negative features were more than compensated for by protection for an infant industry as vital as the extraction of indigo.

A close examination of the economic features of the Sugar Act reveals a strengthening of British manufacturers' grip on the American market at minimal cost to the colonies. Nothing in this aspect of the Sugar Act suggests that punitive or repressive motives were behind British action, or that a constitutional issue was at stake. Richard Jackson saw no basic conflict of interest between his functions as secretary of the exchequer and as agent for Massachusetts and Connecticut when the question of a revenue bill for the colonies came before his desk. That the American duties should support British garrisons in the west did not seem to be in question as far as he and Mauduit were concerned in 1764. Neither man had the slightest expectation that Parliament would find funds from other sources, and were not disturbed by this means of extracting them.

The concern of the agents, according to their notion of responsibility to their employers in the colonial capitals, was with the amount of the new duties. They vigorously disputed the Treasury's original proposal of fourpence. Four agents—Charles, Israel Mauduit, Sherwood, and John Thomlinson of New Hampshire—banded together to present a memorial to Grenville on the grounds that even a threepence duty would be distressing to the colonies, and would have negative results for the empire, since the high duty would encourage foreigners to set up their own distilleries in the sugar islands of Holland or Spain, which in turn would ultimately disturb the serenity of Britain's African trade.

While only four agents bestirred themselves to speak out in this manner, they represented the major colonies involved; and in no case did any one of them receive instructions on the subject before they issued the memorial. As noted earlier, the Assemblies were slow to respond to the challenge, and when Massachusetts Bay did wake up, its response was churlish. The Assembly rebuked Mauduit unfairly for being too mild in his reservations about the Sugar Act, insisting that "No agent of this Province has power to make concessions in a case without express orders." But at least the agent did act in an emergency.

Only in retrospect was his action too weak. In any event, what could he have done legitimately in the absence of any orders at all from Boston? Apparently nothing that would satisfy the Assembly.

Unlike the colonial legislators the agents understood the political realities of London, paramount among which was the power of the West India lobby in Parliament. Before succumbing to wounded pride over the attacks of Massachusetts Bay, Mauduit made as good a case as he could for a minimal duty, warning Britain eloquently that anything higher than twopence would signal the destruction of New England's fishing industry. Despite the support of Charles Townshend, president of the Board of Trade, the agents lost the battle of the pence. Basically, the British government believed that the colonies would prosper even if the threepence duty were imposed; and if they showed signs of suffering they could always pass along the duty in the form of higher costs for the consumer of rum.[4] Lawrence H. Gipson summed up the case for optimism with the observation that "The whole history of the distilling industry in America down to the present day provides evidence of the ability of the industry to prosper while paying excises infinitely greater than that set by the Molasses Act."[5]

What the ministry and most of the agents overlooked in their considerations was that the colonial protest was essentially not based on the economic dangers of the new law, even if the rhetoric of their protest was clearly economic. The rhetorical alternatives inevitably would have embraced political and constitutional issues which even the most emancipated or most unhappy legislature would be unwilling to confront in 1764. To question the right of Parliament to enact such legislation would

[4] Jack M. Sosin, *Agents and Merchants: British Colonial Policy and the Origin of the American Revolution, 1763–1775* (Lincoln, 1965), p. 45, accepts Whately's opinion that the final figure of threepence was a compromise between the fourpence of the West Indians and the twopence of the agents. Edmund S. and Helen M. Morgan, *The Stamp Act Crisis: Prologue to Revolution* (Chapel Hill, 1953) and Allen S. Johnson, "The Passage of the Sugar Act," *William and Mary Quarterly*, Third Series, XVL (October, 1959): 511, Sosin notes, interpreted the threepence figure to be the product of the Treasury's expectation that it would yield the most revenue.

[5] L. H. Gipson, *The Coming of the American Revolution, 1763–1775* (New York, 1954), p. 63.

have meant a direct challenge to the rationale of British imperial control. No Assembly had proceeded consciously to that point at the time of the Sugar Act. But the seeds of the ultimate challenge were present in colonial reactions, when the Massachusetts House of Representatives could approve a remonstrance to the king in the fall of 1764 which looked "upon those duties as a tax, which we humbly apprehend ought not to be laid without the representation of the people affected by them."

It did not matter that the Massachusetts Council rejected the address as too strong; the importance of the House action lay in the fears that animated it and the direction its opposition would take. The revenue issue and the damage it could do to the economy seemed relevant only as an identifiable element in the British plot against American liberties. The concurrent tightening of regulations against smuggling, which was a necessary part of enforcing the new lower sugar duties, was equated with the hitherto relatively private controversy over writs of assistance. Together they seriously undermined the cherished British right of trial by jury. Such was the view from the General Court in Boston on the part of an increasing number of legislators.

The Sugar Act would also breathe new life into the longstanding and largely ineffective vice-admiralty courts, which presumably would be Britain's instrument of repression to try putative offenders against the new laws. The specter of a vice-admiralty system with continental jurisdiction both frightened New Englanders and permitted them to exploit their fears in parts of America unaffected by the sugar trade. This was a constitutional issue on which they could stand as Englishmen concerned with basic rights, without directly threatening the authority of Parliament.

To England the vice-admiralty court was merely incidental to the enforcement of the revenue law, part of the general overhauling of the administration of colonial affairs that would accompany the new laws. The decision to broaden the vice-admiralty system was a direct consequence of one more failure of the Molasses Act of 1733; the old courts did not work, and when they did function, the jurisdictional claims of colonial courts frequently nullified their findings. As a result officials had been reluctant to make charges which would end in acquittal for the defendant and in a charge of false arrest for the arresting officer. Under the new dispensation the customs officers not only could take their cases to a court outside the colony in which the offense took place but could also remove the burden of proof from themselves and place it on the claimants of seized property. Thus the new west and the revenue measures to pay for its acquisition unleashed a chain of related actions which would give a patina of credibility to colonial cries of "Star Chamber" and "Inquisition."

Aside from the obvious hyperbole employed in colonial intercourse with the mother country, there was a genuine threat to the colonial economy in ministerial tinkering. The rum trade was only one of its faces. Another was the currency legislation enacted by Parliament in 1764, the Currency Act that prohibited all colonies from issuing paper money as legal tender after September 1, 1764. Any governor failing to enforce this law faced dismissal, lifetime exclusion from future posts, and a thousand-pound fine. To New England merchants already disturbed about the future effects of the Sugar Act the currency restrictions were obviously directed against themselves. They would have to pay all British debts in specie at a time when shrinking postwar markets had accentuated the chronic shortage of sterling. If all duties under the Sugar Act also had to be paid in specie their burden would be the more difficult and their conviction of a British conspiracy against their welfare the more credible. Even if the funds expended under the new revenue law were supposed to return to America in the form of supplies and equipment for the army, how much of these monies would return to the hard-pressed New England trader and how much to British contractors and manufacturers who would outfit the troops? The coincidence of the currency and sugar acts may not have been malignant design on the part of Britain, but their combined effect was undeniably if inadvertently harmful to Americans.

The fact that the currency legislation represented no break with past British policy accounts in large measure for British callousness about American feelings. Had the extent of the damage been recognized it would not have been out of order for

British merchants to feel that the tables were properly reversed. For years they had complained about the laxity in the Navigation System which permitted sterling debts to be paid in depreciated paper currency to the advantage of the colonial debtor, despite clear cut instructions to governors of ten colonies in 1720 forbidding passage of currency laws without a suspending clause. The familiar colonial disregard for inconvenient Parliamentary laws followed in the next two generations.

It was Virginia's truculent behavior during the French and Indian War that aroused Parliament to give teeth to currency legislation. In the sense that the Grenville actions were all reactions to colonial behavior in that war, the 1764 law was indeed part of a British plan. Over a ten-year period Virginia had issued 440,000 pounds in paper money with the empty caveat that any subsequent depreciation would be taken into account in the payment of sterling debts to English creditors. But the ministry's timing could not have been worse. It came at a moment when an economic recession required inflationary not deflationary measures, and it invited Virginia's support for New England's troubles, which might not have been forthcoming otherwise.

Colonial agents in London were sensitive to the depressing effects on the colonial economy that would follow from the enforcement of the Currency Act. While recognizing the propriety, and even the expediency, of such legislation, Richard Jackson and Thomas Penn had asked the Board of Trade at its February meeting to postpone action until the colonial Assemblies had an opportunity to express their views. Six other agents went further in their requests. After asking for a year's delay until they could receive instructions from their constituents, they suggested they would settle for a law that permitted limited circulation of paper currency to serve as legal tender within each colony. When neither recommendation received consideration, two of the six agents—Garth and William Knox of Georgia—proposed that Parliament allow local emission of paper with the clear stipulation that it would not satisfy debts owed a British creditor. Nor would it even be legal tender for discharge of intracolonial debts until the Privy Council had approved the legal tender laws of the individual colonies.

Superficially it would seem that the colonial diplomatists had failed to draw the teeth from the Currency Act. But when the bill finally became law its provisions embodied some of the major arguments put forward by the agents and their allies among the British merchants. The law extended the Currency Act of 1751, which had applied only to New England. By assuming this form it avoided immediate and drastic removal of paper money; currency then in the economy could continue to circulate. As a result of this partial opening, which was expanded in practice by the relatively large quantities of paper left over from wartime issues, the Currency Act did not draw the emotional reactions encountered by the Sugar and Stamp acts in this period.

Such colonial protest as there was in 1764 originated mostly in Pennsylvania and New York. The latter's Assembly lumped the Currency Act with the Sugar Act and the proposed stamp duties in its petition to Parliament; and in both colonies the currency discomforts provided a point of identification with New England. Richard Jackson, an early antagonist of the new currency program, complained about the "indecorum" in the British government's policy of making laws "respecting people so remote without their even knowing what we are about." Perhaps there may be in these sentiments a germ of the constitutional issue which bloomed so rapidly and so potently from other laws, but in 1764 and 1765 this particular area of the Grenville program lacked the heat and pressure identified with other acts.

Nominally, a serious currency shortage in the later 1760s revived colonial protest when the supply of paper had diminished. In fact the financial issue was by that time only a small part of the problem as the colonial confrontation with the mother country had developed along lines that neither the Assemblies nor the Parliament had anticipated in 1764. For what it was worth the agents had won a genuine victory in postponing the crisis over currency for a few years. But it was an unnoticed and unappreciated victory for the agents. In the early part of the decade agents had been ahead of the Assemblies in anticipating and taking action against unwise Parliamentary proposals. The colonial Assemblies had frequently underreacted to the dangers. In the later years the Assemblies overreacted to Britain's actions in the eyes of many of the agents. The agents in turn were slow to recognize the fears aroused in Americans after 1765; and many of them as Englishmen and Londoners would never recognize them. A communications gap developed between Assembly and agent in many colonies. Their respective responses to the Stamp Act might have exposed the gap in 1765 had not colonial success in securing its repeal—itself the partial product of the agents' labors—obscured the differences for the moment.

It was fitting that the Stamp Act, the culmination of Grenville's American program, should have been the focus of colonial protest. But the fitness is largely in retrospect. Had the Stamp Act not been the last in a series of measure plaguing America it would be reasonable to assume that no Stamp Act Congress would have followed its passage. Neither the British ministry nor the American agents in London had expected the conflagration the act set in motion because too few on the eastern shores of the Atlantic had appreciated that fires were already smoldering and that the Stamp Act was precisely the kind of fuel that would spread the flames from colony to colony. Had the Stamp Act not been postponed a year, it is possible, as Gipson suggested, the duties would have been embodied in the other revenue proposals of 1764 without exciting as intense criticism as they were to meet in 1765. The purposes of the revenue laws made stamp duties a necessary means of reaching the level of financial returns sufficient to care for British forces in America; and agents such as Richard Jackson had anticipated a step of this sort.

Yet Grenville was willing to postpone final enactment of a stamp act in the event the colonies wished to provide an alternative way of raising the funds. Without doubting at any time the right of Parliament to enact stamp duties, Grenville realized that the British stamp duties had never applied to the colonies in the past. Such taxes as the colonies paid derived from the actions of the colonial Assemblies, and there was a question even in Parliament whether stamp duties represented internal taxation. By inviting American commentary the chancellor of the exchequer felt he would be disarming critics. Certainly there was no special pride of authorship involved in the Stamp Act. His advisers deserved the credit or the blame. Henry McCulloh, a former supervisor of royal revenues in the Carolinas, outlined the financial advantages the duties would provide Britain, complete with optimistic estimates of the amounts the Treasury might expect to collect. Charles Jenkinson may have been displaying the authority of the author when he claimed in 1777 "that the measure of the Stamp Act was not Mr. Grenville's; if the Act was a good one, the merit of it was not due to Mr. Grenville; if it was a bad one, the errors or ill policy of it did not belong to him."

In deferring the stamp issue for a year, was Grenville genuinely seeking more information from the colonies, offering the colonies an option to raise the money in some other way, and in general, in Jasper Mauduit's words, willing "to consult the ease, quiet, and good will of the colonies"? Or was he setting a trap for the colonies in order to compromise their position and force them into an unreserved acceptance of his program? The answers to these questions are as elliptical as Grenville's behavior appeared devious. He seemed at this time to be toying with agents and compelling them to play his game. In a conference with colonial agents in May, 1764, Grenville couched his offer in such a way that it was hardly more than a meaningless gesture. He never suggested a figure that would be an adequate equivalent of the amount to be raised from stamp duties. And without a copy of the bill to consult, the agents were helpless to oppose any detail of Grenville's plan. But even if they had the information at hand, it is unlikely that they could have come up with something better than the Stamp Act. It was even less likely that thirteen separate colonies would come up with a common plan acceptable to each of them and to Parliament. Grenville had done his duty, according to his own lights. Having given the colonies a chance to speak out and having charmed their agents into silence or into frustration, he proceeded to go ahead with the plans presented to him by his subministers.

It is doubtful if the colonies could have offered a satisfactory alternative. There is no doubt, however, about their ability to produce a united front against the Stamp Act, based on the denial of Parliament's right to tax them without appropriate representation. Their modes of expression differed somewhat, but not their message. Virginia's House of Burgesses protested in a letter to its agent that requisitions rather than an internal tax would have been acceptable, although Virginia's sacrifices in the "late American war" should have been sufficient contribution in itself to the welfare of the empire. At any event, the Committee of Correspondence was careful to note it "had not the least disposition to any sort of rudeness," but still insisted on observing that "no Subjects of the King of Great Britain can be justly made *subservient* to Laws without their personal Consent or the Consent by their representatives." The difference between the Virginia remonstrance and those of New York and Massachusetts was primarily one of tone. Both colonics put into explicit language what Virginia did by implication. The New York Assembly's challenge in fact was so sharp that its agent in London, Robert Charles, refused to present it to Parliament. He could not defend the New York claim to "an exclusive right of taxing themselves."

Charles' negative response to his employer's instructions was not unique among his colleagues in London. It was not that the agents had adopted intact the British position, or that they were frightened by the unusual move toward unity implied in the Assembly requests for cooperation among the agencies. Having practiced informal cooperation over the years they had no problem in continuing their attempts to modify British policy. Their efforts did not end with the interview with Grenville in May, 1764. In December of that year four agents speaking for all met for two hours with Grenville in a session that had been scheduled for only thirty minutes. But their rebuttals were modest and uninspired.[6] The best they could come up with to divert Grenville was the tired old plan of requisitions, which they abandoned quickly when he forced them to admit that the colonies could not agree on equitable quotas, let alone an equitable method of meeting them. Their difficulty stemmed

[6] Merrill Jensen, *The Founding of a Nation: A History of the American Revolution, 1763–1776* (New York, 1968), pp. 61–62, insinuates that all four agents were sufficiently obligated to Grenville in one way or other to make them kept men.

from their knowledge that whatever they might say the colonies would have to live with the new stamp duties. That the Assemblies would shortly question the right of Parliament to pass such laws did not cross their minds.

Even a man with antennae as sensitive as Benjamin Franklin's was circumspect in his words and temperate in his behavior on the issue. Like the British-born agents he was disposed to accept as legitimate the basic argument that colonial defense required the raising of new monies and that this was the proper function of Parliament to consider. In a way Grenville appeared to gratify a hope Franklin had long been identified with: the idea of a colonial consensus in advance of Parliamentary legislation. Franklin's caution may also have arisen from other hopes involving speculations in western land, which made mandatory amicable relations with British authority.[7]

Perhaps the most concise presentation of the agents' views was that of Jackson who acknowledged that "Parliament is undoubtedly the universal unlimited legislature of the British dominions, but it should voluntarily set bounds to the exercise of its powers." This was the sort of language that would appeal to such friends in Parliament as Pitt and General Henry Conway. When this argument failed to persuade Parliament to accept their particular wishes, then the agents hoped to make the laws as painless as possible for the colonies to bear. The money raised, as they saw it, was to be spent in America, and the best way of assuring its proper administration would be to place the collection of duties in the hands of well-disposed administrators.

The agents' own roles in the naming of collectors was ample evidence of their assessment of the colonial cause in the matter of the Stamp Act. Having done all in their power to postpone Parliament's action and to ameliorate its effects, they were willing, even anxious, to become a part of the new program. In accepting the office of stamp distributor, Jared Ingersoll, the Connecticut agent, felt he was serving the colony as well as himself. And Franklin had no hesitation about recommending a close friend, John Hughes, for the position in Pennsylvania. In

[7] See, particularly, Cecil B. Currey, *Road to Revolution: Benjamin Franklin in England, 1765–1775* (Garden City, 1968), pp. 132 ff.

fact, when Grenville asked his advice on suitable candidates for the position, Franklin regarded it as an opportunity to score an advantage over the Penns and his political enemies who had opposed the stamp duties. Such was the extent to which Franklin had misjudged the mood of his colony.

When the storm broke in America the agents were caught by surprise as much as the British, and were closer to its vortex than any of the ministry. For Franklin, who had hoped to win royal government for Pennsylvania and who had accepted the stamp duties with apparent equanimity, the colonial reaction could have destroyed his political career, as it did his client's, John Hughes. That Franklin survived the clamor to go on to new labors for America was a tribute to his good luck, his shrewdness, and to his eye for the main chance. The colonial agent of Massachusetts, Dennys DeBerdt, claimed that Franklin "stood entirely neuter till he saw which way the cause would be carried, and then he broke out fiercely on the side of America."

Whether or not he placed expediency ahead of principle, Franklin had little choice in the matter if he hoped to have a voice in future colonial affairs. The emotional outburst spared no colony. From New Hampshire to Georgia the tax and its distributors were declared unwelcome, and in the leading colonies hostility was translated into mob violence. New popular leaders, taking the name "Sons of Liberty" for their informal organizations—a term borrowed from Isaac Barre's supportive speech in Parliament on February 6, 1765—emerged in every colony, and the aggression against the persons and properties of the governor, the chief justice, and the stamp distributor in Boston was merely the most dramatic example of their protest. Stamp Distributor Andrew Oliver was hanged in effigy; Chief Justice Thomas Hutchinson's handsome home was pillaged; and Governor Francis Bernard was forced to flee the wrath of a Boston mob.

As ugly as those passions were on the streets of American towns, they were lttle more dangerous in spirit to the royal presence in America than was the verbal aggression of the Assemblies against Parliament's authority over the colonies. Virginia and Patrick Henry led the way. The hero of the Twopenny

Act consigned the images of the crown and of the empire to the same flames that were to consume Stamp Distributor Oliver's effigy in Boston a short time later. In seven resolutions the eloquent young firebrand purportedly went to the brink of treason in defying Parliament's right to legislate for America and hinting strongly at conspiracy against Americans' enjoyment of the rights of Englishmen, equating the situation with those in the past which produced a Brutus or a Cromwell. Granted that two of the most vehement resolutions were rejected by the Burgesses, and a third rescinded, the House did pass four of them and all were published and circulated throughout the colonies, rejected or not. The distinctions between the Virginia Resolves and Henry's Resolutions appear, therefore, to dissolve in the face of general colonial approval; but it would be a mistake to suggest that the differences between what was acceptable to the Burgesses and what was not were deep. True, the discarded seventh resolution had an offensive ring to it when it pronounced that "His Majesty's liege people, the inhabitants of this Colony, are not bound to yield obedience to any law or ordinance whatever, designed to impose any taxation whatsoever upon them, other than the laws or ordinances of the General Assembly aforesaid." Still, was there a substantive difference between the above and the acceptable fourth resolution which asserted that "His Majesty's liege people of this his most ancient and loyal Colony have without interruption enjoyed the inestimable *right*[8] of being governed by such laws, respecting their internal policy and taxation, as are derived from their own consent, with the approbation of their sovereign, or his substitute"? Parliament was clearly the target in both resolutions.

The summoning of a continental-wide Stamp Act Congress at the behest of Massachusetts preceded news of Henry's resolutions and demonstrated the widespread acceptance of the Henry thesis among men of influence in all the colonies. The stamp duties, aside from any constitutional issue, directly affected the most articulate professions in all the colonies—the courts, the church, the journals—whose operations in the future

[8] Italics added.

would require the purchase of the new stamps. Unlike the year before when the Massachusetts House of Representatives had presented a circular letter to all the Assemblies asking for united action against the Grenville programs, its letter of June, 1765, yielded immediate results. Nine colonies attended the meeting in New York and those which failed to send delegates blamed their failure on their early adjournments and the subsequent refusal of their governors to convene them for the purpose of choosing representatives to an extralegal congress.

Although conservative Timothy Ruggles of Massachusetts presided over the Congress and the accents of its deliberations were purposely muted, the product of its deliberations was no less inflammatory than Virginia's Resolves. Even more than the latter the Congress maintained that the right of taxation was the inherent right of Englishmen, and that no taxes could be imposed on them except by their own consent. Since no representation was really possible in the House of Commons, according to the fourth resolution, the only "constitutional" source of taxation was the legislature of each colony. The Congress also took the occasion to remind Parliament of the right of trial by jury which had been abridged in the new court structure and of other burdens imposed by its recent acts relating to colonial problems.

If there were differences among delegates in the Congress, whose majority were moderates, they pertained not to the legality of the Stamp Act but to the cognate question of the explicit right of Parliament to impose duties on colonial trade as well as to supervise it. This line of reasoning went beyond the matter of internal taxation and remained unexplored for the time being. So did the matter of the constitutionality of the Stamp Act itself. The delegates refused to make the final connection between their protest that only their legislatures may tax them and the denial of the right of Parliament to make a Stamp Act. They pointed out, at least *pro forma*, that they have "the most unabounded affection for his majesty's person, family and government, as well as for the mother country, and that their subordination to the parliament is universally acknowledged."

Accompanied by news of legal protest to the crown, mob violence against royal officials, and nonimportation agreements against British merchants and manufacturers, such professions of loyalty were less than credible to a confused and angry Parliament. The response was predictable. When DeBerdt attempted to present a memorial from Massachusetts embodying the recommendations of the Stamp Act Congress, the Commons objected to its introduction on the ground that the Congress was an improper assembly asking intolerable questions subversive of Parliament's fundamental authority over the colonies. The agents' response that Parliament's lack of attention to earlier petitions had made such a Congress possible did nothing to appease the temper of that body.

Actually the reports filtering across the ocean in the summer and fall of 1765 were almost as confusing and disturbing to the agents as they were to Parliament. Constitutional challenges no more than anarchy in the cities reflected their advices to their constituents. But the abnormal and unexpected consensus underlying the behavior of Congress did galvanize the agents into activity which led to an unanticipated success: the repeal of the Stamp Act. Much of it had little to do with their persuasiveness and a great deal to do with circumstances beyond colonial control. Grenville fell in July, 1765, for reasons unrelated to colonial problems and before the Stamp Act Congress had met. The succeeding ministry had a record of opposition to the Stamp Act and to Grenville's general approach to colonial problems. Its nominal first minister was the Marquess of Rockingham, young, inexperienced but well intentioned. Real power devolved upon Henry Conway, leader of the House of Commons and secretary of state for the southern colonies, who was sympathetic to American complaints.

Although neither a Conway nor a Pitt could condone the riots in America or the blocking of officials from their posts, they sought a genuine way out of a situation they inherited. To the Rockingham government the Stamp Act did indeed sin against the rights of Englishmen, even if it accorded with the power of Parliament. In this context the petitions and prodding of agents were useful in providing the ministry with the egress it wanted. Rockingham was prepared to use the agents as "experts" whose experience with colonial problems deserved close attention by Parliament. And in this colloquy the ministry and the agents discovered that British merchants would be closely allied with their efforts to repeal the Stamp Act.

The community of interest between agents and merchants had not always been so close, although ties between the two were old and interlocked. As has been noted earlier, merchants themselves frequently welcomed appointments to colonial agencies. What reinvigorated these connections was simply the dangers, actual and potential, in the burgeoning nonimportation and nonconsumption agreements. Less than a year earlier the wooing of merchants by agents in connection with the Sugar Act had little effect, since many of them sensed increasing advantage to themselves in measures designed to force the colonial trade into the London orbit. Their cool appraisal of imperial relations had depressed the agents' spirits. But Franklin was aware that continuing cultivation of merchants was not futile even if it paid no dividends at the moment. He was confident their good will would be useful in future crises.

The occasion undoubtedly appeared sooner than Franklin had expected. Nonimportation was a serious threat and required active countermeasures. Under the leadership of Boston-reared Barlow Trecothick a group of London merchants set out in December of 1765 to mobilize mercantile opinion against the Stamp Act, with the blessings of the Rockingham ministry. Their committee wrote to mayors of manufacturing and commercial cities throughout Britain as well as to their representatives in Parliament, advancing a purely expedient reason for repeal; the duties "have so far interrupted the usual and former most fruitful branches of their commerce, restrained the sale of their produce, thrown the state of the several provinces into confusion, and brought on so great a number of actual bankruptcies that the former opportunities and means of remittances are utterly lost and taken from them." Here was a *cri de coeur*.

Concurrently Franklin and other agents reinforced the merchants' appeal with letters to newspapers, articles in journals, tales of colonial suffering frequently joined with veiled threats. Nonimportation if continued for long could have serious consequences for the woolen industry should it induce Americans to exploit their own resources rather than buy British products—that is, if one believed Franklin's story about the tails of American sheep being so heavy with wool "that each has a little cart or wagon to keep from trailing on the ground."

The Rockingham ministry was willing to use agents and merchants, and any other intermediaries whose assistance would be consistent with the dignity of Parliament, to end the controversy with the colonies. Franklin's testimony before the bar of the House of Commons in a secret session that was almost immediately made public was an exercise in complicity between the agents and the ministry. In a carefully staged examination in January, 1766, Franklin the master propagandist had ample scope to dramatize the evils of the stamp legislation, and made the most of it. In answer to a question about the differences between external and internal taxation, he explained that an external tax was a duty on imported commodities which could be refused if the price were too high. "But an internal tax is forced from the people without their consent, if not laid by their own representatives. The stamp act says we shall have no commerce, make no exchange of property with each other, neither purchase, nor grant, nor recover debts; we shall neither marry nor make our wills, unless we pay such and such sums; and thus it is intended to extort our money from us, or ruin us by the consequences of refusing to pay it." If the Parliament failed to understand these differences or refused to recognize them, then America might not accept them either, he warned. In other words, which he chose not to use, Americans would resist both internal and external taxes unless redress were given them.

The manoeuver worked because all sides had suddenly become aware of how great a crisis the Stamp Act had provoked. They looked together into the pit of civil war, and drew away—the Rockingham ministry, the British mercantile community, the spokesmen in London for the colonists. What the ministry faced at least in imagination was the horror of rebellion without adequate British military force to suppress it, of a war with the colonials that would invite renewed war with France and Spain. The Grenville program had led to the brink of revolution and the new government, fully supported by the agents, desperately pulled the parties back from the brink. To succeed, the solution had to protect the *amour propre* of Parliament as well as of the colonial Assemblies, and the Declaratory Act proclaiming Parliament's ultimate sovereignty over the colonies served that purpose.

The crisis passed in 1766. The fears of merchants and shippers subsided. The diplomatists for America had done their work well, but, as Gipson concludes, they had all participated in "a fatal breach of the constitution of the Empire."[9] Parliament was able, with the help of the Declaratory Act, to ignore the violence in the colonies and to brush aside the challenge to its authority; but they could not return the past intact. The government had committed the crime of Lot's wife in looking back into the nature of its Navigation System and ultimately it would have to pay the price of its action. And when it did, all the accomplishments of agents, merchants, and ministers in 1766 would have been in vain. Once challenged it was impossible to prevent future challenges.

The irony of the agents' experience was that their very success accelerated the decline of the institution of the agencies. At their best the agents represented an efficient diplomatic corps serving both colony and mother country within the framework of the British Empire. In future crises the agents would face the agonizing dilemma of refusing new American instructions incompatible with their own consciences as British subjects, and thus antagonizing their colonial employers; or of speaking for a new colonial constituency and risking hostility and bewilderment of their Parliamentary and mercantile connections. No matter what their decision was, it signaled loss of influence, and to this extent the diminished effectiveness of diplomacy helped to divide the empire.

[9] Gipson, *Thunder-Clouds Gather in the West*, X, p. 411.

CHAPTER III

Colonial Agents and a New Constituency

☆ 1766-1774 ☆

RARELY HAS the art of statecraft been more effectively practiced than it was by the diverse groups which coalesced to bring the colonies back from disaffection in 1766. The repeal of the Stamp Act was the consequence of the adroit management of the Rockingham ministry, British merchants, and colonial agents turning both the colonial Assemblies and the British Parliament away from an issue none of the parties had truly faced before: namely, the practical source of authority in the governance of the colonies. Although troubled members of Parliament needed the ministrations of a Declaratory Act to reinforce their old perceptions of colonial relations, they shared in the general relaxation of tensions throughout the empire that accompanied the repeal of the Stamp Act.

Hoping to avoid a renewal of the American challenge with its concomitant destruction of law, order, and property, the ministry made a sincere effort to display its zeal for reconciliation by removing much of the revenue legislation of 1764 and by abstaining from punitive measures against the rioters of the year after. Yet no amount of good intentions could contain the forces of division that underlay American unrest. The recent past could not be undone. Such explosive matters as the political future of the Stamp Act radicals in America, the ultimate disposition of troops in America, and the persistence of currency and quartering problems, pointed to the fragility of the grounds for reconciliation. Any imprudent action, American or British, could easily rip apart the thinly mended ties that bound the colonies to the crown.

Given this uneasy balance of powers the colonial diplomatists found their working conditions more difficult than in the past. The agents did succeed in maintaining cooperation within their own ranks, which had produced such spectacular results in 1765 and 1766, but their lines of communication in the next decade with British merchants and with sympathetic politicians became increasingly strained as Britain recognized more clearly the gulf between colonies and mother country. And as the agents too saw this gulf deepen and widen, their own voices were often confused in their correspondence with the colonial capitals. They had doubts about their constituencies and about what the Assemblies wanted of them and of Great Britain. Was their allegiance to the radicalized minority which gradually asserted its authority in every colony within the next decade? Could they reconcile instructions which offended them as British subjects, as supporters of the empire, and as defenders of colonial rights within that empire? The America that was unfolding between 1766 and 1775 bewildered them as new men rose to power in the colonies whose links to the empire were only nominal. Those agents who were American by birth and inclination, such as Franklin and Arthur Lee, joined the new forces at the sacrifice of influence with Parliament and with British merchants. Those who failed to make the adjustment, such as Richard Jackson and Edmund Burke, found they had no constituencies left in America.

At the same time that traditional imperial diplomacy was losing its grasp on affairs and drifting into apathy or despair, a new diplomacy was at work in America bringing together colonies, or at least like-minded leaders of colonies, which had never acted more than momentarily in concert before. Ironically, the spectacle of colonial Americans coming together in a way that fostered a coherent American policy had formerly been the aspirations of agents in England exasperated by the provincial visions of their employers across the Atlantic and knowing that their own services would be much more useful if presented in common rather than separately. But the ferment behind the American movement was subversive of the empire's survival, since the men promoting it were the same leaders who had sparked the Sons of Liberty movements in 1765. While intercolonial rivalry appeared stronger than ever—in the Wyoming valley between Connecticut and Pennsylvania, or in the upper Ohio valley between Pennsylvania and Virginia—Samuel Adams of Massachusetts, Isaac Sears of New York, Charles Thomson of Philadelphia, Patrick Henry of Virginia, and Christopher Gadsden of South Carolina were fashioning new alliances based on a common attitude toward Great Britain. Their new "foreign policy" toward the mother country would follow the completion of the internal alliances at home. Eventually the Continental Congress would be the focus of their activities from which would flow instructions to agents, not from thirteen separate colonies, but from a confederated America. The final step between an agent of a colonial congress and an ambassador of a new nation was a short one. By 1774, Franklin and Lee, alone among the agents in London, were prepared to take that step when they spoke to Parliament in the name of all the colonies.

The impossibility of restoring the equilibrium of the past was apparent almost from the moment of repeal. Rockingham himself was indirectly a victim of the Stamp Act, since the failure to secure monies from America to defray the costs of empire led to new taxes in Britain and to his own removal from office in the summer of 1766. The Stamp Act haunted America too in 1766, but in a very different way. The controversy and the violence attending it had brought to the fore new men who had no intention of returning to obscurity once the furor had subsided. Their instruments were the Sons of Liberty units which had sprung up like so many Cadmean dragon seeds in the previous year to serve as shock troops of the Stamp Act opposition. Although the rhetoric of the day branded their leaders as social revolutionaries, they were in fact closer to the hierarchies which controlled the Assemblies than they were to the proletarian mechanic or the subsistence farmer. Occupying a rung or two beneath the colonial elite, they were usually lawyers, merchants, and even occasional planters with ambitions to share power with those on top as well as to accelerate the tradition of gathering authority for the colonies at the expense of Great Britain. While they would reduce the British factor in colonial governance, most of them did not intend to alter substantially the social fabric of colonial life. When tenant farmers attempted a jacquerie in New York in the midst of the stamp crisis, they looked for support from the Sons of Liberty and did not find it. On the contrary, one of the members of the court which condemned the rural agitators was John Morin Scott, a leading Liberty Boy.

The opponents of the Stamp Act had realized from the beginning the importance of continuing communications with like-minded men and the establishment of some kind of continental association to sustain the initial impetus. Such was the wish of Samuel Adams even before the crisis when he became moderator of the Boston town meeting in 1764. In eastern Connecticut, a center of radical activities, the Sons of Liberty pressed for concerted actions in all the colonies at their meeting in Hartford to keep alive the spirit of 1765. They did not progress to the point of urging separation from the mother country, but William Pitkin, clerk of the meeting and son of the deputy governor of Connecticut, did not rule out such thoughts in warning Parliament: "The Americans have been firmly attached to Great Britain; nothing, I trust, but severity will dissolve the Union."

Adams and Otis of Massachusetts took the longest view in this period and did everything in their power to exhort their colleagues in other colonies to promote an intercolonial unity of spirit. They welcomed the proposal of the Providence Sons of Liberty to create a "union of writers" who would keep alive vigilance after the Stamp Act issue had evaporated. Most of the hopes Adams and his colleagues had raised had little basis in reality for the moment. The secret agreement between the Sons of Liberty of New York and Connecticut to provide mutual aid in the event of military attack had the ring of an alliance about it, but it was hardly an instrument one could take seriously. The movement for a united front against Great Britain failed—at least in 1766. Feuds within colonies, in which Liberty Boys themselves played prominent roles; rivalries between colonies, which hobbled the efforts of Pennsylvania in particular to join other colonies; and a natural recession of anger following the repeal of the Stamp Act all helped to minimize diplomacy of this kind in 1766. But the seeds of future cooperation had been implanted in fertile soil, and British policies were to play into the hands of the new leaders sooner than anyone but a Samuel Adams had anticipated. Adams himself as clerk of the Massachusetts House of Representatives would be able to speak for Massachusetts when the time came by his authority to communicate with the colonial agent when the General Court was in recess.

New York rather than New England gave British skeptics the first opportunity to claim that colonial agitators would interpret the repeal of the Stamp Act as an act of weakness and would press ahead the more vigorously in their encroachment upon the sovereignty of Parliament. If ever the Declaratory Act was needed, according to British observers of all persuasions, it was to block the shocking petition of 240 New York merchants against the revenue policies of both the Grenville and the Rockingham ministries. Instead of showing gratitude for Parliament's benevolence toward the colonies, they now complained that Parliament had not done enough to relieve their distress: "It seems," the petition of November 28, 1766, read, "therefore consistent with sound policy to indulge those colonies in a free and unrestrained exportation of all the lumber and produce they raise and can spare, and an ample Importation of sugar, rum, and molasses, to supply the various branches of their trade." Only a penny-per-gallon duty on molasses would satisfy them. Coming at a time when it did, the New York complaint embarrassed London merchants who had been instrumental in securing the repeal of the Stamp Act and annoyed American friends in Parliament, including the new first minister, William Pitt, now Earl of Chatham. The merchants' petition gave substance to British suspicions of insubordination and ingratitude in the colonies, which had been growing since the end of the war with France.

Upsetting as the businessmen's grievances were to Parliament, the behavior of New York's legislature in 1766 on the matter of quartering British troops was a more heinous offense. It involved not greed for profits, but usurpation of authority which undermined the work of the colonial agents attempting to reduce from the constitutional to the economic all Angloamerican differences. New York as a major entrepot for troops and supplies felt the burden of the Mutiny Act of 1765 that required Assemblies to provide bedding and incidentals such as candles, firewood, and vinegar for troops stationed there en route to the west. The demands on New Yorkers were not new ones; during the critical days of the French and Indian War they had accepted a similar arrangement for British soldiers, which was embodied in subsequent legislation in that period. But they were New York's legislation, not Parliament's; and the mood of the 1750s was very different from that of the 1760s.

Ever since 1763 when the issue of British troops became a part of the general colonial malaise, the Assemblies had steadily denied the British argument that the Mutiny Act of Great Britain automatically applied to the colonies. Responding to American sensitivities, colonial agents and their merchant friends had congratulated themselves on their success in modifying the new Mutiny Act of 1765. Charles Garth and Richard Glover, a member of Parliament and interested merchant, had convinced Grenville that troops would be housed in inns or stables, and in unoccupied barns and houses only if existing barracks were inadequate. They managed to put an end to any idea the ministry may have had of imposing soldiers upon private householders. After Welbore Ellis, the secretary of war, had removed the most objectionable clauses from the Mutiny Act, the agents felt their work was done and the problem solved. Therefore, when New York's Assembly, along with Georgia's and South Carolina's, refused to comply with the pruned and relatively inoffensive legislation the agents were distressed. The resisting colonies, according to them, were discrediting their most effective levers in the struggle with Parliament, rendering the work of agents all the more difficult in such other important campaigns as the repeal of the Currency Act. In their zeal to remove the constitutional component from Angloamerican relations, as they had helped to do in resolving the Stamp Act crisis, the agents missed the fact that Parliament had raised it again by requiring the colonies to take steps which the Assemblies regarded as infringements upon their own powers.

On the surface everything was still a matter of money; the New York magistrates refused to pay for supplies under the Mutiny Act until the Assembly had assured them of reimbursement. When the Assembly finally granted funds for the provisions, the amount was so spare and the manner so grudging that the harassed general, Thomas Gage, complained as much of the niggardliness of New York's contribution as he did of the colony's implementing the Act in a way the Parliament had not authorized. New York's Assembly willfully defied Parliament by refusing to permit the governor and the council to supervise the disbursement of the monies, and so called down on itself the wrath of the parent body. In taking their stand the assemblymen insisted on regarding the Mutiny Act as a requisition, and by presenting the issue in the form of tax vs. requisition, they provided the Sons of Liberty with a popular cause. Parliament did its share to raise emotions by suspending the Assembly until it showed willingness to abide by the laws of Great Britain.

Actually, the ministry's riposte was milder than many of its members wanted. Charles Townshend, the leading cabinet figure in the Chatham ministry, suggested in April, 1767, that Parliament withhold approval of all laws passed by the Assembly until the Mutiny Act had been obeyed. The final form of the Restraining Act held out some hope of accommodation by coupling it with the express promise of a quick repeal if New York should recognize its errors. New York subsequently accepted the Parliament's requirements and the Restraining Act was not enforced. But it was a bad omen for future relations with the colonies that the Englishmen most aroused by New York's behavior were those who had the deepest faith that the Declaratory Act would never be invoked—Chatham, Shelburne, and even Barre. Shelburne went so far as to recommend a military governor for New York with powers to quarter troops arbitrarily in private homes.

While New York was providing its own special challenge to Britain, Massachusetts was not a colony to lag behind. Concurrent with New York's protest, the Assembly, spurred by Adams and Otis, refused to grant appropriate compensation for those who suffered losses in the Stamp Act riots, an action designed to antagonize Parliament. Although the majority of the Assembly agreed on the propriety of compensation, the imposition of the entire burden on Boston brought the opposition support. Ultimately, as in the case of New York on the quartering of troops, Massachusetts provided reparation for damages but with such poor grace that the efforts of Dennis DeBerdt, the agent in London, to use her compliance to win favors in Whitehall antagonized rather than placated British authorities.

The Massachusetts bill was an implicit challenge to Parliament in the guise of repaying obligations. Not only was amnesty for all parties included as a condition of payment, but an *obiter dictum* was added voiding the Declaratory Act. Not surprisingly the Privy Council disallowed the action, although the disallowance had little meaning, since the principals were reimbursed and the offenders of public order overlooked. Had Governor Bernard not been shrewd enough to disarm the colony on the quartering problem, by noting that in Massachusetts the authorization for barracks had always included incidental needs of the troops, Massachusetts might have occupied the place in British thoughts that New York had in the winter and spring of 1766 and 1767. Massachusetts' primacy was still in the future, but the combustible materials of incidents and leaders were present in abundance to make that future near rather than distant.

In retrospect, events seemed to conspire as they had a few years earlier to raise tensions between the colonies and Great Britain and to give radicals in Massachusetts and elsewhere opportunity to reopen fissures which had been superficially closed by the repeal of the Stamp Act. Continuing complaints about the Revenue Act of 1764 and continuing refusal to accept the Proclamation of 1763, New York's reaction to the Mutiny Act, and Massachusetts' treatment of the victims of the Stamp Act all made understandable hostile British sentiment which would manifest itself in assertion of the principles of the Declaratory Act. In this situation the plight of agents trying to span the two continents would have been extreme even if the Chatham ministry had been more effective. As it was, Chatham's abdication of power to Charles Townshend permitted that ambitious chancellor of the exchequer to sponsor legislation reminiscent of the Stamp Act in its impact.

The immediate setting for Townshend's inflammatory program was the pressure of the continuing drain on British finances created by the high cost of maintaining troops in America, the same problem that had set in motion Grenville's program of a few years before. In fact, it was Grenville himself who precipitated the Townshend laws by his suggestion of January, 1767, that the frills in expenses of the military forces in America be reduced in half and that the balance be defrayed from revenue paid by Americans. Townshend agreed in principle with this proposition, and went on to suggest that Britain's heavy land tax be reduced as well. Professing to accept the colonial argument that distinguished internal from external taxation, Townshend presented a series of new duties on British manufactures and on products entering the colonies from Great Britain—tea, paper, and lead. The revenues from these duties would be employed for the support of courts and civil government as well as for the protection of the colonies. A new American Board of Customs Commissioners, aided by four American vice-admiralty courts, each to have original jurisdiction, would enforce the Sugar as well as the Townshend duties. Unlike the Stamp Act, the Townshend legislation of 1767 passed with little opposition and even less concern for the feelings of the colonies.

American response was not slow in coming, and while its most significant expression was from Massachusetts, the resistance was continental in scope. But there were important differences between the attitudes and actions of 1767 and those of 1765. Not least among them was the relative ineffectiveness of the colonial agencies in this crisis. The protests of New York merchants and the pardoning of Stamp Act rioters had alienated many of the agents' friends in Parliament and among the merchants. Townshend, in his speech mocking the distinctions between internal and external taxes, threw a barb at the agents in the galleries that would not have won approval earlier. Looking at them directly, he proclaimed publicly that his acceptance of "external taxation" was a cynical exploitation of Benjamin Franklin's and the Stamp Act Congress' positions and made no effort to conceal his contempt for them: "I speak this aloud, that all of you who are in the galleries may hear me." The agents had lost face.

Not until shortly before he presented his program to Parliament on May 13, 1767, did Townshend even permit private consultation with agents, and then it was only to repeat that he was indulging the colonists by calling his duties external; he personally recognized no such distinction. On the day of the presentation of the program before the Commons, he underlined his opinion of the agents and their clients by deliberately excluding them from the House, excepting of course the important agents who were also members of Parliament. The only concession won by the agents was the removal of salt from the tax list, and this must be balanced against the failure not only to assert their influence in Parliament, but the larger failure to understand what was at stake in the Townshend laws. Misunderstanding of their constituents, not ill will or incompetence, explained their complacency about the new vice-admiralty courts. They were relieved to observe that the jurisdiction of the Halifax court would be reduced so that offenders might be tried in Boston or Philadelphia or Charleston instead of having to travel to Nova Scotia to defend themselves. Richard Jackson was even pleased to find that the judges of the new courts were to receive fixed salaries, preferable in his view to their taking fees from condemnations. None of their observations struck at the heart of the colonial fear: namely, that the removal of officials from dependence on Assemblies for their salaries threatened self-government in the colonies.

In some ways the results of the Townshend laws replicated those of the Grenville program. Nonimportation was revived, agents and some merchants spoke for repeal to anyone who would listen, and most of the duties were repealed by a new ministry which replaced the leadership responsible for the laws before they could be tested. Death rather than royal displeasure, however, was the agent of removal in the case of Townshend. Just as the Declaratory Act cast a shadow over Rockingham's unraveling of much of Grenville's schemes, so the retention of the duty on tea, of the new vice-admiralty system, and of the civil list freed from colonial control, guaranteed to the new North ministry difficulties in the future.

But this analogue had some definite limits. The colonial forces which had mobilized in the face of the Stamp Act threat were in disarray in the wake of the Townshend duties. Substantial mercantile opinion joined by many in the governing hierarchies of the colonies demonstrated far less enthusiasm for either constitutional challenges or economic thrusts against Great Britain. Their genuine concern for Parliament's disturbance of the colonial political structure coexisted with new fears that the violence generated by the Stamp Act had been directed against their position in society as much as it had been against British usurpations. Which was the greater danger to the public order—the British without or the radicals within? Such questions dampened their ardor for renewed economic reprisals and angry legislative memorials.

Additionally, the Townshend actions came at a time when colonial jealousies functioned with greater heat than had been the case two years before, as New York fought with New Hampshire over the Green Mountain country, Connecticut with Pennsylvania over the Wyoming valley, and Pennsylvania with Virginia over the forks of the Ohio River. For the gratification of colonial claims, notably the claims of powerful businessmen with land investments at stake, the benevolence of the British government at every level was important; and jockeying for preferment among colonial competitors undercut common opposition to the Townshend program or to its modifications under Lord North.

Finally, the new crisis revealed the colonial agents to be less confident of their own powers of persuasion in their dealings with Parliament and with the Assemblies. On the one hand, they were uncertain about the direction of colonial actions which with increasing frequency conflicted with their own conception of the proper functioning of colonies within the empire. On the other hand their ties with merchants suffered both from the latter's anger over renewed nonimportation and from the freedom from colonial dependence the opening of new markets in other parts of the world gave to British manufacturers. Such was the unwitting contribution of the Russo-Turkish war to Great Britain's relations with her colonies.

Despite the handicaps confronting radical leaders in the years after 1767, they were able to exploit the Townshend duties to sharpen the sense of division between Europe and America by articulating the colonial sentiment that taxation was the business of the colonies exclusively. This sentiment, amounting to a near consensus by the end of the decade, taunted the Declaratory Act and forced Parliament to face the very constitutional issue which the wiser leaders had hoped would have been buried in 1766.

The colonial position was clearer than in the Stamp Act crisis, and the most influential expression of it in 1767 was that of a conservative Philadelphia lawyer, John Dickinson, in his twelve *Letters from a Farmer in Pennsylvania to the Inhabitants of the British Colonies*, which appeared in the winter of 1767–1768. Without equivocation he asserted that external duties were no more acceptable than internal if they represented taxation, since Parliament lacked the authority to levy taxes of any kind upon the colonies. The Townshend duties therefore became an "innovation, a most dangerous innovation," to be combatted for their fundamental subversion of the British constitution. At the same time Dickinson conceded that Parliament had the right to pass navigation laws to regulate colonial commerce and to prohibit manufactures of competing articles in the colonies.

Whether Dickinson's position was entirely logical was doubtful.[1] It certainly exposed him to the kind of ridicule heaped upon him by William Knox, former colonial agent for Georgia, who struck hard at the Pennsylvanian's distinction between Parliament's right to regulate, and even to suppress trade and industry in the course of regulations, and its inability to levy a tax on them. Yet the inconsistencies inherent in his acceptance of regulation and his rejection of taxation were of little concern to the colonies. What mattered, and what agents, merchants, and Parliamentarians alike failed to perceive, was that a cautious Pennsylvanian, not a New York or Massachusetts radical, was going beyond the argument of the Stamp Act resisters to attack the rationale of the Sugar Act as well. Radical-

[1] Gipson, *The Rumbling of the Coming Storm*, XI, p. 147, notes that "most political scientists of today would question the soundness" of Dickinson's argument.

ism loses its stigma in a situation where it can be subsumed under a growing continental unity.

The results of the *Letters from a Farmer* were immediate and dramatic, particularly outside Pennsylvania. Seven editions of the work in America in addition to one in Dublin, two in London, and a French translation for Europe, set the scene for the return of Samuel Adams to the forefront of anti-British agitation with the formulation of his "Circular Letter" of February 11, 1768. Sponsored by the Massachusetts House of Representatives, the circular was designed specifically to propagate the sentiments that underlay the Dickinson *Letters*. Like the latter, it recognized the Parliament as the "supreme legislative power over the whole Empire," and then proceeded to denigrate this power by claiming that "the acts made there, imposing duties on the people of this province with the sole and express purpose of raising a revenue are infringements of their natural and constitutional rights." Speaker Thomas Cushing of the Massachusetts House distributed a copy to the Speaker of every colony, urging him to join Massachusetts in petitioning the crown for repeal of the Townshend laws. He made sure to include Governor Bernard among the recipients. That the governor would send the letter back to England and to the new secretary of state for the colonies, the Earl of Hillsborough, was neither a surprising nor an unwelcome event. Hillsborough's response, requiring the governor to have the House rescind the act and apologize for producing it, or face dissolution, fitted well into the hopes of Samuel Adams and other radical leaders seeking issues with which to arouse the colonies.

Adams had assistance from other sources as well in his campaign to forge a colonial unity against the mother country. British treatment of the sloop *Liberty* in that same spring of 1768 provided a useful occasion for a display of colonial solidarity centered on the unpopularity of the new vice-admiralty courts and especially the new Board of Customs Commissioners with its seat in Boston. They were a standing invitation to insubordination. On paper the Townshend plan to enforce laws so frequently violated in the past and to use the revenue from duties for the salaries of royal officials seemed reasonable. In practice the stationing of the Board in Boston, the hub of so many of

Britain's troubles in America, was a serious error. When customs officers attempted to seize the *Liberty* they precipitated an open breakdown of royal authority.

The crisis did not materialize in 1768 despite the extravagant efforts of the Liberty Boys and the usual cooperation of British insensitivity. The high hopes invested in the Circular Letter were realized only in part. Speaker Peyton Randolph of Virginia greeted it warmly, and hailed the people of Massachusetts as "very vigilant and steadfast guardians of American rights." Indeed, Virginia went further than Massachusetts in promoting colonial unity by inviting the Assemblies to work out a common pattern of dealing with all provocations from Parliament. But Virginia's reaction was the exception. Elsewhere the counterweights of intercolonial rivalries and intracolonial problems tended to obscure recognition of the external danger. Rhode Island was so consumed by a heated battle for the governorship that its Assembly postponed consideration of the Circular Letter until the fall, although when considered the letter won full approval. In South Carolina an odd combination of mechanics and planters revived the Sons of Liberty and put pressure on reluctant merchants to take up the cause of Boston.

The Circular Letter became peculiarly embroiled in the murky politics of New York. To force a new election the DeLancey faction hoped its approval of the letter would result in the dissolution of the Assembly. The ensuing backing of the Sons of Liberty would improve their chances of unseating the Livingstons. The latter, then in control of the legislature, opposed a response to the Boston proposal in order to avoid exactly what the DeLanceys wanted. The Livingston compromise was to place New York's opposition to the Townshend laws clearly on the record without a specific reference to or acknowledgment of the Circular Letter. Their plan failed, and Governor Moore dissolved the legislature in 1769 after the DeLanceys had forced the letter on the Assembly. The DeLancey faction did win the subsequent election, but with the Liberty Boys divided in their support. As Roger Champagne explained the Byzantine behavior of New York: "In a real sense, the actions of the New York politico-patriots, including the Sons of Liberty, clearly suggests that a local victory was just as important as a defense of American constitutional principles."[2]

Dickinson's own colony raised the greatest obstacles to the intrusion of the Massachusetts letter into local politics. The Quaker faction in control of the legislature was anxiously awaiting news of Franklin's petition for royal government, and wished to avoid ruffling feelings in Whitehall as long as there was a chance of removing the Penn proprietorship. Although legislative anger over Hillsborough's countercircular letter to governors placed the Assembly squarely behind the sister colonies in raising objections to the Townshend laws, Pennsylvania managed to avoid a direct answer to the Massachusetts Circular Letter.

The mixed reception of Dickinson's and Massachusetts' constitutional challenges to British authority pointed to something more than the habitual bickering within the colonies. It reflected the concern among influential merchants which muted their resentment of British actions. They had learned since 1765 to suspect that the Liberty Boys would use nonimportation as a weapon against themselves as well as against overseas rule, and if merchants in Assemblies voted for such measures it was with restrained enthusiasm or under compulsion of a more radical constituency that pushed the Assemblies into motion.[3]

Still, it is doubtful if even a more cohesive society retaining the vitality of the Stamp Act emotions would have succeeded in breaking with Britain at this time. Merchants' caution cannot be blamed for the recurrent outbursts of intercolonial recriminations which stood in the path of effective confrontation. Georgia was convinced that South Carolina pressed her into faithful observance of the nonimportation agreements and then proceeded to violate them herself. Massachusetts was subject to criticism for leading the movement and then dallying in the execution of its promises. Even among the Liberty Boys them-

[2] Roger Champagne, "Family Politics versus Constitutional Principles: the New York Assembly Elections of 1768 and 1769," *William and Mary Quarterly*, Third Series, XX (January, 1963): 79.

[3] Jensen, *The Founding of a Nation*, p. 265, concludes that political leaders rather than businessmen took the initiative at all times in nonimportation planning. For the major opposing view note Arthur M. Schlesinger, *The Colonial Merchants and the American Revolution, 1763–1775* (New York, 1918).

selves the intercolonial suspicions reared on occasion; New York Sons of Liberty were scornful of their Boston counterparts' failure to resist the imposition of British troops on that city in 1768. And the North ministry's removal of most of the duties on American imports and the consequent reduction in tension in 1769 contrasted with the sustained virility of colonial disagreements with each other.

Of all the elements involved in the imperial governing process, the one most bewildered by developments since 1765 was the colonial agent in Great Britain. He could take comfort neither in the prospect of future separation, or independence, of his colony nor in the expectations of a genuine reconciliation that would revive his own lines of influence with officials. There was no mistaking the dismay of many agents, faithful to their duties to their employers and also loyal to their conception of the empire, who could no more accept abridgment of Parliament's power to govern than the ministry itself. DeBerdt, for one, was shocked by the argument of Dickinson's *Letters*. The bypassing of Parliament in favor of direct appeal to the king was no less shocking. It assumed that the king was the only proper link between America and England, a federal notion that was heresy to such devoted Parliamentarians and friends of America as Edmund Burke and Charles Garth.

Understandable as the agents' distaste for colonial behavior was, their conditioning as Englishmen in a Whig tradition deadened their sensitivities to the American view of the Declaratory Act. When conflict moved from taxes to sovereignty the agents found themselves poorly prepared to speak for their colonial constituents. This is not to say that the agents as a body were unregenerate Englishmen whose sympathies for their clients' cause ended with the first major challenge to their loyalties. They were in a genuine quandary. As a matter of good tactics as well as a matter of conscience the colonies should be circumspect in contending with Parliament over the source of power. Their hope was to keep Parliamentary power as dormant as possible, but to effect abstention in its exercise required studied avoidance of any "ostentatious parade" in the colonial demands, as DeBerdt phrased it in a letter to Speaker Cushing. Any overt link of economic pressure to a political philosophy abhorrent to most Englishmen, including the agents themselves, would negate the advantages of nonimportation.

Given this view from London, colonies began to speculate on the usefulness of their agents in the Townshend crisis. Georgia's Speaker of the Assembly felt that Americans were so alienated from the mother country that agents would have to be Englishmen to win any successes. Other colonies drew the opposite conclusion, that only Americans could represent the ideas and emotions of the American colonies. Still others, seeing the diminished influence of the agents, wondered about the value of the agency as an institution. If America was to make its message understood perhaps the colonies would discover or create new channels of communication and new modes of intercolonial cooperation.

As was so often the case, Benjamin Franklin was the barometer by which change could be measured. Hardly an abrasive antagonist of Great Britain in the past, Franklin's pragmatic approach to colonial problems reflected concern for private as well as public lobbying; his plans for Pennsylvania's interests included the wooing of such ministers with western responsibilities as Shelburne and Hillsborough for the benefit of speculating land companies in which he had an investment. In the Treaty of Fort Stanwix, the Iroquois were to cede land to compensate colonial traders for earlier damages, thereby opening opportunities for Franklin's Illinois Company. That year was 1768, also the year when the prospects for a colony developing out of his enterprises which had advanced under Shelburne's secretaryship of state for the Southern Department were dashed by the arrival to power of Hillsborough, an opponent of expansionism as secretary of state for the colonies. Franklin's manoeuvers on behalf of land companies continued to the eve of the Revolution and must have had a cautionary effect on his relations with the successive ministries.

Franklin's views had undergone serious changes since his brief on the distinctions between internal and external taxes. Perhaps his exasperation over the sudden shifting of his personal fortunes in speculation which he could rightly blame on ministerial moods helped to account for his movement to the left.[4] More likely his recognition of the cynical game Townshend had played with his own arguments in 1766, twisting them to serve further exploitation of the colonies, determined his new course. Without giving up hope of influencing Hillsborough on behalf of his western investments, Franklin emerged a full supporter of nonimportation, willing to raise the question now of Parliament's right to make any laws for the colonies. Either Parliament had the power to make all the laws, he wrote his son, or it could make no laws for the colonies. By the end of 1768 he found "more numerous and weighty" arguments for the second position in which "the colonies would then be so many separate states, only subject to the same king, as England and Scotland were before the union." Franklin had reached the point in Angloamerican relations that most future leaders of the Revolution were not to find until 1774. The distance between him and the majority of agents was now unbridgeable.

From the standpoint of the empire's future it was a pity that Great Britain was at last prepared to establish appropriate machinery for imperial coordination at a time when agents had either lost their influence with Parliament or with their colonial employers. It was equally unfortunate that the first secretary of state for the colonies and president of the Board of Trade was temperamentally unsuited to his task. Lord Hillsborough, governed both by resentment of colonial behavior and acceptance of the old mercantile policies, was hardly the man to devise a new and more rational system which would satisfy the needs and pride of both sides of the Atlantic. Still, the demands of the office might have been too much for any man, whatever his attitudes or abilities may have been, to fill with distinction. The secretary's authority itself was open to question, since he would be the third man, after the secretaries of state for the Northern and the Southern departments.

In the long run Samuel Adams could not lose. The course of collision within the empire was too fixed to be diverted in 1768.

[4] Currey, *Road to Revolution* builds a plausible but not wholly convincing thesis around the theme that Franklin's frustrations over the fate of his land speculations in England accounted for his increasing radicalism.

For effectiveness in America, British policy needed a sense of direction and a sense of strength, both of which were lacking at this time. How credible was Parliament's prohibition of western migration when the troops to maintain the prohibition were removed to eastern cities to contain potential riots there? How credible were Parliament's decisions for raising revenues in America when extralegal activities against them could modify or destroy the revenue measures? And when military force was employed against the colonies in the 1760s it emerged only strong enough to provoke mob violence that it could not control. Whether or not the mobs of seamen or unemployed artisans were large or small, "ideologically inert," as Bernard Bailyn saw them, or motivated against social injustice as Jesse Lemisch found, was of less magnitude than the inability of constituted authority to contain them.[5] The rioting accompanying the Grenville and Townshend laws encountered either no opposition by intimidated civil authority or insufficient response by inhibited or undermanned military forces. Witness the inordinate difficulties Justice Hutchinson and other sufferers from Stamp Act disturbances had in winning compensation for their losses; witness also the ease with which the perpetrators of the *Liberty* affair could act with impunity.

These marks of British weakness alone should have instilled confidence in the Liberty Boys. But they had other weapons to frighten their adversary beyond taking to the streets. Among them was their awareness of urban violence in the mother country itself and their ability to exploit it to their own advantage. England was scarcely a nation to fear if she could not contain her own disorders following the expulsion from Parliament and imprisonment of the London journalist John Wilkes. It did not escape American attention that the electors of Middlesex County, petitioning the king in May, 1769, against the vacating of Wilkes' seat in Parliament, linked their grievances to Amer-

[5] Bernard Bailyn, *Pamphlets of the American Revolution, 1759–1776*, I (Cambridge, 1965): 582; Jesse Lemisch, "Jack Tar in the Streets: Merchant Seamen in the Politics of Revolutionary America," *William and Mary Quarterly*, Third Series, XXV (July, 1968): 371–407; Gordon Wood, "A Note on Mobs in the American Revolution," *ibid.*, XXIII (October, 1966): 639, feels that the most noteworthy aspect of mob action in America was "the almost total absence of resistance by the constituted authorities."

ica's complaints. Americans promptly elevated Wilkes to martyrdom, seeing in his defiance of the king and ministers a defender of their own cause. American towns, counties, and children subsequently bore the name of Wilkes. Although Franklin clearly saw distinctions between "Wilkes and Liberty" —the popular toast of the day—and Wilkes and America, the rioting in London on behalf of the peoples' hero facilitated rioting in America.

There was still another side of American strength in its contest with Great Britain that both Englishmen and Americans were aware of, although it lurked in the shadows during much of this period: namely, the role of France in Angloamerica in the years after the Treaty of Paris. All three parties were conscious of a French factor in the imperial problem even though its potential was not to be realized until after the Revolution had taken place. There was no doubt of France's attraction to the colonial cause. From the Stamp Act onward it was inevitable that French statesmen still smarting from the humiliations of the recent war would have seen in American unrest a possible source of revenge against Great Britain. France's Foreign Minister Choiseul in particular foresaw the beginnings of revolution even before the Stamp Act. Encouraged by the advice of the French ambassador to London, Choiseul dispatched a knowledgeable naval officer to America who quickly came to the conclusion that the colonists were "too rich to be obedient, eager to be the sole masters of their fur trade, and restive to shake off the fetters and restraints on their commerce." Such observations were welcome to the foreign minister, since they not only confirmed his predispositions but fitted into his schemes for the rebuilding of the French navy and for an ultimate attack on England. If France were to become a world power again America had an important part to play in her renascence. Outside the circle of *Machtpolitik*, influential liberals such as Diderot, who shared a Whig view of America, and physiocrats such as Turgot, who admired the agrarian order of American society, provided a sympathetic atmosphere in which Choiseul could operate.

Great Britain herself was sensitive to these currents in French thought. General Conway, the powerful secretary of state for the Southern Department in Rockingham's ministry, had recognized the French menace as a reason for patching up the Stamp Act rifts as quickly as possible. British and American writers played on the theme. In two books with a similar note the American Nicholas Ray and the Englishman Stephen Sayre warned Great Britain of the consequences of American discontent with British legislation. The price would be the disruption of the empire abetted by the aroused Bourbons. Arthur Young, then a youthful follower of Chatham's approach to empire, urged his country to defer to the wishes of the Americans, or else risk a second-class status in the world when the empire was disrupted. He was convinced that in the event of a rupture Britain's enemies would promote American independence. Naturally, Franklin was cognisant of this line of reasoning and made his own modest contribution to British insecurity by arranging for publication in Paris of pro-American pamphlets. Rumors of impending war between Britain and the Family Alliance left him with the hope that Parliament would be shocked into concessions. And if the mother country failed to heed this counsel, Franklin could still enjoy the "satisfaction in seeing that our part is taken everywhere."

Americans of all walks of life appeared to sense that the outside world was on their side. The account of a Frenchman who overheard backwoodsmen talking about France in a Williamsburg tavern shortly after Patrick Henry's bold speech in 1765 is instructive: ". . . Come to the worst we'l Call the french to our sucour; and if they were in Canada the British parlem't would as soon be Dd. as to offer what they do now." Discounting some exaggeration or imprecision in this account owing to the language barrier or to the hazy atmosphere of a tavern, the sentiment was not unusual. Durand, the French ambassador to England, reported to Choiseul of an emissary from an American secret committee who conferred with him in London during the Stamp Act controversy about colonial willingness to return Acadia to France in exchange for French intervention in the crisis.

There is no doubt that France was titillated by the prospect of a division of the British Empire, and was willing to stoke such fires as she could find. But her conclusion was that Britain was not yet in danger, that the colonial resistance was waning rather than increasing, and that interference in America entailed more risks than it was worth. One secret agent, Jean de Kalb, traveling extensively in the colonies in 1768, found no genuine revolutionary spirit abroad and no military preparations to accompany the vocal resistance to British actions. Even Durand, when directly confronted with a *quid pro quo* proposition from uncertain American sources discouraged hopes for intervention.[6] There were too many obstacles within France herself to permit such a commitment. When Choiseul fell from power, his successors, particularly Comte de Vergennes, were more cautious. Vergennes played for a time with the possibility of a genuine rapprochement with Great Britain when in the early 1770s he considered the revival of France's colonial system less important than the development of new commercial outlets. His later conversion did not include interest in the re-establishment of a French empire in America.

Americans and Frenchmen were still far apart in this period, although sympathies were growing on both sides. But most of France's gestures belong to a familiar tradition of international politics in the eighteenth century which fostered secret assistance to the enemies of one's enemies. Just as Britain expressed interest in Corsican independence in this period, so the French would even the score in America. They were not ready to go beyond this point until new colonial grievances against the mother country reopened the matter.

Choiseul rather than his critics was right about Britain's future in America. New grievances were inevitable. The elimination of most of the Townshend duties in the reforms of the new North ministry was not tied in any way to an appreciation of the American constitutional argument. It reflected, rather, the older mercantilist belief that taxation of British products of the

[6] Durand referred to an emissary of "their secret committee" who presumed to speak for the colonies. The parental body of the secret committee is as cryptic as is the spokesman whom it sent. See Durand to Choiseul, December 1, 1767, *Archives des affaires étrangères*, *Angleterre*, vol. 474, p. 234. Richard W. Van Alstyne, *Empire and Independence: The International History of the American Revolution* (New York, 1965), p. 52, identifies the emissary with the Stamp Act Congress.

order of glass, paper, and paints were, in Hillsborough's words, "contrary to the true principles of commerce." While the retention of the tea duty was in apparent violation of these principles, it did conform to the even higher principle of asserting Parliament's legislative authority, and thereby assured continued strife with the colonies. By 1770 articulate colonial opinion had shifted to the position that Parliament could not enact laws for America. All that was needed for a revival of passions was a provocation, real or imagined, which could be exploited by the new breed of colonial leader.

Boston was a logical site for the staging of conflict, and the Boston Massacre was a useful, though not immediately successful, vehicle in 1770. The ability of an imaginative politico like Samuel Adams to take advantage of the combustible potential inherent in the presence of oppressive British troops and an insecure civil government made the ultimate confrontation only a matter of time. Even if the Massacre failed to ignite America, John Adams, who defended the British soldiers charged with the crime, claimed years later that the retirement of two regiments from the city laid the foundation of American independence. If an aroused citizenry was able to force hostile military forces out of Boston, how much longer could Great Britain herself remain in Boston?

Such a question may have seemed rhetorical in the wake of the acquittal of the soldiers and the exposure of the "Massacre" as a pious fiction of radicals. Similarly, the return of prosperity to America in the early 1770s and the acceptance by the merchant class of the new civil list paid out of revenues raised in America indicated a new period of calm on the horizon, particularly in New England where the sugar duty had been reduced to a bearable level. Massachusetts' emergence from debt at this time, which rendered provincial taxes unnecessary, was a useful check on rebellion. In this setting the nonimportation movement faltered and died, and the brave talk of convoking a congress of merchants of the commercial colonies to work out a uniform and equitable pattern of enforcement never went beyond the discussion stage. But this retreat from militancy was only a temporary respite for both sides, and must have been an illusion at all times if a relatively minor incident could undo in a moment the complacency of those who hoped for reconciliation.

The attack on the revenue cutter *Gaspee* in 1772 was just such an incident. Patrolling the waters of Narragansett Bay, a notorious center of smuggling, the *Gaspee* had a reputation for excessive zeal in exposing violations of the Navigation laws. When it ran aground near Providence it was not surprising that it received unwanted attention from hostile Rhode Islanders who promptly set upon the vessel. The ship was burned, the commander wounded, and royal authority in the person of royal officers was grievously affronted. The outrageous assault was all the more galling because of the subsequent false arrest of the unfortunate British commander by civil authorities, and the inability of anyone to identify the American culprits behind the action. As everyone knew, they were leading men of business in Providence.

Essentially the incident was not different from a number of other clashes in the preceding decade; and essentially British response was similar to earlier responses. In the first instance the colonial provoked by a British regulation and recognizing limitations in local British power strikes out at an exposed extension of authority. In the latter Britain promises punishment which she is unable to deliver. The major difference on this occasion was in the aftermath of the affair. In the past the colonies had spoken vaguely of future concert against British policy, but never fulfilled their pledges. This time Samuel Adams and his network of colleagues in other colonies established a continental Committee of Correspondence with the objective of circulating information quickly about future British abuses and of addressing the world with a single American voice. The *Gaspee* affair revealed how much the events of the previous decade had radicalized the colonies.

Reaction to news of a royal commission interfering in the Rhode Island case was immediate. The commission became a court of the Inquisition in the rhetoric of its opponents, who claimed that its purpose was to compel Americans to bow before alien and illegal jurisdictions. Anticipating the summoning of troops in January, 1773, in consequence of the investigation, the *Boston Gazette* conjured up slaughter worse than the Boston

Massacre, and asked itself how long the patience of the colonies would last before an effective riposte was made. It came within two months as Virginia, spurred by Richard Henry Lee, took the initiative and appointed a standing committee of eleven to keep watch over the acts of Parliament and to correspond with the other colonies. The motion of the young Virginian found a response first in Boston and then within a year in all the colonies except Pennsylvania, which delayed the appointment of a committee until after the Boston Port Bill had passed in 1774.

While a Continental Congress would soon overshadow the Committees of Correspondence, they symbolized a spirit of union which had not been present in the previous crises. Here were permanent units different from the ad hoc basis of the Stamp Act Congress or from the unstructured reactions to the Circular Letter. New leaders emerged inside and outside the legislatures who could give currency to the language of conditional independence. Not only did the *Boston Gazette* deny Britain's right to make laws for the colonies but it warned that "if Britons continue their endeavors much longer to subject us to their government and taxation, we shall become a separate state." And the state would be strong enough to be a "guardian of the rights of mankind throughout the world," according to the *Providence Gazette* in 1773. Certainly it would be confident enough to dispatch its own ambassador to Parliament, if not to the Court of St. James.

The passage of the Tea Act in the same year illustrated Parliament's insensibility to the extent of the ferment in the colonies. By permitting the East India Company to market its product directly in America through company agents rather than established tea merchants, Parliament unwittingly stimulated a continental-wide reaction, centering about the physical rejection of the tea in American ports. The most notable clash was in Boston, where Samuel Adams, leading his followers into a direct contest of wills with Governor Thomas Hutchinson, staged the Boston Tea Party. The impudent and daring dumping of tea into Boston harbor resulted in punitive measures which in turn converted the committees of correspondence into a Continental Congress of united colonies. Samuel Adams had won his fight.

From the Townshend laws of 1767 down to the Coercive Acts of 1774 the colonial agents in England had followed closely the deepening crisis, some with horror over the course America was taking, a few with appreciation of the rebuffs to the ministries, almost all with insufficient understanding of the changes taking place in the colonies. They continued to intervene as intermediaries with Parliament on behalf of the colonial legislatures, but they had lost heart for their work as well as effectiveness in it. They were still given audiences in Great Britain, and many of them felt with good reason that they retained more influence with their British connections than they had with their American clients.

The only colonial agent to whom the Assemblies would give their trust in the 1770s was Franklin, who had been the most suspect of agents during the previous decade when he had been accused repeatedly of serving his private interests at the expense of Pennsylvania's. These suspicions had waned after 1768, almost in proportion to Franklin's increasing identification with the American popular cause. Georgia engaged him as agent in 1768, and Massachusetts followed in 1770. He achieved his greatest acclaim in the midst of the storm over the Boston Tea Party. Like many agents he supplied Assembly leaders with illicitly acquired correspondence, asking in return anonymity to protect his position in London.

Among letters that fell into the hands of the legislative radicals was the correspondence of former Chief Justice Hutchinson and former Stamp Distributor Oliver with Secretary to the Treasury Whately during the Stamp Act controversy. The correspondence revealed them to have urged strong measures against American licentiousness, thereby assuming a position which would have embarrassed them in 1765 and did compromise them in 1773. Instead of keeping the letters confidential the House leaders had them read publicly, and then printed, in order to provide grounds for impeachment of the two men for betrayal of their colony. The attack backfired at the hearings in London when Franklin's role became known. In view of Parliament's indignant reaction to the Tea Party reaction, Hutchinson and Oliver became victims of the radical plot against British authority and Franklin became one of the conspirators. In

January, 1774, Solicitor General Alexander Wedderburn denounced the Massachusetts agent before the Privy Council in language more violent than the Boston radicals had applied to Hutchinson and Oliver. Boston had a hero, if not quite a martyr; but it certainly had in Franklin no influence in Parliament.

Humiliated as Franklin was, he had not lost his sense of reason or of proportion. He foresaw disaster for the empire and clearly knew his own future course. But decisive action was still in the future. In the meantime, he was wary of the account sent to him by the Massachusetts House committee which blamed the destruction of tea solely on the refusal of the consignees to send their cargoes back to England. The privileges accorded the East India Company, according to the committee, were such a threat to the colonies that only extreme countermeasures could cope with them. In his capacity as agent Franklin was disturbed by this interpretation and its implications. Privately he wrote to Speaker Thomas Cushing of Massachusetts that the Tea Party had united all Englishmen against Boston. Only some genuine reparations on the part of Massachusetts for the destroyed property would appease Parliament.

Franklin was not misreading British opinion; if anything, he understated British anger in his communications with his Massachusetts correspondents. The Coercive Acts were more than punishment of Boston's offenses. They were Great Britain's revenge for America's subversive conduct. In striking at Boston, Parliament struck a blow against traitors who had been "levying war against His Majesty," according to a report of Crown Law Officers in 1774. Each of the measures against Massachusetts—closing the port of Boston, uprooting the offending political establishment through the Massachusetts Government Act, assuring suitable quarters for troops, and protecting royal officials from prejudiced juries—helped to discharge the pent-up frustrations from which Englishmen had long suffered in their dealings with the colonies. Justice for Massachusetts was a simple matter. Either the colony repaid the cost of the lost tea or it would remain deprived of its political and civil liberties.

That the other American colonies would rally to Boston's defense hardly seemed to occur to the ministry. That the savagery of the assault on the city played into the hands of radicals by fulfilling the direst predictions of Anglophobes did not appear relevant to Parliament at this moment. Indeed, the outrage of Englishmen extended to many of America's familiar friends, not excluding Isaac Barre. In this situation it was remarkable that any moderating voice would dare to assert itself in London. Merchants, or at least a portion of the larger body who spoke out so clearly ten years earlier, did attempt to prevent the restraining legislation against Boston from going into effect. Their motives were not political sympathy but fear of a resumption of nonimportation and of the effect of the closure of the port of Boston upon their businesses. They asked for a delay of six months to give the Massachusetts Assembly a chance to reconsider, while they would help in the restitution of the lost property. The Lord Mayor of London offered to cover the amount if the ministry would withhold a punitive bill. But the economic issue was subordinate to the political, and the merchants themselves were not unaffected by the constitutional problem at stake. So when North refused their propositions they retired from the fray.

The official agents of the colonies were no better equipped to influence the ministers than were the merchants. Their zeal was equally open to question. The division between "Englishmen" and "Americans" that had occasionally come to the surface in past crises now curtailed any united front. In fact, some colonies —Maryland, Delaware, Virginia, and North Carolina—had no agents at this time. And two others—Rhode Island and Connecticut—had failed to complete arrangements to replace agents who had departed from the service. The most effective of the men had defected from the colonial cause: Richard Jackson to become government solicitor to the Board of Trade; Charles Garth, demoralized by American behavior, to inactivity; Edmund Burke to his primary function as a leading member of the opposition in Parliament. Jackson spoke for the majority when he admonished Connecticut not to participate in such crimes as the Tea Party and to avoid identification with any defiance of Parliamentary authority. And when a man of Burke's well-known sympathies could not understand New York's anxiety over the Quebec Act, since it did not materially affect that colony, the alienation of the agencies from their constituencies appeared almost complete.

The only agents remaining in London who appreciated and shared, for the most part, the colonial apprehensions were those least influential in London and most vulnerable to British recriminations against America. They were also the spokesmen for the colony which was the focus of Parliament's attention—Massachusetts. Franklin was the most distinguished of the "American" agents, representing now Pennsylvania, New Jersey, and Georgia as well as the Bay Colony. Additionally, Arthur Lee and William Bollan served Massachusetts as agents of the House of Representatives and the Massachusetts Council respectively. Inasmuch as Franklin was virtually *persona non grata* in early 1774 and Lee was away on the Continent, Bollan alone was in a position to combat the punitive legislation. He attempted first to address an appeal to the king and, when that failed, he induced the Lord Mayor of London, a member of Parliament, to present a petition against the Port Bill in the House of Commons. The House refused to hear him. When the Lord Mayor himself presented a petition composed by Americans living in England, few listened. Bollan was dismissed on the specious grounds that he was not the official agent of Massachusetts Bay. Such official agents as Garth and Burke were either silent or tepid in their commentaries in the Commons, although the latter did charge that the ministry was rushing the bill through the House, and later felt the legislation was tyrannical.

The Coercive Acts of 1774 were a watershed for the agents as they were for the colonies themselves. They completed the metamorphosis of those agents who accepted the colonial outlook into Americans serving the colonies united rather than a specific colony or even a group of colonies. The Pennsylvania ties of Franklin and the Virginia origins of Lee had lost their significance, at least for the years of crises between the Coercive Acts and the Declaration of Independence. As noted earlier, the process in the case of Franklin was already some years old in 1774. He had observed to his son in 1772 that he was identified as a colleague by the diplomatic corps in London, and he was particularly impressed with the fact that other diplomats courted him, "partly, I believe, from the desire they have, from time to time, of hearing something of American affairs, an object become of importance in foreign courts." The Earl of Buckinghamshire later confirmed Franklin's perceptiveness in suggesting that Franklin "was here, not as an agent of a province but as an ambassador from the states of America. That he could not compare his embassy to anything but that sent by Louis XIV to the republic of Genoa, commanding the doge to come and prostrate himself at Versailles, to appease the resentment of the grand monarque."

There was hyperbole in this comparison, but not as much as Buckinghamshire himself may have intended. It was slightly premature. The colonies had not yet submerged their separate identities in a higher sovereignty sufficiently to permit Franklin to display quite the pride in nationhood connoted above. Nor were the colonies individually prepared, except for a distinct minority, to examine fully the implications of their discontent with British laws. Had it not been for Boston's unusually provocative action and Parliament's unusually repressive reaction, the Tea Act of 1773 might not have led straight to the Continental Congress of 1774. In Charleston the Sons of Liberty had been unable to prevent the importation of tea; in Philadelphia there was little but docility to greet the law; and in New York the dispirited radical leader Isaac Sears informed the Boston Committee of Correspondence that talk of an absolute boycott of English tea was consolidating conservative strength in that province.

Boston's initiative gave the radical minority its opportunity, or at least it unleashed the kind of emotions in the mother country which played into the hands of those who worked to destroy the ties with Great Britain. To cope with the effects of the Coercive, or Intolerable, Acts, the Committees of Correspondence agreed to call a Continental Congress which would express an American backing for the victimized citizens of Massachusetts Bay. But even at this congress John Adams made clear that he was present as an ambassador of his state, not his country. The colonies were still separate entities groping toward union. Only from London was the picture of the future relatively clear, and in that imperial capital the surviving American agents, Franklin and Lee, anticipated their countrymen both in addressing England as servants of a united America and in addressing their correspondents at home as advocates of a united America.

By the time the Continental Congress convened in September there was little room for diplomatic manoeuver between the colonies and Great Britain. The gulf was now wide, and the help proper language might provide toward its bridging was limited. In light of these dismal circumstances the amount of time both sides expended in the effort was all the more remarkable. The roles of Franklin and Lee were active ones. But it was obvious that they regarded themselves after 1774 as envoys of a foreign country, even if the country they represented was not quite France of the Sun King. The tragedy of British conciliatory endeavors in the next two years lay first in their chronic inability to recognize Franklin's and Lee's real position in England, and then in their unwillingness to accept this position.[7]

[7] Sosin, *Agents and Merchants*, p. 187, is sympathetic toward Britain's problem. With all its faults the "ministry was not culpable of attempting to subvert representative government in the colonies or depriving individuals of rights, but of trying to maintain its authority . . ."; Kammen, *A Rope of Sand*, p. 314, is less benign in his judgment: ". . . British politicians, particularly Grenville, Townshend, Hillsborough, and North, lacked the judgment and generosity needed to resolve the crisis that began in 1764."

CHAPTER IV

Independence and Alliance: The British Reaction

☆ 1774-1778 ☆

THE EMERGENCY meeting of a Continental Congress in Philadelphia to protest against the Coercive Acts should have been an occasion for Parliament to reassess imperial relations. It did give Parliament pause for reflection, but in no way deflected its resolution to bring the colonies to heel. Rather than interpreting the significance of the Congress to be a call for radical change in relationships, Great Britain labeled the Congress a sinister force which unchecked would destroy the empire. Whatever efforts Parliament made subsequently to ameliorate colonial grievances have to be weighed against the more powerful determination to maintain at all costs its ultimate authority over America. The result was failure; war and independence followed.

British policies were not frivolous, vindictive, or ignorant, although elements of all three qualities were present.[1] The men who formulated legislative proposals in the 1770s for Amer-

[1] Ira D. Gruber, "The American Revolution as a Conspiracy: the British View," *William and Mary Quarterly*, XXVI (July, 1969): 360–372, challenges Bernard Bailyn's thesis, as expressed in his *Ideological Origins of the American Revolution* (Cambridge, 1967) and *The Origins of American Politics* (New York, 1968), that belief in a conspiracy animated both sides in the imperial conflict. Gruber claims that the British may have indulged in that rhetoric, but did not believe in an American conspiracy until after the bloodshed of Lexington in 1775.

ica were for the most part administrators of considerable experience in these matters. A coherent colonial office had been functioning since 1768, and after the departure of the Earl of Hillsborough in 1772 it was held by the sympathetic if not perceptive Earl of Dartmouth. The sketching of major policies, including the Coercive Acts, was the work of well-trained colonial hands. Subministers John Pownall and William Knox had been responsible respectively for the planning of the Port Act and the Quartering Act. Unlike George Grenville and Thomas Whately in 1763, they knew exactly what they were doing; they were saving the empire by exposing and neutralizing the radical conspiracy in America. Their diagnosis may have been an error but their direction was clear.

America's traditional friends in Parliament had difficulty in restraining the ministry. To begin with, they were few in number. The largest contingent was a group of sixty mavericks who joined from time to time the twenty members of the Rockingham faction and the ten or twelve members grouped around the mercurial Chatham. More important, they were divided in their feelings toward each other and toward America. The larger of the organized opposition forces, Rockingham's, was exceedingly sensitive to the question of parliamentary sovereignty, and this sensitivity inclined them toward acceptance of strict colonial accountability for the Tea Party outrage in Boston. The Declaratory Act was their particular lodestar. The Tea Party directly affronted their claims, forcing the Rockingham men to awaken their preferred "sleeping sovereignty," which, as Bernard Donoghue understood it, was "a supremacy that is tacitly accepted without being tested and demonstrated."[2] Chatham's disciples, however, maintained that parliamentary supremacy was constitutionally limited in that Parliament lacked the right to impose internal taxes or a standing army on the colonies without the approval of their Assemblies. While Rockingham could not accept this qualification on the powers of Parliament, both factions abhorred the notion of American

[2] Bernard Donoghue, *British Politics and the American Revolution: The Path to War, 1773–1775* (London, 1964), p. 132. He notes that Lewis B. Namier claims that Rockingham was as authoritarian as George III and Lord North on this subject.

independence, either as a separate nation or as separate units within a federal empire free from any control by Parliament.

Even had pro-American Parliamentarians worked more harmoniously, the dissipation of their former harmonious community of interests with merchants and manufacturers would have damaged their efforts on behalf of the colonies. The unfortunate combination of the relative decline of the American trade and the rise of American radicalism in this decade had cooled the ardor of merchants for the colonial cause. Moreover, the informal collaboration of Wilkes and his supporters in the City of London had lost its strength in 1774. Whereas the links between Chatham and Wilkes were reparable, the diminishing role of merchants in American affairs appeared more permanent. It is worth observing that between 1771 and 1775 British trade with America had declined by over 25 percent from that of the previous decade while the Russian market rose over 300 percent, and the Swedish, African, and Flemish markets over 100 percent in each area. When merchants realized that the colonies wanted, among other things, free trade with the non-British world, their disaffection deepened.

Oddly enough, in their refusal to countenance the removal of Parliament's authority from America the reputed friends of America were not far apart from many of the moderates in the North ministry who continued to seek accommodation with the colonies. Notable among the latter were Lord Dartmouth, the colonial secretary, and Thomas Hutchinson, former governor of Massachusetts, newly arrived in England to report on the meaning of the Tea Party. Their objective was to separate the loyal citizens from the radicals, to bring relief to those who suffered unjustly from the effects of the Port Bill, and to find some semantic device to evade open avowal of Parliament's power to tax. Although events had outdated his evaluation of American temper, Hutchinson appeared to understand the heart of America's grievances. He had won Dartmouth's confidence by the time the Continental Congress had assembled. If only the colonies would apologize and make amends for their unacceptable treatment of the Tea Act, they might then petition to be exempted from Parliament's taxation on grounds of traditional usage.

It was this element of generosity among British policymakers that made rejection so difficult to bear. Pure malevolence on the part of the ministry might have quickened the pace of the opposition's acceptance of the evolving American positions. The Declaration of Independence and the state of war would have been an appropriate confounding of evil, and the enemies of North might have brought him down long before 1782. What the liberals did accept in 1782 might then have been acceptable in 1774. This was not to be. Instead, a series of reluctant retreats from fixed stances characterized British policy, with each move coming too late to serve its purpose. American terms for remaining in the empire always seemed to be one step beyond the most recent British concession. Such was the pattern of Angloamerican communication from the Congress of 1774 to the alliance with France in 1778.

British expectations in the fall of 1774 were buoyed by news of bickering between radicals and conservatives in the proceedings that led to the meeting in Philadelphia. It confirmed the judgment of Hutchinson that, given suitable concessions, the hitherto passive majority of conservatives would overwhelm the transitory influence of the radicals.

There was no doubt of the seriousness of colonial divisions over the course America should adopt. The consensus among American merchants was that while the Port Act was too severe, the provocations made it understandable. In this context the struggle against it and the companion acts of Parliament should be carefully waged, rather than be subjected to the sledgehammer approach of the Boston Committee of Correspondence. The latter's simplistic solution was to initiate and to enforce an abrupt and complete cessation of trade between America and the mother country until Parliament offered redress. Samuel Adams' complementary plan for a Solemn League and Covenant to coerce nonconsumption of British products increased the uneasiness of merchants and led many to wonder if the radical passions which would be aroused by such a covenant would be as dangerous to the welfare of the colonies as the loss of trade would be itself. The memories of the past decade were strong on both sides; radical political leaders remembered how much cheating there had been on the nonimportation agreements that had followed the Townshend laws.

As it became apparent that most of the Committees of Correspondence were divided on the shape their counteraction should take, radical politicians gave up their plans for an immediate blow and acceded to the idea of a continental congress. It was not that the more conservative influences found any absolute values in a congress as such; it was simply their vehicle for delaying movement and for draining the energies of the popular leaders. With conservatives fully in control of the delegation from Pennsylvania and with the DeLancey faction allied with the merchants of New York they were willing to take their chances of controlling the congress and modifying its decisions. The actual inspiration for the congress itself emerged from the interplay of ideas stimulated among the Committees of Correspondence, with the major impetus in support of Massachusetts coming from Virginia. Samuel Adams and Joseph Warren of Boston had been important advisers to Richard Henry Lee on this occasion, and he in turn had been much impressed with advice from his brother, Arthur Lee, and from Franklin in London who had emphasized the value a united colonial front would have for their labors at Whitehall. The Continental Congress was the fruit of this activity.

When it finally met in Philadelphia in September the conservatives failed to realize their hopes. Radicals outmanoeuvered them in the control of the meeting when Charles Thomson of Philadelphia assumed the office of secretary. Adams shrewdly kept silence, encouraging an Anglican minister to conduct prayers and southern fireaters to make the most damning accusations against Great Britain. The Congress also gave an opportunity to radical leaders who had never been introduced before—Adams of Massachusetts, Gadsden of South Carolina, Henry of Virginia —to fraternize, compare views, and generally to invigorate each other's determination to make a strong stand. Moderates may have been present in large numbers but they lacked the verve, and ultimately the logic of their opponents' stance.

The trouble with American conservatism was partly a problem of definition in 1774. How did one distinguish accurately a Joseph Galloway of Pennsylvania whom Gipson identified as holding "somewhat conservative views" from moderates of the stamp of John Dickinson or John Jay? If the criterion was an unwillingness to leave the British Empire, the moderates and conservatives might be lumped together. As far as Parliament was concerned it was unable to grade the variations of opposition to British policy or the differing degrees of intensity in feelings about the Coercive Acts. Certainly the measure usually identified with the conservatives, the Galloway Plan, would be unacceptable to Great Britain even if it had won approval in the Congress. Built around the conception of an American Parliament chosen from the colonial Assemblies, Galloway's plan would have endowed that new body, a Grand Council, with authority over civil, criminal, and commercial affairs of America and with the right of veto over Parliament's legislation affecting the colonies. Admitting that it would be an "inferior" branch of the British government, the delegates might well have asked if it would be inferior enough to satisfy the mood of Parliament. The question became academic when the Congress rejected the plan.

If Great Britain's acceptance of Galloway's proposal, or of any proposal that qualified Parliament's power or did not make amends for the Tea Party was questionable, it was certain that she could not agree to the conclusions of the Congress. The declaration of rights assumed the applicability of the laws of nature behind the American cause and referred to the British government as a "foreign power" despite the latter's authority to regulate genuinely external trade. To inflame British passions further the Congress dismissed the Declaratory Act as unconstitutional. The accommodating spirit of the Galloway Plan was replaced with the Suffolk Resolves which replicated the spirit of Adams' Solemn League and Covenant in applying economic pressure to Great Britain, and enhancing it with a continental approbation that might have been lacking under the latter scheme. An Association accompanied the Resolves which would police the embargo on British trade relations until colonial grievances had been remedied. Finally, a petition to the crown, a body now thoroughly diminished in scope, completed the labors of the Congress.

At this point the ranks of radicals were much expanded. No

longer did that label adhere to a handful of demagogues seeking a violent overturn of relations with the mother country at the risk of internal convulsions. Independence in all but name was the mood of the majority in the Congress, and this majority included names which had not previously been identified with the radical leadership. The implications of the denial of Parliament's powers pushed them all togeher. Men such as Jefferson of Virginia and John Adams of Massachusetts Bay moved into radical ranks without full recognition of the change, as their terms for reconciliation projected a British Empire based on a federal membership. This conception was incomprehensible to even the best disposed of Englishmen in 1774. The only difference between them and Samuel Adams at this moment was that the latter had no interest in reconciliation. What kind of citizenship was John Adams displaying a few months later in his "Novanglus Letters" written for the *Boston Gazette*, when he claimed: "We owe allegiance to the person of His Majesty, King George III, whom God preserve, But allegiance is due universally, both from Britons and Americans to the person of the king, not to his crown."

Adams' reasoning was ingenious. Since Massachusetts underwent its own revolution in the previous century and made its own oaths of allegiance to the crown, its link to the king was not derived from any act of Parliament. That America's sympathizers in the Parliament and in the cabinet could not understand the notion of a "King of Massachusetts" was at the heart of the Angloamerican dilemma. They preferred to ignore as long as they could everything that was coming out of the Congress at Philadelphia. They could not cope with it. Instead, such friends as still remained in London instinctively went to their traditional sources of American advice and information—the colonial agents. They found no comfort there. Franklin and Lee were in the advance guard of the new America, and had been prepared to serve as agents for an American Assembly long before the Congress itself had convened.

The agents welcomed the task Congress had imposed upon them: namely, to present the petition to the king protesting the Parliament's actions and defending the work of the united colonies. Indeed, one scholar is convinced that the agents may have been prematurely loyal to an American constituency. They had misrepresented to their Assemblies in America "the nature and the intent of the Massachusetts Acts, the political situation in England, and the course of action most likely to force the imperial government to accommodate the colonists."[3] In so doing they had confirmed the convictions of the radicals at home that their plight was a consequence of a conspiracy to destroy American liberties. Although this indictment has some merit, it places too much responsibility and influence upon the agents. Franklin and Lee had made their choice of loyalties and were bound to act on the instructions of the Congress even if they knew that the tone and language of the petition doomed their chances in the Parliament. Actually Lord Dartmouth was courteous in his reception of Franklin, Lee, and William Bollan and suggested that the king would receive the petition since it contained "nothing in it improper." The king, however, laid it before the Parliament where it died before the American agents could argue its virtues.

The fate of the petition in January, 1775, did not mean that all negotiations had terminated. Dartmouth and his colleagues in the Colonial Office continued to ignore all the evidence that poured out of America and still hoped for a reconciliation in which the colonies would accept their subordination to the Parliament. The message of the Congress went unheeded, as did the frantic requests for help from General Thomas Gage, the military governor who succeeded Hutchinson in Massachusetts Bay. Gage shrilly asked either that the Coercive Acts be suspended or that twenty thousand troops be dispatched to Boston immediately. Perhaps the dissolution of the Parliament in September, 1774, and the call for new elections, an event unconnected with American developments, obscured both the significance of the Continental Congress and the ominous warnings of General Gage.

Undistracted by the clamor around him, Lord Dartmouth took the initiative in opening quiet negotiations with Franklin through intermediaries, Dr. John Fothergill, physician to both Dartmouth and Franklin, and David Barclay, a merchant and

[3] Sosin, *Agents and Merchants*, p. 187.

a Quaker. Out of these private meetings came Franklin's outline of terms under which the American colonies might resume their former place in the empire. Or, as Franklin himself phrased it: "Hints for Conversation upon the Subject of Terms that might probably produce a durable Union between Britain and the Colonies." Although necessarily elliptical in his hints for fear of appearing to be in conflict with the wishes of the Continental Congress, Franklin's first "hint" could not have been more explicit: "The tea destroyed to be paid for." But the price Britain would have to pay in exchange for this concession in the other sixteen hints was too high, even for Dartmouth who never openly rejected more than three of them. The hints ranged from the repeal of the tea duty act to the disclaiming by Parliament of its right to enact internal legislation for the colonies. Hint No. 7 would permit the retention of the British monopoly of American commerce if the British surrendered their practice of requisitions in times of peace. Conversely, No. 17 stipulated that if Parliament opened possibilities for American trade with the rest of the world, the colonies would freely provide requisitions in peacetime as well as in war. In other conversations with Richard, Lord Howe, over the advisability of the ministry sending a commission to America, Franklin was even firmer in his demands on Great Britain. After receiving the specific petition he was to present to the king on behalf of the Continental Congress, he included a requirement that Parliament must sanction the establishment of an Assembly along the lines of the Continental Congress.

Whatever the results of Franklin's ploys, they indicated a remarkable personal recovery from the ignominy over the Hutchinson letters just one year earlier. Franklin was all the ministry had to work with if it wanted accommodation. It is equally remarkable that so much optimism could be generated from such a small hint as Franklin's statement on the payment of the lost tea. The North ministry seized on this straw and added to it Franklin's warm reaction to Dartmouth's proposal that the government send commissioners to America to investigate grievances. Both Chatham's and Burke's gallant attempts at reconciliation in their speeches of February and March, 1775, respectively, owed some of their inspiration to Franklin's hints. At least Franklin thought they did. Among Chatham's marks of favor toward him was an extraordinary visit to the House of Lords and a more conventional one to Chatham's country estate four days before the famous speech.

Chatham was the Pitt of old in his encomium to America as preserver of British liberties. Denouncing at last the Declaratory Act, he could not bring himself to ask for its repeal, but he would suspend it for all practical purposes. In effect, he would efface the years that had passed since 1763. The innovating features of his proposals would be the perpetual free grant of revenue provided by a Continental Congress which would fix the amount for each province. The subordination of the colonies to the crown and Parliament remained, and was so stated in his first clause, but it would be irrelevant to the actual governing process in America. Despite some appreciation of the plan on the part of Dartmouth, the North ministry found it unacceptable. The bill failed, and failed badly. It was "treated with as much contempt," observed Franklin, "as they could have shown to a ballad offered by a drunken porter."

Franklin understandably overstated the ministry's response. Parliament and the ministry wanted reconciliation only if it would avoid a humiliating retreat from their hard stand of 1774. They would not allow the rebellious colonists to go unpunished. Chatham's willingness to denigrate Parliament's power, to withdraw troops from America, to confer legitimacy upon the Congress all went against the grain of the vengeful atmosphere in both Houses of Parliament. So when North tried his own hand at reconciliation three weeks after Chatham's effort, his apparent permissiveness in forbearing to tax Americans "except for duties designed for the regulation of commerce" had some important caveats. Merrill Jensen claims it was "fraudulent in its conception" because North's primary purpose was to win support in Parliament for the repressive legislation against Massachusetts that he had presented only three days before his speech.[4] His plan was to divide New England from the rest of the colonies and from its friends in Great Britain by coupling the New England Restraining Bill, which would cut off those

[4] Jensen, *The Founding of a Nation*, p. 581.

provinces' commerce with the British Isles and the West Indies, with a suggestion of tax freedom to the colonies which agreed to respect the Navigation System. It should be noted that all New England was to share Massachusetts' punishment and that the punishment would extend to deprivation of fisheries. Concurrent increases in the size of land and sea forces in America consistent with Gage's appeals rendered absurd the idea of conciliation advanced by North on February 20, 1775.

To their credit America's friends promptly seized on the weaknesses in North's propositions—its deviousness, its cognate threats, and its blatant attempt to divide and rule. Chatham was sure they "would be spurned in America, as well as laughed at by the friends of America and by the unrelenting enemies of that noble country." Although North's gesture found no positive response except for the ever optimistic Dartmouth, who sent the plan on to the colonial legislatures, it did spark another round of liberal speeches, pleas, and motions on behalf of the colonies. Urging repeal of the remnants of the Townshend duties as well as most of the Coercive Acts, Burke insisted on March 22 that Great Britain take steps to mollify, not to punish, the colonies, suggesting as a possible way out of the tangle an arrangement whereby they would make mutually agreeable settlements of salary on superior court judges. The king would not remove them except on complaint of the legislature or the governor. As for the provision of monies for the imperial welfare he averred that the fourteen Assemblies were the appropriate instrument to determine the manner in which this would be done, rather than a ministerial "ransom by auction," as North had proposed. Five days later David Hartley, a close friend of Franklin, pursued Burke's line of reasoning when he recommended that the colonies fulfill their fiscal obligations by freely granted requisitions fully sanctioned by Parliament. And as a sop to Parliament's self-esteem he pressed for suspension rather than repeal of Coercive legislation. Both Burke's and Hartley's proposals went down to defeat.

Whether or not the colonies would have approved these impassioned pleas for understanding even if Parliament had accepted them is doubtful. America's mood had advanced far beyond a status quo ante 1765, and none of her British supporters had caught up with it. The North ministry, far more than Chatham, Burke, or Hartley, had recognized the central fact that the rebellious colonies unequivocally denied the right of Parliament to legislate for them in any capacity. When North's critics finally faced this fact squarely, the sharp differences between their positions melted; they were differences largely in attitude and manner rather than in interpretation of the British constitution. Without deprecating the importance of their conciliatory dispositions there was no alternative for the liberals in the circumstances of 1775 but to join their Parliamentary opponents in facing the new America across a gulf of independence.

Perhaps the only truly constructive move at this time emerged from the office of Dartmouth, the most ingenuous of North's ministers. The peace commission, blessed earlier by Franklin, proceeded across the Atlantic to investigate at first hand the possibilities and terms of a reconciliation. The subsequent histories of such missions as those of Howe and Carlisle in the next few years were as barren of results as were the speeches of Burke or Chatham; but at least they had the virtue of seeking out middle ground instead of taking fixed positions in advance which the colonies could not have accepted in 1775.

The explosive incidents at Lexington Green and Concord Bridge in Massachusetts in April, 1775, punctuated the Anglo-american division and accelerated the decomposition of the empire. For Parliament they made punishment and retribution all the more vital now that open rebellion had resulted in the bloodshed of British troops. For the colonies, now gathered in a Second Continental Congress, the need to continue the fight for their conception of membership in the empire was no longer a matter of debate. The issue was not immediate independence, although John Adams wrote in his *Autobiography* that he had determined by this time that the Congress should "recommend to the people of all the States to institute governments for themselves, under their own authority, and that, without loss of time. That we ought to declare the colonies free, sovereign and independent States, and then to inform Great Britain we were willing to enter into negotiations with them for the redress of all grievances, and a restoration of harmony between the two countries, upon permanent principles." This posture was a step beyond that of the "Novanglus" papers, and yet it was one into which even reluctant conservatives at the Congress were pressed in the summer of 1775. Fighting British troops as they were, their state of discontent had changed considerably from that of the previous winter. So while John Dickinson hoped that the object of war would be to fix America's proper position in the empire, he was responsible, along with Jefferson, for the "Declaration of the Causes and Necessity of Taking up Arms," whose invitation to world opinion was subversive of those intentions. Despite his moderation of Jefferson's more vigorous language, the Dickinson document clearly anticipated the Declaration of Independence in the following year.[5]

Dickinson's conservative hopes were probably better expressed in the last major colonial petition to the king, the American Olive Branch Petition, on July 8, 1775, two days after the Declaration, in which he blamed the ministry not the crown for America's difficulties with the mother country. Never once was Parliament mentioned except by implication as the king's evil advisers. The petition sought royal intervention to remove not only the laws that had plagued the colonies but all other obstacles to reconciliation. Dickinson managed to have this mild request accepted over the opposition of many radicals.

Had the radicals been willing to assess the petition soberly they would never have exercised themselves over it. The King of England could not separate himself constitutionally from his Parliament in the manner outlined in the Olive Branch even if he had been personally so inclined. Richard Penn, serving as special agent of the Congress, carried the document to London to lay before the crown. Officially it never went beyond the American Department; but the press had it in the first week of September and ultimately Parliament gave it desultory notice. Burke's reaction held the key. When Arthur Lee asked for his help before going to Lord Dartmouth, Burke turned him down for lack of authorization from his New York employers. Upbraided by a friend for this pusillanimous response—"You are the agent of New York alone. Is Mr. Garth agent for any

[5] *Ibid.*, p. 617.

other colony but Carolina? Mr. Bolland [*sic*] and Mr. Lee for any but Massachusetts-Bay, and Virginia? Is Mr. Penn the agent for any province whatsoever? And yet to them equally with yourself is the letter of the congress addressed"—Burke replied that no action he might have taken would have an effect at that moment.

Dartmouth's behavior seemed to confirm the correctness of Burke's sense of the situation in the ministry. Plans for punishment which had been initiated since the shocking news of Lexington Green and the even more shocking challenge at Breeds Hill were too far advanced to be reversed. The Olive Branch Petition became another piece of effrontery demonstrating that the rebellion was a continental plot rather than primarily a New England phenomenon. The ministry had already made up its mind to treat the uprising as a foreign war and to hire twenty thousand troops from Europe to suppress it. On August 23, two days after the petition reached his office, Dartmouth under pressure from Knox and Pownall issued a formal proclamation of rebellion in America. It followed logically that Parliament at its fall session would implement it with a Prohibitory Act barring all trade and intercourse with the colonies until they had made their submission to British authority. In spite of vigorous dissent from the opposition on the part of those who saw only tragedy and ultimate separation in this proposal, it became law in December, 1775. Thus had the Boston Port Bill of 1774 expanded to cover all the thirteen colonies of North America. Notwithstanding elaborate provisions for setting aside this draconian law, Great Britain had declared a state of war to exist between herself and her colonies.

Charles James Fox was speaking for more than the left wing of the Whig opposition when he asserted that the Prohibitory law "should be entitled, a Bill for carrying more effectually into execution the resolves of the Congress." Certainly, the two documents of justification issued by the Second Continental Congress in July, 1775, had provided enough hints as to the course of action America would take if their appeals failed. Essentially it was a course just short of complete independence, but not necessarily bound to an unregenerate empire. Congress was well aware that an outside world was watching the conflict between Britain and her colonies. French or Spanish help was expected. As Dickinson had expressed it in his Declaration, "Our union is perfect. Our preparations are nearly completed. Our internal resources are great; and our assurance of foreign assistance is certain." The latter point gave strength to all the others. Similarly, the Olive Branch Petition stressed that the success of Angloamerica had been an object of envy of other nations, who, observing the "happy connection" between mother country and colonies, had attempted to check the growth of settlement. Might not these same rivals be tempted into the service of America at a time when the relations between the two parts of the empire were less than happy? Franklin, back in Philadelphia since May and a member of the Continental Congress, not only thought so but endorsed Richard Henry Lee's proposal that if the restraining acts were not repealed American ports be opened to foreign commerce duty free.

The above implications and recommendations belonged to the summer of 1775. They remained in abeyance pending Parliament's response. The Prohibitory Act therefore was just the vehicle to bring them to the fore. What was considered too radical in July became imperative six months later after Parliament's measures were promulgated in America. America had new governing instruments. For one, an American government was emerging from the Second Continental Congress which, when reassembled in September, 1775, after a month's recess, identified itself as the custodian of colonial sovereignty for an indefinite future. For another, the Congress spawned organs capable of carrying out separation from England and management of a foreign policy.

A "Secret Committee" of the Congress, chaired by Thomas Willing and later Robert Morris, both Philadelphia merchants and partners, was established to buy military supplies. This meant links to Europe where arms, ammunition, and supplies were to be found. Later known as the Committee of Commerce, the Secret Committee laid groundwork for the more important Committee of Secret Correspondence created on November 19, 1775, a committee of five to act on its own initiative "for the sole purpose of corresponding with our friends in Great Britain,

Ireland, and other parts of the world." It became the Committee on Foreign Affairs in 1777 and took responsibility for controlling foreign policy of the new nation until a secretary for foreign relations replaced it in 1781.

Continuity with past experience was obvious in the habits and conduct of the new committee. Just as the Committees of Correspondence of the Assemblies had dealt with agents and merchants for specific tasks, so the new Committee of Secret Correspondence commissioned agents and merchants for its diplomatic assignments. It was fitting that the most important members of both the Committee of Secret Correspondence and the Committee of Commerce were Benjamin Franklin, the former colonial agent, and Robert Morris, an active member of the international business community. Their initial action was to open correspondence with Arthur Lee in London and with Charles William Frederick Dumas in The Hague, the latter another intellectual on Franklin's long roster of friends.

Confidence in their powers of persuasion as well as in the future of the war developed early in the history of the committees when they met with unexpectedly eager suitors. Achard de Bonvouloir, Vergennes' special agent fishing in the troubled waters of British America, assured the Committee of Secret Correspondence of France's interest in having an American agent in Paris after it had convinced him of the seriousness of the Congress' determination for independence. And shipmasters of many nationalities—French, Spanish, Dutch, American —seeking a profit from gun-running as well as from trade out of the American rebellion offered their services to the Secret Committee. Before the end of 1775 some forty American merchants had signed contracts with the committee to deliver gunpowder and other supplies to the troops of the new nation. Aside from the lure of patriotism, merchant-politicians of the rank of Morris and Silas Deane, the first agent to France, were aware of the profit margin in a shipment of a boatload of grain from the Connecticut valley to Amsterdam. Robert Morris in particular discovered in the American Revolution a happy union of public service with private profit.

At the opening of 1776 every sign pointed to a complete break with the mother country. Continental forces under George

Washington held Boston under siege, while a full-scale invasion of Canada begun in the fall of 1775 was to reach its climax on New Year's Eve with the unsuccessful assault on Quebec. Yet the Continental Congress was strangely reluctant to ask the question which Franklin had put to Dumas on behalf of the Committee of Secret Correspondence on December 19, 1775: How many European countries "would enter into an alliance with us"? Such a question presupposed the existence of an independent state, a condition a majority in the Congress was still unwilling to face. To Franklin, however, if successful prosecution of war with Great Britain depended upon foreign aid and trade, and if the latter depended on American independence, he had no doubt about the course America should follow. Victory was more important than accommodation with the mother country, a sentiment the Congress did not accept the winter of 1776. As late as February 16, 1776, moderates led by John Dickinson managed to table Franklin's proposal to open American commerce to the world for a two-year period. Dickinson was afraid that passage of this proposal would undermine his and other moderate attempts to respond to the king's address on the Olive Branch Petition of October 26, 1775. The hope was to convince Parliament that while the colonies denied its claim to authority they also denied any intention of establishing an "independent Empire." News of the Prohibitory Act made this response irrelevant, but opponents of independence still managed to hold off opening of ports until April, 1776.

Actually, the formal announcement of freedom of trade was an anticlimax when it was finally proclaimed. Over a month earlier Congress had authorized the privateers to operate under letters of marque, and the Committee of Secret Correspondence had sent Silas Deane to France on a purchasing mission. More important, the powerful influence of Thomas Paine's *Common Sense* had begun its work in January of that year to express in words what a majority in the country had sensed: reconciliation with Great Britain was now impossible. But the common sense of the public and of Paine went beyond this evaluation to announce that reconciliation was also undesirable. America was fighting for the rights of all mankind in destroying the unnatural institution of monarchy and, accordingly, he was convinced that peoples around the world should applaud America's struggle.

Paine's message to the Congress was clear: declare independence immediately and reap all the advantages separation from Great Britain would secure to the United States. First, it would radically transform American thinking about the Bourbon powers; "France and Spain never were, nor perhaps ever will be, our enemies as Americans, but as our being subjects to Great Britain." Why should Americans be yoked to Europe's quarrels, he asked, as submission to Great Britain had required in the past? Second, Paine suggested that America's interest in Europe should be confined to its markets for American trade, but not to a political entanglement with any European country.

Paine performed a more striking service to his newly adopted country than his patron Franklin could ever have anticipated. *Common Sense* not only quickened the impulse toward independence but underlined the importance of diplomacy in winning the war against Britain. The weapons of commercial opportunity which would flow from a declaration of independence would permit diplomatists to secure such foreign assistance as might be necessary. All without cost, since Europe would compete for America's favors. Nothing in the American experience with French agents in Philadelphia or with Dutch bankers in Amsterdam contradicted this assumption. Indeed, the announcement of independence in July should have facilitated the work of Silas Deane in Paris.

Such was the sentiment that characterized the views of John Adams when he drafted a "Plan of Treaties" in conformity with Richard Henry Lee's motion of June 7 which linked independence and confederation with the making of "foreign alliances." Adams' Model Treaty entailed full support of France without any concomitant political connection or hint of submission to a French patron, without military control or even a request for French troops. The connection desired was purely commercial, and for this a treaty with France must permit American ships free entry into French ports while French arms, ammunition, and supplies poured into American ports. Even when France enters the war as a consequence of her new American interests, the most the United States should concede would be a promise not to exploit an Anglo-French war to achieve better terms with Great Britain. Given these expectations Adams' use of the term "alliance" to describe American relations with France must be interpreted, as Felix Gilbert suggested, "in a sense different from the present-day meaning of a close political bond."[6] An alliance merely had to be a treaty of commerce for Adams to speak, at one point, of making a foreign alliance and, at the next, of assuring his readers that it would contain no political commitment. The internal evidence could not be plainer. Writing on June 23, 1776, Adams said, "I am not for soliciting any political connection, or military assistance, or indeed naval, from France. I wish for nothing but commerce, a mere marine treaty with them."

Language of this kind may have sounded presumptuous to those reared on the balance-of-power statecraft of the eighteenth century. The Plan of 1776 could appear to be the mouthings of colonial bumpkins innocent of the realities of international politics, or empty bravado of a frightened government pinning its hopes on impossible dreams to divert itself from its perils. Yet France's interest had been unmistakable, from the cautious soundings of Choiseul's envoys a decade before to the probings of Bonvouloir in 1775 and to the welcome accorded Deane in 1776. The Americans could see as readily as the French the benefits which would accrue to France in a disruption of the British Empire. Those benefits could be substantial, particularly if Vergennes pursued a lead contained in the instructions of the Committee of Secret Correspondence to Deane, to the effect that the trade which had made Great Britain rich "will naturally fall to the share of France." They should also be sufficient to allow Silas Deane to win more than contracts from French merchants.

Even before Deane had arrived in Paris, Vergennes appeared to have been adopting the role the Model Treaty had planned for his country by becoming a patron of the playwright and adventurer, Caron de Beaumarchais. The author of the *Barber of Seville* took up with British and American radicals in a visit to London in 1775, and returned to Paris an enthusiast for the colonial cause. Seeing in it advantages to his own country, he

[6] Gilbert, *To the Farewell Address*, p. 46.

urged on the Ministry of Foreign Affairs full endorsement of the American rebellion. Whether or not his voice was the most important in making up Vergennes' mind, he joined other advocates in warning the foreign minister that failure of the American insurrection might lead to a joint Angloamerican assault on the French sugar islands.[7] The result of his importuning and of Bonvouloir's commentaries was the royal decision for secret assistance to the colonies in May, 1776, by means of a fictitious business concern, Rodrigue Hortalez and Company, with Beaumarchais as the middleman supplying the colonies with munitions. The French king provided a million livres in secret and persuaded the Spanish sovereign, Charles III, to match the amount, all of which would be distributed through Hortalez. Arthur Lee in London described in detail his dealings with Beaumarchais to the Committee of Secret Correspondence, but most of the information was contained in a report that was lost at sea. Unfortunately, lack of precise information encouraged misunderstandings about the nature of France's assistance, which led to severe damage to the careers of Lee and his successor, Deane. But no matter whether it was a loan or a gift, French aid in massive amounts was en route to the American consumers by the time the Model Treaty was framed.

France's disposition toward the colonies was manifested openly in the spring of 1776 by the permission granted American merchant ships to sail into French ports on equal terms with other flags, and by the denial to Great Britain of her demand to search French ships in French territorial waters for evidence of contraband goods. Nor would she allow British sea power to interfere with her own colonial commerce, thereby encouraging the clandestine mission of Rodrigue Hortalez and Company. Underscoring the policy of assistance, France stationed naval squadrons off the Channel ports and in the French West Indies with specific instructions to help American vessels in distress.

All the foregoing events took place on the eve of independ-

[7] Van Alstyne, *Empire and Independence*, p. 91, feels that Beaumarchais "gets more credit than he deserves" as a policymaker. See Samuel Flagg Bemis, *Diplomacy of the American Revolution* (Bloomington, 1957), pp. 20 ff., for a different view.

ence, and made reasonable the optimism of the signers of the Declaration of Independence. But the self-assurance of so many of the framers of foreign policy at this time grew out of more than an acute analysis of the stakes Europe had in reducing British influence in the New World. It stemmed also from their participation in the *Weltanschauung* of the philosophes, the influential, loosely defined, international band of intellectuals who postulated a new world order in which war would be an irrelevant relic of a barbarous past. The philosophes, many of them French in culture if not in origins, assailed power politics and the traditional statecraft that served only dynastic interests. To them the balance of power was wasteful and destructive as well as immoral, and the system of alliances a conspiracy against the natural order. In a world ruled by reason secret diplomacy would disappear, to be replaced by an international structure that recognized the interdependence of all members.

The philosophes inevitably differed widely among themselves on how to realize this new world, but all could agree with the sect of physiocrats in believing that the removal of artificial economic barriers between nations would accelerate change. The physiocrats sought to convince sovereigns that an unrestricted exchange of goods would increase the wealth of all. Free trade was their slogan and conventional statecraft their *bête noir.* As Felix Gilbert concludes about the cumulative effects of all the philosophical schools, "the logical consequence was that in a reformed world, based on reason, foreign policy and diplomacy would become unnecessary, that the new world would be a world without diplomats."[8]

The appeal of the ideas of Europe's philosophes was natural for Americans. They were tempted to see in America the archetype of the ideal society Europeans were groping toward. Their own union of colonies in a free association of states was one example of reason in politics; the American conception of commercial alliances with the rest of the world could be another. Without illusions about the amorality of the diplomatic arts at the Court of Versailles such American envoys as Lee, Deane, and Franklin self-consciously employed the language and sym-

[8] Gilbert, *To the Farewell Address*, pp. 65–66.

bols of the new diplomacy in their labors among old-fashioned diplomats. There was some guile in their manner—in the image of the Pennsylvania Quaker that Franklin was to project in Paris, and in the assumed humility of Deane apologizing for manners natural to a "new-formed people." But there was also a genuine disdain for what underlay the diplomatic etiquette in Europe. The idea of a *novus ordo seclorum* had a reality for Americans abroad that no European could appreciate.

That idealism coincided with self-interest was not a matter the Committee of Secret Correspondence or its agents wished to conceal. They made sure that all Europe would understand that the service the American Revolution rendered mankind also benefited the nation state, particularly the small vulnerable nation. By defending a strict construction of contraband and blockade they were promoting principles of international law that strengthened all small maritime states, not exclusively the fledgling United States. In the philosophes they apparently had allies who could be useful in assuring wise decisions on the part of French policy toward America. The old diplomacy would serve the new, conferring for the time being the advantages of the traditional alliance without imposing any of its obligations.

Against these massive American expectations derived from credible evidence of external assistance, the British ministers responsible for the pacification of America had little of substance to foster similar hopes of success. Once revolution was an established fact British passions subsided to some degree, sufficient to permit a careful assessment of their opportunities. Swift military victory was not one of the assets, since rumblings against the war effort in Britain combined with excessive reliance upon foreign mercenaries created doubts of a military solution from the outset. The longstanding internal weaknesses of the former colonies offered a better case for optimism. The ministry was fully briefed on the internal divisions still alive in the colonies: the intercolonial rivalries over land claims from the Connecticut River to the Ohio River and competing pressures of speculating land companies for control of western territories. They were also sensitive to the conservatives' uneasiness over the prospects of social revolution producing chaos in place of the Angloamerican community. Buoyed by reports of continuing stresses of this kind, the North ministry felt in 1776 that promises of reform should be raised once again as long as submission to Parliament's authority accompanied them. Such was the background of the Howe mission, appointed on May 3, 1776, and empowered to grant pardons to individuals and groups by proclamation and to arrange for the resumption of trade by town or colony after a pledge of allegiance had been secured.

There were some differences of opinion among ministers about the terms the Howe Commission should offer. Lord Germain, the colonial secretary, insisted on a specific acknowledgment of Parliamentary supremacy as a *sine qua non* of negotiations. Lord Dartmouth preferred to ignore the matter of supremacy altogether. Lord North finally settled the differences by allowing the commission to proceed to America without raising initially the colonial relation to Parliament, but with the understanding that no final reconciliation was possible without appropriate deference to the source of sovereignty. At any event, none of the cabinet was in disagreement over those preliminary terms which required the dissolving of all illegal congresses or committees that had usurped the functions of the "Constitutional Officers of Government."

The appointment of the two commissioners—Lieutenant General Sir William Howe and his brother, Admiral Viscount Richard Howe—created consternation in many American circles, if only because of their reputations as men of good will and moderation. Not even the signing of the Declaration of Independence a week before the arrival of Admiral Howe on Staten Island reassured the more nervous members of Congress. After some hesitation General Washington was instructed to provide the commissioners with safe conduct passes into American territories. Fortunately for the self-doubters Howe proceeded to make two tactical blunders at the outset of his mission: first, by sending a copy of his commission to each of the colonial governors, all of whom were defunct according to the views of the newly independent states; and second, by addressing a letter to Washington, the commander-in-chief of the Continental Army, with the title of "Esquire." While these actions reflected accurately

Parliament's intentions of ignoring the Congress and the rebels' armies, they damaged the benevolent image the Howes wished to present to America. To his credit the admiral had the grace to see the folly of these gestures, and quickly apologized to Washington for his breach of etiquette. A little more circuitously he opened unofficial communications with the Congress through the captured General John Sullivan of New Hampshire.

Mollified by Howe's amends for his initial indiscretions, moderates in the Congress still hopeful of ultimate reconciliation with Great Britain on terms of equality pressed successfully to grant the mission a full hearing. It was a tribute to the good sense of the radicals that they yielded to this sentiment. They realized that no matter how ingratiating the Howes might be personally, their fundamental requirements for reconciliation were incompatible with American independence. The selection of Franklin and John Adams, two doughty champions of the Revolution, to be the spokesmen of the Congress banished their lingering reservations about meeting with Englishmen.

Anglophobes had little to fear. When Lord Howe confided his deep feelings of affection for America, and confessed that "if America should fall, he should feel and lament it like the loss of a brother," Franklin as usual had the appropriate response. With unaccustomed admiration for his colleague, John Adams recorded Franklin's answer: "Dr. Franklin, with an easy air, and a collected countenance, a bow, a smile, and all that *naivete*, which sometimes appeared in his conversation, and is often observed in his writings, replied 'My Lord, we will do our utmost endeavors to save your lordship from that mortification.' "

Their colloquies could not advance beyond such pleasantries because Howe could not promise even freedom from Parliament's interference in the internal affairs of the states, let alone recognition of an independent United States. Franklin, speaking unofficially, informed the commissioners that it would be easier for them to secure new instructions permitting them to concede independence than it would be for the former colonies to renounce what they had already achieved. He pointed out that the United States had declared its independence only after Parliament had declared war on America. On this note the conference adjourned.

The Howes did not give up their efforts immediately. The admiral went over the heads of the Congress in an appeal in September to the public at large to reject their representatives and to reinstitute a "Constitutional Government" which would remove without difficulty all the obnoxious legislation of the recent past. He also tried to enlist the captured General Charles Lee to arrange another meeting with the Congress. Both efforts failed. The next time Great Britain was to send over a mission she gave her negotiating team powers to offer everything, or almost everything, short of independence itself. The time was then 1778, on the eve of the French alliance and much too late for serious consideration by Americans. In fact, it was too late in 1776. But all these motions of conciliation had the beneficial side effect of straightening the tortuous path of a Franco-American entente which had taken a different turn from that anticipated by American diplomatists in the summer of 1776.

The making of an alliance, old style or new style, proved to be much more arduous than the Committee of Secret Correspondence had anticipated. The Declaration of Independence did not usher in the new era of statecraft influenced by the ideas of the philosophes. France's decision to extend secret assistance to the Americans could lead reasonably to a French war with England alongside the Americans, which Vergennes was willing to risk. But it need not lead to war. France was not so committed, and there were serious obstacles in the way of a complete military alliance. Among them was the powerful argument of Turgot, the controller general of finances and a leader of the physiocrats, that the nation's financial structure could not bear the load of a war with Great Britain. Besides, he wondered if war were necessary to achieve France's purpose of humbling the British Empire or America's purpose of maintaining independence. He felt that no amount of British effort could win back their lost colonies. Vergennes' elaborate plans were therefore unnecessary.

Although Turgot resigned after his advice was ignored, the continuation of the Hortalez scheme still did not mean that France had committed herself irrevocably to the American cause. There were other problems. Her Bourbon partner was reluctant to extend more than grudging assistance to the American Revolution. Spain, in the words of Samuel Flagg Bemis, "had too many hostages of her own on the other side of the Atlantic to allow her to champion American independence."[9] While the Spanish king was more than willing to exploit the fact of rebellion against Britain, he was uneasy about living with its consequences. Would the new nation be a threat to Spain's colonies, either by its role as model or by its spirit of aggrandizement? None of the counterarguments of Vergennes or of Conrad Alexandre Gérard, his principal aide, completely assuaged Spanish fears, but they did manage to convey the impression with some success that the United States would never have the strength to undertake aggression against French or Spanish interests in America. Additionally, Vergennes had been able to frighten Spain with the specter of Great Britain attacking French and Spanish possessions in America to recoup the costs of the pacification campaigns against the United States, or to divert the British public from other failures, or to seal a new Angloamerican bond with blows against the traditional Bourbon enemies. In fact, Vergennes had done his work so well that for a time in 1776 the Spanish were more anxious for war with England than France ever was. Jeronimo Grimaldi, Spain's foreign minister, and his ambassador in Paris, Count de Aranda, recognized in France's importunities a chance to conquer Britain's ally, Portugal. Friction between the two Iberian neighbors over the lands at the La Plata in South America inflamed Spanish tempers and tempted them to take on England and Portugal if France would accept the obligations of an ally.

Spain's overreaction to French overtures was not what Vergennes had in mind when he first approached Spain for cooperation in assisting the American colonies. Although the Portuguese issue had some attraction for him, particularly as a means of holding Spain to other commitments, the French did not want to risk war with Britain while America's fortunes looked as bleak as they did in the fall of 1776. Vergennes wrote his reply to Grimaldi at a time when news of Washington's defeat on Long Island at the hands of General Howe had reached Paris. Vergennes backed off. War at that moment

[9] Bemis, *Diplomacy of the American Revolution*, p. 41.

would fulfill Turgot's nightmares, particularly if the Americans failed to maintain their independence. So, rather than seeking new adventures, it was enough for France that Americans were continuing to engage British troops and that their Declaration of Independence appeared to assure American resolution in their fight. Vergennes was content to encourage that resolution without open provocation to the British by making alliance with the Americans or by joining Spain in a war against Portugal.

For the British part, the information from the spies of Lord Stormont, the British ambassador to France, combined with complaints from merchants victimized by privateering, made Whitehall fully cognizant of the "secret" role of France in the American war.[10] British reactions varied. On the one hand, the ministry was inclined to wink at French assistance to the colonies if by so doing it could avoid an open confrontation with France. On the other hand, the opposition forces in Parliament which had regretfully turned their backs to America on the issue of independence looked with some sympathy on a British struggle with France, hoping that the nation in peril would reunite Americans and Britons. On "the principle of self-preservation," as Camden put it, the Chathamites could bring themselves to live with an independent United States, provided it rallied to the support of the mother country in a crisis.

Much of the foregoing was unknown to Americans and perhaps irrelevant to their troubles in the hard winter of 1776 and 1777. Military reverses led to diplomatic reverses and both produced a revaluation of their relations with Europe. They had to reckon with the mood of Vergennes, who paid more attention to continuing American defeats in the middle states and to the destruction of New England fisheries than he did to the theoretical benefits America was supposed to confer on the grateful Europeans. Even shipments of supplies arranged through Beaumarchais were discreetly stopped in the fall of 1776, as the

[10] Samuel Flagg Bemis, "British Secret Service and the French-American Alliance," *American Historical Review*, XXIX (April, 1924): 474–494, emphasizes the success of British spies in providing the North ministry with full information on American diplomacy in France. Van Alstyne, *Empire and Independence*, p. 118, claims British espionage was unnecessary. The ministry learned all it needed to know through merchants victimized by French and Spanish seizures of their ships.

French awaited an American collapse. Instead of repeating the conditions of the Model Treaty, American diplomatists began a hasty scaling down of their demands upon potential European benefactors.

There were now three Americans in France representing the foreign policy of the new republic, each of them sensitive to the disillusionment in France. They were prepared to go to considerable lengths to win back French confidence. Silas Deane went so far as to suggest the appointment of a French leader, Marshal Broglie, to command American armies and thus tie the French more closely to the American effort. Franklin, armed with the latest instructions of the Committee of Secret Correspondence, sailed for France in November, 1776, with full knowledge of the dependence of the United States upon sustained French assistance. He was empowered to offer American support to the reconquering of France's lost West Indian islands and a declaration of war on Portugal if such acts would bring France and Spain over to an open alliance. The latter had cooled considerably in its appetite for war when the crisis in Latin America subsided. So Arthur Lee, the third American in France, discovered when he crossed the Pyrenees in March, 1777, to press personally the case for alliance.

It was obvious that the Model Treaty devised by John Adams in the early summer of 1776 was obsolescent by the time the Congress adopted it in September. The summer's events had overtaken it. Such bargaining power that the United States now had was not in its discretion to present or withhold special privileges to one or another European country, but in its confession that the failure of France to make an alliance could produce reunion with Great Britain.

Despite the gloomy prognosis in the difficult year following the signing of the Declaration of Independence it would be an error to claim that either the Congress at home or the diplomatists abroad had abandoned all hope of survival. Franklin, the dominant envoy in France, recovered upon landing what little composure he had lost on the high seas, and immediately proceeded to hedge on the concessions Congress had permitted him to make in return for an alliance. Much of his sang-froid derived from his conviction that in the long run the American break with Britain was of itself sufficient to induce French intervention; the loss of the commercial monopoly in America was a crippling blow to British mercantile interests, and France had the opportunity to replace those interests with her own. Furthermore, Franklin realized that excessive impetuosity was poor tactics. America must negotiate from at least the appearance of strength. He opposed consequently Deane's shrill insistence on demanding an immediate answer of the French, or else threaten openly to make an accommodation with Great Britain. In the autumn of 1777, before learning of Burgoyne's defeat at Saratoga, Franklin could say calmly that "we shall derive resources from our distress, like the earth-born giant Antaeus, who derives strength from his falls." The Franco-American alliance of 1778 vindicated his faith.

Perhaps as much difficulty for the American commissioners arose from their own personal differences as from rebuffs they met at the hands of France and other European powers. There was ample excuse for strained tempers. The Continental Congress, itself a weak and uncertain source of authority, did nothing to relieve them. Although the Committee of Secret Correspondence, unlike other organs of the Congress, was able to act on its own initiative with the help of a separate payroll, it had no single locus of responsibility and was subjected to all the pains of government by committee—factionalism, inefficiency, and lack of direction.

The inadequacies of the central administration were directly accountable for the lamentable spectacle of the triad of American diplomats in France and later others wandering all over Europe uncertain of their assignments and jealous of their colleagues. The very choice of agents was the product of the kinds of pressures one would expect to be exerted upon the Congress. Silas Deane was a close business associate of Robert Morris, the most powerful single figure in both the Committee of Commerce and the Committee of Secret Correspondence. Arthur Lee owed his position less to his slender diplomatic talents than to his membership in the influential Lee family of Virginia, while Franklin arrived in Paris direct from seats in the Continental Congress and Committee of Secret Correspondence.

The personality differences, hazy responsibilities, and overlapping missions reflected the divisions within the Congress itself. Arthur Lee the radical was to balance Deane the moderate. Similarly, committees balanced each other, and frequently duplicated each other's work, as in the examples of the Committee of Secret Correspondence, the Committee for the Drafting of the Model Treaty, and the Committee of Commerce. Frequently the only escape from chaos was the presence of the same men on more than one of these committees, and even this was insufficient. Franklin ruefully recognized the dangers and frustrations of diplomacy in this situation in a lament to James Lovell, leading figure in the Committee of Foreign Affairs in 1778:

> Speaking of commissioners in the plural puts me in mind of inquiring if it can be the intention of Congress to keep *three* commissioners at this court. . . . But as to our number, whatever advantage there might be in the joint councils of three for framing and adjusting the articles of the treaty, there can be none in managing the common business of a resident here. On the contrary, all the advantages in negotiation that result from secrecy of sentiment and uniformity in expressing it and in common business from dispatch are lost. In a court, too, where every word is watched and weighed, if a number of commissioners do not every one hold the same language in giving their opinion on any public transaction, this lessens their weight.

The plight of the envoys of the United States was reminiscent of the troubles of the old colonial agents seeking to influence the British court, each identifying his own and his patron's welfare with the common welfare. While the new agents were not speaking for state interests specifically, they reflected biases and attitudes of competing political and economic sections of the country. The dangers potential in these tensions presented themselves most sharply in the quarrel between Deane and Lee over the Beaumarchais operation. It almost aborted the mission and did split the Congress into hostile factions. Elements of personal pride were fundamental. Arthur Lee from his London base had initiated dealings with Beaumarchais only to find that Deane was to replace him in the task. The Frenchman quickly dropped Lee as soon as he realized Deane's greater access to power and greater sophistication in matters commercial. Franklin having displaced Deane in turn was in a position to correct the political naïvete of the latter and the anti-French animus of the former. His own mild sympathies went out to the more personable Connecticut entrepreneur.

Lee, sensitive to French favoritism toward Deane, accused his rival of engaging in his own business ventures in France and using public funds to advance his enterprises. And the public funds supposedly misapplied related to the workings of Rodrigue Hortalez and Company. The question was whether the monies channeled through that bogus company were intended to be gifts or loans. Deane claimed that they were to be charged against the United States, while Lee insisted they were granted gratis, and assumed that Deane in some manner or other had profited from the arrangement.

That Deane was connected with entrepreneurs engaged in privateering operations out of French West Indian and European ports was undoubtedly true. He was closely associated with Robert Morris and those Philadelphia trading houses working in harmony with French counterparts. Whether this tie adds up to peculation is quite a different question; many of the leading Revolutionary figures in the United States saw no conflict of interest in securing financial advantages from their public positions. Deane's attitude toward Beaumarchais suggested that he had contempt for the business sense of the romantic Frenchman and had dealt with him solely because Gérard, undersecretary of state for foreign affairs, had designated the playwright as France's liaison agent with Americans. There is no proof that Lee's charges were valid. What counted was the success of the embittered Lee to win the attention of radicals in the Congress, notably the suspicious New Englanders who were willing to risk a damaging split in that body over the credibility of Lee's cause. When the divided Congress did not respond to Deane's demand for a hearing, he went over its head and pleaded his case to the press.

After his return to America in 1779 Deane did not stop with protestations of innocence. He proceeded to accuse the Lee partisans, who included Paine and John Adams among their number, of being pro-British and of seeking reconciliation with the mother country. Regrettably for French interests, the new minister, Gérard, who had accompanied Deane to Philadelphia, damaged Deane's credibility by supporting him against Lee. Gérard hoped to have John Jay, a certified moderate and friend of France, replace Lee on the commission. Ultimately Congress compensated Deane's estate for the costs of his services, but not before his estrangement from his own country which led him into a treasonable relationship with Britain before the war had ended.

So much for ironies. Much of this tale of course had significance after the signing of the French treaties. But this imbroglio was symptomatic of the trials of policymaking generally, and they applied to military and financial affairs as well as diplomatic. A logical solution would have been an administrative reorganization of the foreign office establishing clear lines of authority and responsibility. A stronger foreign office might have prevented the outbreak of the Deane-Lee feud and saved the careers of both men for further service to the nation. But such an arrangement assumes a different and presumably more centralized national government which would have run afoul of the emotions of those fearful of sapping the autonomy of the states. Not until a more conservative Congress emerged in 1780 was a Department of Foreign Affairs possible, and this was merely a halfway station toward a genuine Foreign Office.

When the long-awaited alliance finally matured on February 6, 1778, the virtues of all the negotiators—Deane and Lee as well as Franklin—triumphed over their administrative handicaps and personality defects. This happy outcome was abetted by the course of events in the war which justified Franklin's practice of refusing to play the suppliant before the French benefactor. On the contrary, the familiar gambit of a rapprochement with the British became all the more credible after news of the smashing American victory at Saratoga in October, 1777 found its way to Europe two months later. Vergennes was genuinely worried about British reaction to Burgoyne's disaster. It could create such panic that Britain might grant acceptable concessions to her former colonies. Consequently, the French foreign minister put the matter plainly to the Spanish king when he asked how he should deflect the American commissioners from further conversations with Lord Germain's agents: "If we dissuade them from listening, what shall we give them as an equivalent? Would it not be time to enter the breach and make an engagement?"

Vergennes seemed to have reason to be disturbed. The disclosures of Edward Bancroft, secretary of the American commissioners and a British spy, combined with the reports of Lord Stormont, had reinforced the complaints of British merchants about Franco-American collaboration in privateering and other activities in behalf of the new nation. Knowing the extent of their danger from a potential alliance the British finally determined to make a substantial bid for reconciliation before it was too late. But since the decision came after Saratoga it was already too late. Celebration of the capture of Philadelphia or of the defeat of Washington at Brandywine could not efface the symbolic importance of Saratoga to the American cause. Alliance with France quickly followed. French fears over Britain's counteroffers to America were as much an inducement for complete identification with the United States as American victory over the British army.

Franklin made the most of the distress of both parties. In asking the American commissioner if he could accede to reconciliation short of independence, British agents sensed that he was using the specter of a French alliance to force England to grant more favorable terms. At the same time, they knew that their conversations and Franklin's cryptic responses were being used to exacerbate French fears, and sweeten the terms of French assistance to the United States. In their view, what else could explain Deane's and Franklin's spurning of bribes? The North ministry was in a genuine dilemma. Opposition to conciliation had always been strong, as North recalled in 1775, and the new prospect of fighting France as well as the United States would only enlarge this opposition. When the alliance became known in England in March, no less a figure than Pitt himself expressed his anger over America's affiliation with Britain's traditional foe.

The inevitable conflict with France after the alliance stimulated North to override his own pessimism and brave the wrath of his enemies on the left and on the right by proposing a new plan of conciliation. On February 17, when the Franco-American alliance was only unofficially known in England, the prime minister offered to repeal the Tea Act and yield the exercise of the Parliament's right of taxation in exchange for simple regulation of trade. As for the internal affairs of the colonies, they would return to the normality of 1763.

What might have ended hostilities in 1775 would not suffice in 1778. Nothing less than complete independence would satisfy the United States. Not even the visions of Camden or Hartley, wherein Americans and Englishmen (with the former independent but fraternal) would reunite in a war against the Bourbons, could find a response in 1778. Still, Parliament, hoping to delay war with France and to divide the new allies, appointed peace commissioners to carry on negotiations with the colonies.

The commission of three men—the Earl of Carlisle, nominally the chairman; William Eden, one of the Lords of Trade and the real leader of the commission; and George Johnstone, ex-governor of Florida—had far broader powers than the Howe Commission of 1775. While insisting upon restoration of Loyalist properties and the redemption of colonial paper money, they could accept popular election of governors and veto of customs officials. Additionally, the Americans could have representation in Parliament. Their own Congress would have legal jurisdiction over American affairs. Tactfully, the commissioners could avoid the question of revoking the Declaration of Independence. It need not be announced publicly. So flexible were the instructions to the Carlisle Commission that they might have yielded on the matter of Parliament's official position on legislative supremacy.

It was all too late. The French alliance was being rapidly implemented at the time of their embarkation in mid-April, 1778, and the turn of events in the war had worsened their position upon their arrival in May. At Philadelphia they discovered that General Clinton, Howe's successor, was to evacuate the city. Psychologically it was a defeat of the first magnitude and was open to interpretation as an early fruit of the French connection. The Carlisle commissioners recognized immediately that there was little incentive for the United States to respond to their overtures.

Congress regarded the commission warily. Its president, Henry Laurens, halted his reading of its instructions when he came to the passage that referred to the "insidious interposition of a power" in Angloamerican affairs. The "power" of course was France. Having just ratified the terms of the alliance, Congress had no wish to risk an insult to its new partner. Thus America's answer was predictable to any observer in 1778. It was negative. Officially peace negotiations required Great Britain's formal acceptance of the Declaration of Independence and the withdrawal of British armies from America. Unofficially the great expectations arising from the new alliance might have doomed even a favorable British response to these terms. The mission ended in farce, with charges of bribery raised against one of the commissioners, George Johnstone, whose attempts to exert influence in the traditional fashion served merely to compromise himself.

While the presence of the Carlisle mission discomfited some Americans, the motives which had inspired it pointed to the accelerated success of the new republic. Without waiting for Spain, France had made her momentous decision in 1778. The belated flurry of British diplomacy had pushed her into hasty action. With very little strength behind them the American diplomatists in Paris had exacerbated the fears of both parties and made an important contribution to an impressive victory.

CHAPTER V

Independence Secured: The French Factor

☆ 1778-1783 ☆

FRANCE'S DECISION to make a formal alliance with the United States on terms so favorable to Americans was a bold and dangerous departure from the normal course of eighteenth-century statecraft. There were compelling reasons against such a step. The precedent of official, as opposed to informal, recognition of a republic was a serious matter for any monarchy to contemplate. Certainly Prussia, Russia, and Spain, each with some interests at stake in the American war, appreciated the dangers to all monarchies in the success of the American experiment. Although the powers may probe weaknesses within their rivals' domains by means of disaffected minorities, none would encumber itself with the kind of commitment France had made to the United States in 1778. Spain was willing to offer secret assistance to Americans in 1775, as Britain herself had done for Corsicans resisting France a few years before; but they all would draw the line at independence, especially when the new state would adopt a republican government.

France had other reasons for hesitation. American partnership in the expected war with Great Britain inspired little confidence. American military forces had been frequently invisible, the government chaotic, and the finances hopeless without major transfusions from French and other European sources. The vigorous opposition of Turgot to French entanglement with the United States as well as the abortive attempts of his successor, the Swiss banker Jacques Necker, to make peace later at America's expense, reflected the desperate condition of French finances. Could France afford a war even if victory were assured? And victory was not at all assured in 1778. No matter how embarrassing the American rebellion may have been to the British, their navy was in command of the seas. Another disaster of the order of the Treaty of Paris in 1763 was a distinct possibility.

An unexpected opportunity to acquire the Austrian Low Countries from Joseph II further complicated Vergennes' decision-making at this time. The Austrian emperor dangled these territories before the French court to induce its cooperation in his occupation of Bavaria against the wishes of Prussia. Aware of Britain's involvement in America and Russia's in Turkey, he hoped to secure twenty thousand troops from France and would pay handsomely for this assistance. Joseph had already won from the Elector's heir cession of part of Bavaria in return for recognition of the latter's claim to the rest of the country. News of the death of Maximilian Joseph reached Paris two days before the Royal Council was to meet on January 7, 1778, to conclude the alliance with the United States. Vergennes could not have both the Low Countries and the alliance, and he knew it. He turned his back on Joseph's temptation in order to assure a peaceful continent at his rear while he went ahead with his American plans. Austrian resentment was one penalty France would have to pay later for Vergennes' decision. Joseph blamed France for the Treaty of Teschen in 1779, at which he had to retreat from his Bavarian pretensions. Austria's subsequent interest in mediating between France and England was in part revenge for France's betrayal.

Vergennes' initiative was made in the face of the hostility of France's old ally, Spain, as well as her new ally, Austria. Earlier, under Grimaldi's indecisive leadership, Spain had flirted with the notion of war against Britain, and had made half-hearted gestures of aid to the American cause. The Spanish king had contributed half of the initial expenses of Beaumarchais' enterprise, and had dispatched an agent to Philadelphia to deal directly, though unofficially, with Americans. At one point in 1776 Grimaldi had even consented to France's request to use

New Orleans as a supply depot for colonial forces. The arrival to power of the Francophobic Count de Floridablanca and the ending of the crisis with Portugal in 1777 ended the close accord with France and the cautious patronage of Americans. Floridablanca was jealous of France and fearful of the United States. He foresaw none of the advantages for the Bourbons which the French had put forward so urgently. Instead he saw the vulnerability of Spanish possessions in America to both British and American designs and was determined to protect the monarchy from the dangerous blandishments of his ally. Against such convictions American attempts to woo Spain never had a chance. Arthur Lee had been rebuffed at the border even in Grimaldi's day, while Franklin's offer of aid in conquering Pensacola in return for free navigation of the Mississippi was left unanswered by the Spanish. France fared little better in 1777, although in the long run Vergennes was optimistic. He could always play on Spain's sensitivity about Gibraltar and on her obsession about British aggression in the Caribbean.

Spanish collaboration, therefore, was left for the future. In 1778 France acted alone. What then moved Vergennes to defy doubters at home and friends abroad on behalf of the new republic? Was it the familiar European eagerness for territorial advantage? This would be an unlikely motivation.[1] There is no reason to challenge the foreign minister's own disclaimers on the subject of territorial acquisition, or his acceptance of Article 6 of the Treaty of Alliance, in which "The Most Christian King renounces for ever the possession of the Islands of Bermudas as well as of any part of the continent of North America which before the Treaty of Paris in 1763, or in virtue of that Treaty, were acknowledged to belong to the Crown of Great Britain or to the united states . . ." Two years later when American military men, including Washington, would have welcomed any sort of French expeditionary force, the Count d'Estaing and the Marquis de Lafayette enthusiastically rallied to a Franco-American Canadian venture. While the excessive French ardor for the

[1] Two generations ago Edward S. Corwin, *French Policy and the American Alliance of 1778* (Princeton, 1916), p. 9, scoffed at Frederick Jackson Turner's suspicions, based on the suspect testimony of Manuel de Godoy, that Vergennes wanted to recover Canada and Louisiana.

project dampened Washington's interest, it is worth noting that neither Vergennes nor his minister to the United States gave their blessings to the Canadian campaign.

There was still the question of French ambitions in the West Indies, specifically encouraged in Article 7 of the treaty. It would not be unreasonable to assume that Vergennes would seek the return of the rich sugar islands of the West Indies in the event of victory over Britain. French concern for this region manifested itself in the concentration of French and Spanish naval forces in the Caribbean in 1777 and the subsequent role of the West Indies in French military thinking during the war. But were the West Indies objects in themselves, or were they means to a larger end? Vergennes was less interested in commercial or territorial gains than in a psychic recovery from the traumatic losses of 1763: revenge upon Britain and the reduction of her status in the world, and the corresponding establishment of France in Britain's place. Toward this end the survival of an independent United States, a patronized dependent but genuine beneficiary of French policy, was an essential ingredient. Van Alstyne considers that the point of no return in the formulation of this scheme may have been September, 1777, when French, Spanish, and British forces confronted each other in the Caribbean.[2] After that date the French alliance was only a matter of timing.

It was a matter of military fortune and diplomacy too. Although a case may be made for the relative unimportance of the victory at Saratoga compared with the inevitability of a clash in the Caribbean, the role of diplomacy was of vital significance in making Saratoga advance France's timetable of assistance to the United States.[3] At one and the same time Burgoyne's defeat in the woods of northern New York in September, 1777, indicated to the French that Americans could hold their own against British military forces and aroused fears among Vergennes' ministry that England would thereupon succumb to American terms for a rapprochement. The latter eventually would not only have rendered bankrupt France's investment in the American

[2] Van Alstyne, *Empire and Independence*, p. 133.

[3] This point is elaborated on in masterly fashion in Bemis, *Diplomacy of the American Revolution*, pp. 58–60.

cause over the past two years, but could also culminate in an Angloamerican assault on the Bourbon empires as a by-product of their reconciliation. Such hopes and fears informed French relations with America from the signing of the alliance to the signing of the peace treaty in 1783. The American envoys abroad exploited both throughout the next five years.

American diplomatists in Paris at this moment stoked Vergennes' apprehensions and embellished his nightmares, inducing him to forget the incompatibility between America's passion for complete independence and George III's stubborn determination never to yield on this point. Reflection on this fundamental conflict between America and Britain might have set his mind at rest. But he seemed obsessed with the possibility of a conciliatory Chatham replacing the North ministry and winning the respect of Americans. The American envoys did their best to deflect him from realizing that Chatham would, as he expressed it to Shelburne, "as soon *subscribe* to *transubstantiation*, as to *sovereignty* by right, in the colonies."

Franklin in particular capitalized on this sensitive issue. Talking with Gérard, the future French minister to the United States, he asserted that only France's entry into the war would stave off negotiations between the United States and Great Britain, which might conclude with a joint attack on France and Spain. So Vergennes reported to the king in his petition for action of January 7, 1778. When Gérard countered the next day with the hope of a peaceful solution to the problem of American independence, Franklin responded that only an immediate treaty of "commerce and alliance" would guarantee America's independence and nullify the prospects of a return to the British fold. It is noteworthy that the pace of Franco-American negotiations accelerated rapidly following the arrival of news about Saratoga in Paris on December 4, 1777.

Franklin's shrewdness in his secret negotiations with Britain had its effect. The latter's access to American diplomatic files from the double agent, Edward Bancroft, turned out to be another card in America's hand. The British may have had a complete inventory of French aid to the United States, "down to the last musket ball and bayonet . . . in the hold of the *Amphi-*

trite," as Julian Boyd points out; but they were never sure of Bancroft's integrity, and never sure how to exploit their information.[4] They were correct in their mistrust. Inadvertently the effects of the enormous amount of intelligence available to the ministry through secret agents were those of cleverly calculated leaks. Franklin's terms were so bold and his manner so assured that they wondered if a secret treaty with the French had been signed by the time of the Saratoga defeat. Paul Wentworth, chief British agent and confidant of William Eden, returned to London in January, 1778, without budging the Americans from their positions on independence or on evacuation of troops.

None of these unofficial negotiations, or even private correspondence with influential Englishmen, was kept from the French ministers. By the winter of 1778 the two European powers, each fully aware of the American game, had bid as high as their estimates of the politico-military situation would permit them. France won the prize at the cost of a generous alliance. While her gamble was riskier than Britain's, the price for America's hand was more acceptable than her rival's, which would have been nothing less than a massive transformation of her empire.

Franklin and his colleagues, working in reasonable harmony at this vital juncture, had played off one party against the other in the classic manner of Old World politics, but with the addition of New World symbols. The American commissioners were both guileful and guileless in their statecraft. They genuinely conceived themselves to be the bearers of a new style of national life. To sustain the precarious existence of their society they had to exploit traditional methods. So Franklin found that if the fur cap he had worn during the cold November voyage to Brittany in 1776 had converted him into a Rousseauan sage, he would continue to wear it in the warmer climate of the Paris salons. "Figure me in your mind as jolly as formerly, and as strong and hearty," he wrote in February, 1777, "only a few years older; very plainly dressed, wearing my thin grey straight hair that peeps out under my only coiffure, a fine fur cap, which comes down to my forehead almost to my spectacles. Think how

[4] Julian P. Boyd, "Silas Deane: Death by a Kindly Teacher of Treason," Part II, *William and Mary Quarterly*, Third Series, XVI (July, 1959): 326.

this must appear among the powdered heads of Paris." He played the game magnificently, enjoying it all the while.

Despite the pleasures of role-playing and pleasure-seeking, the Americans in Paris were doing more than using a different rhetoric to win a place for America in the old scheme of international society. Franklin and his fellow commissioners agreed on the objectives of the Model Treaty of 1776 as fully as John Adams himself. They saw as values in themselves the American effort to eliminate war, to promote free trade, and to ensure America from the failings of the outside world by limiting obligations to foreign nations as much as possible. Franklin may have been looking always for self-interest and the national interest in the policies he pursued, but as Gerald Stourzh noted, he retorted "characteristically,"[5] to a skeptic who felt that international disputes could be settled only by war: "Why not by mediation, by arbitration, or by considerate and prudent argument?" They retreated from the high ground of the Model Treaty only after the pressure of events, primarily France's reluctance to provide as much support as they had anticipated and the chronic failure of American arms to cope with British military power, had made a retreat mandatory.

If France and Spain would not assist Americans without entangling alliances the envoys were prepared to make this concession. The survival of the republic was at stake. Without specific authorization from the Committee of Secret Correspondence, the men on the scene took it upon themselves on February 2, 1777, to pledge to the French that

> if France or Spain should conclude a treaty of amity and commerce with our States, and enter into a war with Great Britain in consequence of that, or of open aid given to our States, it will be very right and proper for us, or in the absence of the others for any one of us, to stipulate and agree that the United States shall not separately conclude a peace, nor aid Great Britain against France or Spain, nor intermit their best exertions against Great Britain during the continuance of such war; provided always that France and Spain do on their part enter into a similar stipulation with our States.

[5] Gerald Stourzh, *Benjamin Franklin and American Foreign Policy* (Chicago, 1954), p. 259.

The appropriate synonym for these stipulations was military alliance.

What is significant about this declaration was not simply the initiative of the commissioners in exceeding their instructions from Congress, but the almost concurrent, and quite independent, action on the part of the Committee of Secret Correspondence, in recommending the concession of an alliance to the envoys. A little over a month before the commissioners had made their offer of a triple alliance, the committee had sent them instructions to do precisely what they had done without instructions.

The ultimate results of this practical decision were the two treaties of 1778 with France, signed on the same day, February 6, 1778. One of them, the Treaty of Amity and Commerce, appeared to realize the aims of the "new" diplomacy of the Model Treaty. The other, the Treaty of Alliance was a typical document of eighteenth-century diplomacy in which territorial promises were solemnized and military obligations undertaken. The two countries agreed that their "defensive alliance" included the securing of American independence, France's renunciation of all former continental possessions, and the mutual refusal of peace terms without consent of both parties.

The presence of "two diametrically opposed trends of thought" in these two treaties is a moot point.[6] The Treaty of Amity and Commerce, like the Model Treaty before it, implied a timeless concern for abstract rights for all nations. The doctrine of "free ships, free goods" is easily equated with freedom of the seas. Yet it is obvious that the commercial treaty was far better geared to extract immediate special advantages for the United States than it was to serve as a blueprint for some maritime utopia of the future. The details of commercial links to follow from the treaty may have been portents of a better way of international life. They were also of practical service to a small mercantile power that hoped to profit from trade with belligerents of the Old World. In this light the differences between the Treaty of Commerce and the Treaty of Alliance begin to

[6] Gilbert, *To the Farewell Address*, p. 104.

blur; they were both designed to exploit the French connection for the national advantage. They were both successful. Granting that it would have been preferable if the second treaty had been unnecessary, the commissioners and the nation alike recognized that their world of 1778 was something less than ideal. They acclaimed the treaties, both treaties, and rightly so.

American expectations from the French alliance in the spring of 1778 were as high as their mood of exhilaration. This commitment should open immediate warfare between Great Britain and France, a cornucopia of financial aid and military assistance, and the dispatching of a large army of French soldiers to America to complete the defeat of the enemy. Some of the optimists in Congress of 1776, who had counted on full French involvement without full American reciprocation, revived their earlier hopes. The alliance appeared to make imminent all they wanted: western boundaries at the Mississippi, free navigation of that river and a port facility at its mouth, fishery rights off the Banks of Newfoundland, and possession of all of Canada. France's military might combined with her abjuring of territorial pretensions should permit these fruits to fall at minimal obligation to France's client. Once they were won France would depart, her mission accomplished. This was the meaning Samuel Adams gave to the words of French Minister Plenipotentiary Gérard, whom he credited with saying, ". . . whenever Great Britain should acknowledge our Independence, there would be an end of dispute between her and us, and it would not be the inclination as it was not the interest of France to continue the war."

In early 1778 everything seemed possible. Vergennes purposely tried to project France as the friend of the small powers and the friend of the neutral rights. France's modest requests for herself in the treaties were designed to lend credence to this image. They did. The inevitable war between Great Britain and France fulfilled one major American expectation. If that consequence of the treaty could take place so quickly, the others might be realized just as easily. Actually, the declaration of war could have come at any time, since Britain, as has been noted, was aware of every step toward the alliance, and knew equally well that the signing of an alliance was the equivalent of a French declaration of hostilities. Not that France confided to Whitehall the fact of the alliance; she had no need to do so. If the British postponed the conventional reply to French provocations, it was in the vain hope that a striking military victory or a dramatic reconciliation with the colonies might stay France's hand. These considerations no longer applied after February, 1778, despite the Carlisle mission to America. Great Britain declared war on March 17, 1778, upon formal notification from the French ambassador in London that France had concluded a commercial treaty with the United States.

American visions of triumph were much too grandiose. They were surprising, too, since many of the men who projected them were the hard-headed radicals of the John Adams persuasion who had earlier averred that France would serve America only to serve herself. What they should have appreciated were the obvious limits to the usefulness of America in France's foreign policy as well as the limits of France's abilities to advance American interests. Before the year 1778 was over, disillusionment had set in on both sides. And since the level of emotions and the stakes in the outcome of the alliance were greater for America, the feelings of disappointment were correspondingly keener.

The vaunted French military and naval forces were the first casualty of American credulity. A French naval force at Toulon under Admiral Charles Hector d'Estaing had been chafing for lack of action, and accordingly looked forward to war with England and a challenge to Lord Howe's ships in American waters. When war came d'Estaing departed immediately for Philadelphia, along with the recalled American commissioner, Deane, and the French minister, Gérard. The British Admiralty, fearing an attack on Gibraltar or on Britain itself, was immobilized for the moment by uncertainty and permitted the French flotilla to cross the Atlantic unmolested. D'Estaing had the additional advantage of the decline in British morale in America as a consequence of the recent evacuation of Philadelphia.

None of these assets served the French admiral. Instead of taking on the smaller British force in New York, he found his ships too big to pass the bar at Sandy Hook. He then moved on to Rhode Island where he refused American importunities to capture the British garrison at Newport. Subsequently he sailed for Boston for refitting, to meet a predictably chilly response from the local inhabitants. By the end of the summer of 1778 d'Estaing's opportunities for successful combat had ended. The British navy received sufficient reinforcements to retain its superiority in the western Atlantic, and d'Estaing retired to the West Indies for the winter.

America's performance was no better than that of her ally's. Neither the Continental Army nor the state militias were prepared to coordinate their forces with d'Estaing's either in the aborted siege of New York or in the unsuccessful siege of Newport. General John Sullivan in command of Continental and militia troops blamed his own failure to mobilize Rhode Island militiamen on the ally. D'Estaing was equally quick to place the blame on Sullivan. This dismal beginning to Franco-American military cooperation obscured the very real early dividend from the alliance in the British evacuation of Philadelphia, secured before d'Estaing had arrived in the United States.

Fortunately, American leadership had not lost all sense of proportion. Congressional awareness of dependence upon France helped to mute some of the resentment, and even led to apologies for and by Sullivan after his impolitic outbursts against the French. The old dreams survived. In the fall of 1778 the newly organized Committee of Foreign Affairs attempted to convince the ally to provide massive support for the final reduction of British power on the continent, including such posts as Quebec and Halifax, in exchange for substantial American sharing of fisheries and fur trade. The American planners were convinced that the West Indies would be exposed to easy conquest once their access to supplies from the mainland was shut off. Hence, if a sizable body of French soldiers accompanied by an impressive naval presence were made available to the American cause, the allies could bring the war to an end on most favorable terms. To expedite this objective, the United States would invite Spain to join once again, with recovery of the Floridas as bait. All of these proposals went directly from the committee in Philadelphia to the American commissioners in Paris. The latter now included John Adams, successor to Deane. The tone and content of the instructions were reminiscent of Adams' optimism of two years before.

The reasoning behind these hopes proved faulty again, although in the long run France finally conceded to America a considerable portion of its expectations for the minimal price Americans had always wanted. But in 1779 Vergennes was in no position as well as in no mood to accept such advice from his American client. He did not even reply to Franklin's overtures on the subject. He was out of sympathy with most of the committee's program for a number of reasons. In the first place the Canadian adventures desired by many Americans, ranging from New England radicals to the moderate Franklin, had never aroused his interest. On the contrary, he notified Gérard before the minister's departure from France that it was in the interest of France to see Canada remain in England's hands, since it would make Americans "feel to an even greater extent the need which they have for the friendship and alliance with the King." Second, Vergennes was uneasy over the role of John Adams in the American Commission. He was exercised in particular over Adams' bumptious stand on the future of North American fisheries, which he felt conflicted potentially with France's own fishing rights. Three years later, Chevalier de la Luzerne, Gérard's successor, revealed France's concern in a message to Vergennes recommending that France invade Cape Breton Island if necessary to exclude American claims at the peace conference. Indeed, one of the grievances troubling Vergennes about Great Britain's remarkable concessions in its preliminary negotiations in 1782 with the Americans was her sacrifice of France's exclusive rights affirmed by the United States in the Treaty of Commerce of 1778.

The most painful of the American importunities, however, concerned the western boundaries and navigation of the Mississippi River. Although it did not affect the vital interests of France, it struck at the heart of Spain's fundamental fears about the American connection. French consciousness of Spanish sensitivity about American war aims developed into the major trial of Gérard's mission in 1779. Instructed to protect Spain's American stakes at a time when Vergennes was anxious to push the Spanish king into the war, he had to perform this service without guidance from the Spanish themselves, without knowing in advance Spain's specific conception of her own interest. Basically Spain's objective was to win security from fear that Americans would intrude into her territories in the course of hostilities with Great Britain. Even if the United States did not immediately threaten Louisiana, her presence on the east bank of the Mississippi and her demands for navigational privileges on that river were unpleasant omens of the future. George Rogers Clark's expedition to the Northwest on behalf of Virginia in 1778 signalized American ambitions, but it was not until after the Franco-American alliance that Floridablanca became fully aroused over American claims. His anxieties increased as the war progressed, keeping French diplomats under constant pressure to sacrifice the interests of their new ally for the sake of the Bourbon Compact.

There was no question of priority on France's part. She could scarcely wage war alone for very long, and required Spain's naval and financial assets to achieve her own objectives. Thus Don Juan de Miralles, the Spanish agent in Philadelphia, had a powerful lever in his knowledge that France valued Spain more highly than she did the United States in the struggle with Great Britain. Gérard tried unsuccessfully to allay his suspicions about America, pointing out that the states had reasonable claims to the back country along the river. Vergennes tried his hand at soothing the Spanish by suggesting that republican states were too autonomous to unite and too weak to pose a threat to Spanish territories. When Spanish officials in Philadelphia and in Madrid refused to abandon their fixed positions on American expansion, France was not disposed to argue. Eventually France adopted Spain's own claims to the territories east of the Mississippi and would not interpret Article 11 of the Franco-American Treaty of Alliance to include territories west of the Alleghenies.

France's reward for her persistence was the secret Convention of Aranjuez in 1779, wherein Spain joined France in the war against Great Britain with a guarantee that there would be no suspension of hostilities until Gibraltar had been restored. The convention was preceded by a mock mediation offer which neither Vergennes nor Floridablanca expected to succeed, or even to be taken seriously. By that time Spain's war manoeuvers in the Caribbean and the planning of a Franco-Spanish invasion of England were earnest enough of Spain's real intentions.

In all these secret parlays American interests were disregarded. Not only was France unable to induce Spain to commit herself also to American independence before laying down arms, but she knowingly altered her own commitment to the United States by acceding to Spanish adamancy. Similarly the Spanish ultimatum to the British contained much too generous a solution to the American problem. It revealed the position Spain was to maintain toward the United States throughout the war. Canada would remain British so that a permanent source of friction would remain to divide the United States and Britain. With respect to the British presence in the thirteen states, the principle of *uti posseditis* was recommended, which would leave the enemy in possession of New York as well as other vital areas in 1779. About the only agreeable aspect from the American point of view was an assurance of American independence, and this would be de facto only as far as Spain was concerned. In fact, Bemis notes that even the de facto status during peace negotiations and the phrasing of "American colonies" went no further than the language of the Carlisle commission.[7] What Floridablanca wanted in effect was, as Richard Morris observed, the identification of the American states as "feudal dependencies of England, holding a relationship to George III very much like the states of the Empire did to the court at Vienna," where anarchic internal relations with sister states and hostile external ties with the former mother country would render the new nation impotent.[8]

Most of these nuances went unrecognized in the United States in 1779. Congress still hoped for recognition from Spain to accompany cobelligerency without knowing of the compromises France had made to entice the Spanish into the conflict. Reluctant though the French frequently were to jeopardize American war aims, their collaboration with the Bourbon part-

[7] Bemis, *Diplomacy of the American Revolution*, p. 172.

[8] Richard B. Morris, *The Peacemakers: The Great Powers and American Independence* (New York, 1965), p. 45.

ner inevitably affected their diplomatic relations with Americans. And for the worse. Gérard's primary function came to be the limitation of American objectives in such a way as to conform to Spanish wishes. Even if the Americans did not know the full extent of their problem with Spain, his was a difficult assignment. He made it all the more difficult for himself by his subsequent meddling in the domestic politics of the United States, which he generally misinterpreted, by his protectiveness toward his personal investments in western lands which distorted his views of state claims to the Northwest, and by his reliance upon jaundiced advisers, such as Daniel Jenifer of Maryland who frequently gave him misleading information.

Gérard made the mistake of dividing by region the friendly pro-French southern and middle states from the anti-Gallican north, leaving no room in this simplistic division for the position of Virginia and of Arthur Lee and their dislike of Spanish policies in the west. Gérard's unhappiest moment in his brief tenure was his involvement in the Deane-Lee affair on the side of the Connecticut businessman. By leaking the French government's negative opinion of Lee to friendly congressmen he helped to bring Lee down and at the same time made implacable enemies of such suspicious New Englanders as the Adamses and John Lovell, a leading figure in the Committee of Foreign Relations. If there had been no anti-French bloc in the Congress on his arrival in Philadelphia, Gérard's inept handling of the Lee-Deane controversy helped to create one before his departure. His service, terminated by illness after little over a year in America, was a disappointment, rather than a failure, given the high hopes he had brought with him at the outset of his mission. He never appreciated that the French alliance had the support of many groups besides merchants and moderates, and that they all required cultivation.[9]

With all his shortcomings Gérard had been able to assert French influence in Congress. His strong opposition to John Adams as Lee's successor in France and his championship of John Jay of New York, undoubted conservative and reputed friend of France, led to a compromise in which Jay was given

[9] William C. Stinchcombe, *The American Revolution and the French Alliance* (Syracuse, 1969), p. 46, makes a useful contribution to this issue.

the Spanish post and Adams made sole minister plenipotentiary to negotiate a peace treaty with Great Britain. Both sides of the dispute assumed that Spain would be the more important post, perhaps even the scene of negotiations; and that the recall of Lee and the appointment of Jay, a supporter of Deane, was essentially a victory for the middle states and the French cause. This was not to be the case. Jay in Spain developed suspicions of France as strong as Adams had ever held, while Adams as the American representative in Paris was to be a comfort to New Englanders worried about the fate of fisheries and about Philadelphia's dangerous subservience to France. Vergennes had to console himself with the continued presence in Paris of Benjamin Franklin as the sole American minister to that country in place of the triumverate.

Although the French would have preferred Franklin in Adams' place, they were responsible for creating the occasion of the New Englander's appointment. They had pressed Congress to have a peace commissioner empowered to present American terms in the event of British capitulation or of some success in the Spanish mediation. Congress obliged by setting the American conditions, but they were not the ones Gérard had been pressing for. He had informed Robert Morris, then secretary of the Committee of Foreign Relations, that France and Spain wanted a Congressional resolution condemning any state that sought to extend its borders beyond specific limits. The instructions to Adams, however, repudiated in effect this kind of thinking. The *sine qua non* were: independence, the Mississippi River as the western boundary, and the 31st parallel as the southern boundary on the West Florida frontier. The instructions to Jay en route to Spain expanded on this theme; the Spanish were to confirm the above-mentioned boundary plan and to show their approval by acceding to the Franco-American alliance.

Still, the sense of confidence and national pride that inspired these instructions did not indicate a conscious repudiation of Gérard or of the ties with France. Gérard accomplished a number of the assignments given him. The delicate fisheries problem was removed from America's peace terms as a prerequisite of negotiation, in spite of New England's pressures. Nor were the

Floridas or Canada named among American claims in 1779. Gérard was able to leave an America loyal to the alliance and responsive, if not subservient, to French views.

The diplomatic jockeying between the allies in 1778 and 1779 disclosed general agreement in America over what were the vital issues for the new nation. Unqualified independence was to be the touchstone of all her relations with the outside world. To this precondition all groups subscribed. The peace terms also revealed that the rival land claim did not exacerbate interstate jealousies or bring to the surface selfish private speculations among prominent congressmen, at least not at this time. It was enough for the moment that they could agree on the Mississippi as the natural boundary for the United States. Such sectional jealousies as arose in 1779 pertained to New England's overriding solicitude for fishery rights and the southern states' pressure for navigation rights on the Mississippi. But even these sore points failed to dent the remarkably firm front America was able to present to her French ally.

When internal conflict did erupt in the course of the war, there was the temptation, to which Gérard yielded, to cast the parties in ideological molds. Thus both French ministers tended to find a Francophilic spirit among moderates who feared the social revolution which might accompany independence from Great Britain, and looked upon aristocratic France as an anchor against such violence. Robert Livingston and John Jay of New York appeared to be men of this persuasion. On the other side, they labeled as radical those Americans, mainly from New England, who were hostile to France's advice and suspicious of her intentions. Radicals seemed to want a social order as well as a political order in which Europe would play no part. While Gérard and Luzerne were not wholly mistaken in their evaluation of Francophilism or of Francophobia, they were deluded by a monistic conception of pressure groups in America. The making of a Francophobe or a Francophile had no clearcut social or regional or economic or philosophic base. The division over the merits of the Deane-Lee dispute crossed all the lines. If the majority of Deane's enemies were also anti-French, it was because Lee's paranoia had identified the Connecticut merchant with Beaumarchais' plotting and with Franklin's complaisant relations with Vergennes. Gérard then made the equation more solid by his open espousal of Deane's position.

What is in question was the free use of such evocative terms as "radical" or "moderate." Adams' radicalism was hardly that of a social revolutionary and his expansionism had little to do with democracy. His interests were those of his region, and of his nation, which he felt to be compromised by the way the French connection was unfolding. Adams was far closer in his views on politics and society to such moderates as Robert Morris. And the latter's own friendship to France was definitely finite, secured by the absence of conflict over fisheries or western boundaries on the Mississippi and by a corresponding resentment over New England's or the south's anxieties over their respective preserves. The moderate could afford to be realistic about the benefits of the French alliance as long as there was no immediate conflict of interest with French objectives. All the participants in the debate over France shared an insistence upon independence and none of them would have accepted the categories the French observers wanted to put them into. The hand that wrote the committee report on peace ultimata which demanded absolute and unlimited independence in government and commerce as preconditions belonged to none other than Gouverneur Morris, an identifiable "moderate." In sum, the distinctions between the two become too blurred to be meaningful for more than a brief time.

Although the year 1779 was the high-water mark of radical strength during the alliance, as William Stinchcombe maintains, and the peace terms the symbol of this strength, some serious qualifications should be appended.[10] It is true that radical power was to wane in subsequent years with leaders of the order of Samuel Adams returning to their state governments discouraged over the state of the confederation. But if "radical" was the appropriate description for this faction, was their loss of power in the Congress explained by the superior influence of the financiers of the middle states? Or did it succumb to the wiles of French statecraft? Perhaps the best explanation for the increasing ascendancy of France over the councils of Congress

[10] *Ibid.*, p. 75.

lay not in the political shrewdness of the moderates but in the painful recognition that the ultimate success of the Revolution depended on the good graces of the French patron. This awareness came to moderate and radical alike; service in Philadelphia where one could not be unaware of the near bankruptcy of the American war effort after 1780 was a unifying force in molding attitudes toward France. American diplomats in France, whatever their presumed affiliations may have been, were under much less constraint, and accordingly were far more independent than the men in Congress. For the latter, he who paid the piper called the tune.

The paymaster was Chevalier de la Luzerne, a diplomatic novice but an experienced military officer, who made the ministry in Philadelphia a more effective instrument for the carrying out of France's policy than had his more professional but ill-starred predecessor, Gérard. Flanked by the able assistants François de Barbé-Marbois and Louis-Guillaume Otto, he was able to buy, threaten, or wheedle into relative subservience the Congresses of 1781 and 1782 and the new secretary of foreign affairs, Robert R. Livingston. Luzerne even claimed credit for the appointment of Livingston, a considerable achievement—though not wholly accurate—since Livingston was able to operate a foreign office with a greater freedom than the defunct Committee of Foreign Affairs had enjoyed earlier. Only letters dealing with "great national objects" would have to be examined by Congress. Luzerne's success with Livingston was the result of a combination of assiduous flattery and a common conception of their respective national interests. Perhaps also the overt selfishness and bad manners of the New England enemies of France made Livingston the more receptive to the reasoning of the French minister.

The fruits of Luzerne's warm association with Livingston were to be more modest than Luzerne himself ever admitted, but in general Luzerne's labors in America were a triumph for the man and his country. He had many factors working for him. Among them were the American reaction to reports of a new and large expeditionary force France was dispatching under General Rochambeau, the entry of Spain into the war, and the ending of the Deane-Lee imbroglio, all of which coincided with his arrival in the United States in 1779. The lesson of France's experience with Arthur Lee proved to be useful to Luzerne, who never allowed himself to forget the unfortunate impact it had had upon Franco-American relations. He ignored the instructions of Vergennes to have the troublesome Adams removed from his post for fear of reviving the emotions of the Lee partisans. By realizing that there was no anti-French conspiracy in Congress, he was able to make himself persona grata with most of the factions in that body. His policy of gentle persuasion accomplished his purpose. Long before the war had ended, Congress had effectively turned over the direction of American foreign policy to the French ally.

Powerful as Luzerne's personality was, his success was due neither to charm nor to intrigue. Money explains much of it. From the beginnings of his tenure in Philadelphia he had made a point of emphasizing the necessity of France's financial assistance to the republic and its leaders, partly as a tool of influence, partly to relieve the desperate state of America's economy. His own government, faced with equally difficult financial problems, refused to promise an annual subsidy, but continued to maintain a steady flow of gifts and loans. From 1781 to the end of 1782 France supplied a subsidy of six million livres each year in addition to the expenditure in America of sixteen million livres for the upkeep of the French military and naval forces. The total amount reached an estimated forty-eight million livres, an impressive and indispensable prop to the hard-pressed Americans. Luzerne himself had some access to funds which he put to good use. Over the war years the influential voices in the press and pulpit of Reverend Samuel Cooper, Hugh Henry Brackenridge, and Thomas Paine were rewarded with French gold for their efforts in publicizing the virtues of the French ally. They produced a significant number of articles with the liberal encouragement of both Gérard and Luzerne: Brackenridge with forty-three articles over an eighteen-month period, Cooper with twelve in six months, and Paine with special contributions late in the war. As Stinchcombe phrased it, ". . . the primary sources of news for a majority of the public was the Patriot press, and they read, much of the time, what the French Minister wanted them to read."[11]

Although Luzerne embellished his own role in his correspondence with Vergennes, he had reason for pride in his achievements. Even events apparently harmful to the allied cause proved to be of service to France. For example, Virginia, the home of the Lee family, had been associated with Massachusetts in leading opposition to French influence from the beginning of the alliance. Tension from this hostility lessened noticeably when the south became the major scene of British military operations against America. The fall of Charleston to Cornwallis in 1780 and Arnold's burning of Richmond in 1781 gave Virginians an appreciation of the French ally that had been lacking previously. So complete was the change in Virginia that the inadequacies in France's help—the failure of General Detouches' force to penetrate the British-controlled Chesapeake and the disappointing size of Rochambeau's reinforcements—failed to shake that state's new confidence in the ally. Instead it dramatized the extent of Virginia's dependence upon French aid.

Luzerne exploited American weakness, doing whatever he could to intensify the sense of dependence. He strengthened the hand of Congress whenever possible against the states, particularly those with Francophobic tendencies, and he made special efforts to keep friends in states sympathetic to France. As a consequence of this policy Maryland was the beneficiary of an emergency loan to its treasury and a welcome appearance of a French fleet in the Chesapeake at a time when the future of the Articles of Confederation was at stake. The French minister did his part in making a confederation a reality, since a stronger central body than the old Continental Congress, with authority to dispose of western territories, presumably would be susceptible to French control.

Congress was aware of Luzerne's activities and, given the critical conditions of 1780 and 1781, it was grateful for them. Everything else seemed to have gone wrong in this period. In America the British were making important territorial gains in

[11] *Ibid.*, p. 132.

Georgia and the Carolinas, were threatening to take over Virginia, and remained firmly at their base in New York without serious resistance from either French or American troops. In Europe Vergennes was sufficiently discouraged by the sluggishness of America's war effort, by the inconstancy of her Spanish ally, and by the imminence of bankruptcy in his own country that he was ready to accept outside mediation on the basis of the principle of *uti posseditis* in North America. To effect this solution to the war without technical violation of the Treaty of 1778, the American peace commissioner would have to be carefully controlled. John Adams would have to be disarmed and the peace instructions of 1779 changed.

Luzerne's most conspicuous achievement was to convince a cowed Congress to change the terms of the instructions to the American commissioner it had formulated in 1779. At that time of relative optimism Adams was to have governed himself in all matters not specifically presented "by the alliance between His Most Christian Majesty and these States, by the advice of our allies, by your knowledge of our interests, and by your own discretion, in which we repose the fullest confidence." These pious generalities were not good enough for Vergennes when the man he would have to deal with in the event of an Austro-Russian mediaton had the intractable personality of John Adams. Luzerne responded to this challenge by playing shrewdly on the unpopularity of the outspoken New Englander, feeding suspicions that Adams would be more likely to sacrifice southern-state interests than he would French interests if he had a chance. He succeeded in having Congress by-pass the Committee of Foreign Affairs, dominated by James Lovell of Massachusetts, and appoint an ad hoc committee under the chairmanship of the elderly and moderate John Witherspoon of New Jersey.

This committee promptly boxed in Adams with new instructions which minimized chances of personal independence. Instead of being guided by the "advice of our allies," he would be required "to undertake nothing in the negotiations for peace or truce without their knowledge and concurrence." Luzerne was not yet content. He asked for and received an addendum spelling out Adams' duty that obligated him to be guided by French "advice and opinion."

Note that Adams was no longer alone in his mission. Even bound and gagged he was not to be entrusted with the commission by himself. Originally Luzerne had suggested the advisability of adding two commissioners, although the exact number did not bother him. Congress complied with the selection of a balanced slate of five men, representing a good part of the national spectrum. Of the distinguished new members—Franklin, Jefferson, Jay, and Laurens—only Laurens had an anti-Gallican reputation.

All of these changes were made quickly and with large majorities. Instead of eight months of the sharp internecine combat in the Congress that preceded the instructions of 1779, the changes of 1781 occurred within a week's time after little debate. Virginia restricted its negative commentary to questions about the trans-Appalachian west. The relatively concerted New England bloc dissolved under the impact of the sudden conversion of John Sullivan of New Hampshire, who presented himself as a vigorous partisan of France after his early hostility. Luzerne's special attentions to Sullivan were repaid in full. In the final tally a handful of New Englanders stood apart from the rest of the nation in their opposition to the new stringent wording of the peace instructions.

Because of humiliations at home and his rebuffs abroad, Adams was tempted to resign from his post. Congress did not even allow him to retain his special commission to conclude a commercial agreement with Great Britain, an authority cherished by New Englanders who felt that whatever else might happen, Adams could preserve American access to the fisheries. The arguments of his friends Lovell and Elbridge Gerry and his wife, Abigail, prevailed. Adams remained in Europe to serve as a watchdog for his own idea of American interests. The fact that he remained at his post might well have been a factor in mitigating the vehemence of New England's reactions to the events in Philadelphia in 1781.

If this is true, faith in Adams did not go unrewarded. In fact, the peace commission collectively revealed themselves to be watchdogs of a policy neither Congress nor France approved once they engaged Europe at the conference table and in clandestine sessions. Two of the five never reached the firing line: Jefferson withdrew because of his wife's illness, and Henry Laurens was captured en route to Holland, and not released until most of the work of the commission had been completed. The remaining three—Jay, Adams, and Franklin—on balance operated smoothly as a team in speaking for a nation, rather than for regions or factions.

It was hardly surprising that while the congressmen might propose, the commissioners disposed. Time, distance, and rapidly changing circumstances all conspired to permit a freedom of action whose results they knew instinctively Congress would accept. After all, the Congress of an insecure confederation was not a formidable adversary any more than it was a useful protector. Although it may not have appeared that way in 1871, Luzerne had won a Pyrrhic victory. The optimism emanating from the Franco-American victory at Yorktown, won less than six months after the instructions were rewritten, loosened Congressional bonds and revealed the essential limits of French authority over America. The United States may have been a client of France, but was scarcely a satellite. The commissioners could pursue their own course without excessive fear of retribution. In this their experience differed strikingly from that of their predecessors, the colonial agents.

Their course before Yorktown, however, was far from clear; and what little of it was visible to them presented a dismal aspect. Adams in France as sole negotiator had felt himself to be utterly useless, since Vergennes found him personally obnoxious. He departed for the Netherlands in 1780 to see if he could secure enough financial assistance from the Dutch to reduce America's dependence on France. Although he was finally successful in persuading Amsterdam bankers to provide help, he was initially frustrated by Holland's anxiety to avoid a war with England that would endanger the profitable contraband trade with America, and by the refusal of France to encourage the Dutch to accommodate the United States. Holland persisted in her refusal to make a treaty with the United States long after the British had forced her into the war late in 1780. It is a fitting irony, therefore, that an illegal agreement between a delegate of the Burgomaster of Amsterdam and an informal American agent—William Lee, brother of Arthur—embodying a draft of a treaty similar to the Franco-American Treaty of Commerce should have been the occasion for the entry of the Netherlands into the war. This document, written without authorization by two "dilettante diplomatists," as Bemis calls them, was seized from the same ship that was carrying Laurens to Holland and became a *casus belli* for Great Britain.[12]

John Jay in Spain fared as badly as Adams did in France and Holland. In one respect his experience was worse: the expectations of a Spanish accession to the Franco-American alliance, for which there was a secret provision in the pact, were greater. He shared Adams' sense of rejection at the hands of European diplomatists and was accordingly resentful at his exclusion from the mysteries of European cabinet politics. Floridablanca gave Jay just enough evidence of his awareness of America's interests to keep the envoy from leaving the country in disgust, but not much beyond that. For the Spanish minister, Jay's presence in 1780 was a useful pawn in his elaborate intrigues with Britain to end the war and still regain Gibraltar. Presumably, if the British terms were unreasonable, he could always threaten to move closer to the United States. Not that this feint was ever intended seriously. No matter what Floridablanca might tell British agents he had no intention of granting even formal recognition to the American republic. Occasional patronizing donations of money to Jay could not conceal this truth from the American diplomatist for very long.

Against this setting American ministers abroad were tempted, and frequently succumbed to the temptation, to adopt "militia diplomacy." By abandoning conventional protocols and pursuing recognition aggressively they sought to win by bravado what they had failed to win by tact. Franklin was firmly opposed to this strategy, having warned Arthur Lee as early as 1777 that "a virgin state should preserve its virgin character and not go suitoring for alliances, but wait with decent dignity for the application of others." Besides, this strategy had been tried in Berlin, Vienna, and Turin, and had failed in each instance. But lacking other alternatives militia diplomacy was preferable to passivity in the mind of the impatient John Adams. With the blessings of

[12] Bemis, *Diplomacy of the American Revolution*, p. 158.

Congress he continued his search for counterweights that would free the nation from France as much as from England.

The emergence of the League of Armed Neutrality in 1780 looked to be the answer to the problem of the activists. Dominated by Catherine II of Russia, the League was composed of Russia, Denmark, Sweden, Portugal, Austria, and the Two Sicilies. Its program, centered on the liberal interpretations of neutral rights that would protect small neutrals in their enjoyment of the belligerent carrying trade, was especially appealing to Americans. Since the major antagonist and fundamental object of the League was British sea power, French diplomacy quietly and carefully cultivated the League as a weapon of war. Into this expanding web the United States blundered boldly in the person of John Adams' secretary, Francis Dana of Massachusetts. Congress sent him on a mission to St. Petersburg to extract recognition from Russia and membership from the League, although the latter objective would be difficult for a country that was anything but neutral at that moment in history.

The result was failure again for American diplomacy. Unable to speak either Russian or French, Dana spent two lonely years in St. Petersburg enduring the hostility of the British, the wariness of the French, and the indifference of the Russians. Catherine was no enemy of America; she foresaw independence, or at least separation from the mother country, as inevitable. But Russia was fencing with her former ally and did not want the intrusion of the American issue to upset her balance. Looking ahead to a position as mediator in the war Catherine refused to receive Dana in any official capacity. Furthermore, Russia's dependence upon British markets was hardly an inducement to risk a break for the sake of the United States. Dana did not understand these considerations.

The League never developed into anything more than the "Armed Nullity" of Catherine's description. Its failure to protect the Netherlands from British attack illustrated its weakness as a check on Great Britain's mastery of the seas. The maritime powers confessed defeat when they denied the Netherlands admission to the League although they knew that the British had forced the Dutch into war precisely for the purpose of exposing the League's impotence. Still, France did not regard the League as an unmitigated failure. It revealed how the old Russo-British ties could be loosened, and dramatized Britain's isolation in Europe. Above all, it laid the groundwork for a Russian offer of mediation in the Anglo-French war that both belligerents could accept. As for the United States, armed neutrality had lost its value once peace negotiations had begun. At the war's end in 1783 Secretary Livingston advised that Dana's instructions on applying had been limited to the duration of the war. Congress terminated the flirtation by resolving against any tie with a "neutral confederacy" that would entangle the United States in European politics.

It was France's anticipation of Russian mediation—joined by a less welcome Austrian bid—that accounted for Vergennes' insistence upon new American peace instructions in 1781. He recognized that if a detente should be reached in Vienna, it might have required the United States to terminate her war with British troops still left on American soil, with the new nation cut off from her western claims, and with something less than unequivocal admission of independence by England. Hence the need for compliant American envoys and more pliable instructions for them.

The Austro-Russian mediation never came to pass. The end of Spain's dalliance with England over a separate peace and the success of Franco-American arms at Yorktown made mediators superfluous. Britain and France would find their own path to the peace table, each with reservoirs of bargaining power to give them confidence in a diplomatic victory. What France failed to comprehend was that the United States would also choose a private path to a peace treaty. Firsthand encounters with European statecraft had estranged them from the Francophilic mood of Congress, and distance from Philadelphia encouraged a freedom from Congressional control that made a mockery of Luzerne's mastery over the Congress.

Militia diplomacy finally accomplished what orthodox statecraft had been unable to achieve: a breakthrough in the European conspiracy to ignore America and the successful pitting of Great Britain against France. It was fitting that John Adams, the *bête noir* of Vergennes, should have been instrumental in setting in motion a chain of events that led to unequivocal British recognition of American independence. Long suspicious of French intentions, Adams displayed a willingness to travel anywhere—London in 1779, The Hague in 1780, or Vienna in 1781—to press America's case. When Vergennes reluctantly called him back from Holland to discuss the implications of outside mediations, the American commissioner predictably declared his opposition to any kind of truce, tacit or explicit, which would leave British troops on American soil. Although Vergennes extended no invitation, Adams made it known that he would agree to treat separately with British emissaries at a congress in Vienna provided that "the two Imperial Courts would acknowledge and lay down as a preliminary the sovereignty of the United States, and admit their minister to a congress." He suspected rightly that Vergennes would have permitted the mediators to have Britain treat with representatives of the "American Colonies."

Since neither Austria nor Russia could sponsor negotiations in which Americans would sit as equals, Adams understandably credited the subsequent abandonment of mediation to his own demands. Even if George III's stubbornness and other external factors had a part in aborting the plans of mediators, Adams reinforced Jay's, and even Franklin's, wariness of the French ally, and stimulated a climate for fruitful collaboration among the three leading diplomatists abroad. Small wonder Vergennes wanted Adams removed! Had the French foreign minister waited a little longer before summoning Adams from The Hague, he would have received the news from Philadelphia of the new five-member peace commission with which he would have preferred to deal.

Adams' firmest supporter in his Francophobic suspicions was now John Jay, of all people. The New York aristocrat who had been Gérard's choice to succeed Lee in 1779 had never been known to be partial to the political or economic concerns of New Englanders. His unhappy experiences in Spain, however, had activated his Huguenot heritage of distrust of Catholic France and converted him into an almost xenophobic American by 1781. The collapse of his Spanish mission left him brooding on the perfidy of Europeans in general and on the meaning of

Spain's American policy. Concluding early in his stay at the Spanish court that the exclusion of the United States from the Mississippi valley lay at the center of Spain's ambitions, he accepted hesitantly Congress' decision in 1781 to recognize Spain's exclusive right to the navigation of the Mississippi below the 31st parallel on condition that this concession produce an alliance with Spain. When Floridablanca refused to accept the condition, Jay with some relief withdrew the offer to surrender American claims to the navigation rights. He was grateful for Spanish inaction, as was Congress, which upon reflection approved Jay's withdrawal of the concession. Jay was convinced that mere abnegation on navigation would not appease Spain's real designs of occupying territories on the east bank of the river. And even more serious, his conversations with the French ambassador in Madrid led him to suspect that France would pander to Spain's wishes. In a contest between her two allies the United States was bound to suffer.

By 1781 Jay's attitude toward France was identical with that of Adams', and he made this clear in his protestations against the new peace instructions after he had learned of his appointment to the commission: "As an American I felt an interest in the dignity of my country, which renders it difficult for me to reconcile myself to the idea of sovereign independent States of America submitting in the persons of their ministers, to be absolutely governed by the advice and opinions of the servants of another sovereign, especially in a case of national importance." Adams could not have expressed the case more forcefully.

In light of their adventures the two Americans should have occasioned no surprise in discarding French efforts to control their moves in Paris in 1782. That the third commissioner, Franklin, an indisputable Francophile, should join their ranks appeared to be a genuine reversal in roles. It was Franklin himself who pushed the American delegation down the path of independent negotiation with the British enemy. Approached indirectly by the new Shelburne ministry about possibilities of peace, Franklin seized the opportunity to suggest an American price to the amenable British agent, Richard Oswald. It included the cession of Canada, something Vergennes would not have approved had he known of the details Franklin had listed. Franklin clarified the troublesome question of independence by making this acknowledgment a prerequisite of any treaty that might follow. Such deviations from his celebrated Francophilism occurred before Jay and Adams had come to Paris to add their contributions to peacemaking.

To point out Franklin's eye for the main chance is not to claim that Franklin was considering the abandonment of the alliance, or even a policy of defiance in the spirit of his two younger colleagues. He merely recognized that the interests of the two countries were not identical. When an attractive opportunity arose to the advantage of the United States, Franklin took it. He had no intention of distressing the French, partly because of the genuine gratitude he felt for past French help, partly because of the counterbalance to Britain he anticipated for the future. But on the matter of British propositions, even propositions obviously designed to divide the allies, Franklin did not hesitate to risk the displeasure of both great powers by setting one against the other. After all, he had done this before with great profit to his country in 1778.

What made this gambit possible in the first place was the profound political changes in England in the winter of 1782 which swept out of office the men who had controlled British policy toward America for over a decade and who bore responsibility for the conduct of the American war. Lord North had been in power since 1768; Sandwich had been First Lord of the Admiralty since 1771; Dartmouth, Hillsborough, and Germain had been associated with American affairs almost from the beginnings of the Colonial Office. The only relatively new man in the ministry was Lord Stormont, former ambassador to France, who joined the cabinet in 1779, and his experience with American machinations in Paris before the alliance had made him more unbending in his attitudes than his colleagues. Their collective errors of understanding, of judgment, and of policy, contributed first to the outbreak of rebellion, and then to Britain's inability to suppress it. Their removal had been long overdue. The strong insistence of the king and the illusory hopes of victory in the West Indies almost alone kept them in office after 1779.[13]

While French West Indian operations were no more successful in 1782 than they had been earlier, the king bowed to the verdict of Yorktown and finally released the hapless North from his service. At last the Whig opposition leaders managed to have the country face up to the fact of an American nation living apart from Great Britain. Yorktown then was a psychic rather than a military crisis, inasmuch as the military position of Great Britain looked brighter in 1782 than in the year of Cornwallis' defeat. In ousting North, however, they failed to win office themselves. The king offered the ministry to Lord Shelburne, a faithful disciple of Chatham, primarily because he had rejected American independence in the past, and continued to do so after Yorktown. Shelburne sought instead a new form of Angloamerican collaboration, in the Pitt manner, which would keep the colonies in the empire but with the perquisites of independence. In the absence of support from other factions the ministry went initially to Rockingham, with Shelburne returning to the secretaryship of state for the Southern Department, which embraced once again colonial affairs. His more radical rival, Charles James Fox, an avowed defender of American independence, was in charge of the Northern Department, which now extended to all foreign affairs. Although both men claimed jurisdiction over the American problem, the shrewder Shelburne managed to predominate even before he assumed the prime minister's functions on the death of Rockingham in the summer of 1782.

Shelburne felt the way to a solution was by prying apart France and America through marks of special favors to the Americans. To test American loyalties he sent over carefully selected agents, such as the above-mentioned Richard Oswald, a Scottish merchant and former business associate of Henry Laurens, whose philosophic temperament was intended to appeal to Franklin. Laurens himself was released from the Tower of London and asked to feel out Adams' attitude in the Netherlands. While still a subordinate in the cabinet, Shelburne took

[13] Ian R. Christie, *The End of North's Ministry 1780–1782* (London, 1958), pp. 370–372.

the responsibility for sending General Sir Guy Carleton to talk directly with Washington about an armistice based on evacuation of British troops. At the same time Carleton was to talk individually with state leaders on their reactions to Parliament's peace feelers. Shelburne's cleverly calculated moves to detach the states from Congress and Congress from France subsequently miscarried, but his device of choosing congenial agents succeeded handsomely with Franklin. The success, however, was ultimately Franklin's and America's rather than Shelburne's and Britain's.

Oswald discovered in Franklin a delightful companion interested in reconciliation with Great Britain and possessing ideas about effecting it which deserved to be carried back to Shelburne. To disarm both the British and the French Franklin not only made known to Vergennes the fact of Oswald's visit but requested and received sanction for separate preliminary negotiations with Britain, barring of course any conclusions without French approval. In being so apparently candid in his dealings with France, Franklin spoiled Shelburne's scenario in which France would be blamed for holding up America's independence by her obligations to the Bourbon partner. It did not escape the Americans' notice that the British viewed independence only as a last resort in their negotiations as a price for peace, not a precondition of it.

Fox's removal from office should have increased prospects for peace in the summer of 1782, if only because of lessened friction within the ministry and greater coherence in its future policies. But no matter how warmly disposed Shelburne professed to be toward America, he continued to treat with representatives of "colonies," rather than of a nation. To smoke him out Franklin, continuing his friendly informal conversations with Oswald, had the agent transmit to the ministry terms for ending the conflict which were separated into "necessary" and "advisable." Under the former went, first of all, "Independence, full and complete in every sense, to the Thirteen States, and all troops to be withdrawn from thence." After listing also a Canadian boundary north of the Great Lakes and a guarantee of American freedom of fishing on the Banks and elsewhere, Franklin recommended "as a friend" a number of other concessions "advisable" for the British to adopt—indemnification to Americans whose properties were destroyed in the war, a resumption of American commercial privileges in Britain, an acknowledgment by Parliament of its errors in America, and finally the cession of all of Canada to cement the renewed friendship of the two peoples.

Franklin did not receive all he asked for. Although his new friend Oswald did become an official negotiator, the terms of his commission omitted the issue of independence, and implied something less than equality for American plenipotentiaries. At this point Jay and Adams, both suspicious of Vergennes' permissiveness as well as of Shelburne's manoeuvering, urged their reluctant colleague to suspend talks until the British had presented in writing full recognition of the United States and her negotiators. Jay was of the opinion that Vergennes had encouraged negotiations in the expectation that loopholes, such as the above, would prevent any meaningful action while the French foreign minister continued to accommodate Spanish wishes for continuing the war. France was using the Angloamerican conversations for her own purposes, confident that they would divert American attention from her own questionable activities.

Eventually Jay won recognition from Whitehall in the form of a commission in September, 1782, "enabling Mr. Oswald to treat with the Commissioners appointed by the Colonys, under the title of Thirteen United States." So read the instructions to Oswald. They represented a compromise, a veritable retreat from the earlier demands of the American envoys. The humiliating use of "Colonys" and the equivocal term "Thirteen United States" were actually less than the British themselves were prepared to concede at this time. The precondition of independence was transplanted by mutual agreement into the first article of the future treaty of peace.

Fear of a new betrayal at the hands of France explained Jay's and Adams' acceptance of a flexible position on independence that Franklin had taken weeks before. In early September the fortuitous confluence of an intercepted cipher dispatch from Barbé-Marbois to Vergennes and of musings about conversations with Conde de Aranda, Spain's ambassador to France, inflamed Jay's highly sensitive antennae. The former purportedly advised the foreign minister to protect French rights against American claims in the fisheries off the Grand Banks. The latter fed Jay's suspicions that Aranda and Gérard de Rayneval, Vergennes' aide in the Foreign Ministry, had combined to deny America access to lands east of the Mississippi. Rayneval's plan, Jay had gathered, would place Indians dwelling west of a line south of the Ohio River under Spanish protection, and those east under American influence. News of Rayneval's secret visit to London immediately after the account of the memorandum had leaked out was enough proof for Jay to maintain that France and England would make peace on the basis of a trans-Appalachian west in Spanish and British hands.

Even though Franklin remained unperturbed, Jay's accusations had some substance to them. An Anglo-French entente at America's expense was not just a neurotic's nightmare. Rayneval was indeed in London; Spain would accept reasonable substitutes for Gibraltar; and France was angry over American attitudes toward fisheries. As a result of his conjectures Jay dispatched Benjamin Vaughan, a young English sympathizer with American family connections, to England without informing Franklin of his action. Vaughan was to inform Shelburne of America's mistrust of France's pretensions in the moderator's role and of America's interest in a rapid and equitable conclusion of the war. To spike Vergennes' enticements in the west, Jay held out the prospect of sharing the Mississippi navigation with the British and the restoration of a trading community with the former mother country. All for the price of an explicit admission of independence and equal status in negotiations. Such was the background of the wording of Oswald's new commission.

Jay had hit upon the nerve of a long-standing aspiration of Shelburne's in his hints about a new Angloamerican commercial empire and the dissolution of the Anglo-French link. If the British first minister seriously considered an entente with France, he deemed it was worth sacrificing for the considerations Jay had put before him. Conceivably the separate treaty that followed in the fall of 1782 might have contained more of Franklin's "advisable" articles had not Jay's fright caused talks to be suspended at an inauspicious moment from the American point of view. Reports of Spain's unsuccessful assault on Gibraltar reached London at the end of September, and stiffened British terms to such a degree that its legacy poisoned Anglo-American relations for generations. The murky boundary lines with Canada, vagueness on fishery articles, and the postponement of a commercial treaty could be traced in some measure to Britain's rising confidence in her conduct of the war as it drew to a close. Additionally Jay's near panic over French intrigue contributed to the impolitic secret article in the peace treaty which would have placed the boundary of West Florida at the Yazoo River had Britain retained the Floridas in 1783.

With all its shortcomings the treaty with Great Britain represented a magnificent piece of statecraft whereby a weak republic acquired independence and an empire of its own. And the accomplishment must be set against the backdrop of Europe's active disapproval. Fox, no more than his predecessor Shelburne, voluntarily granted America her demands. Vergennes was shocked almost as much by the willful disobedience of France's tutelage as he was by the amazing results of the final treaty. Floridablanca looked upon America's independence as the symbol of the bankruptcy of the Spanish war aims; it foreshadowed the survival of a British Gibraltar in the Old World and the arrival of an American menace in the New World. Even Congress mingled misgivings with its jubilation, wondering how the diplomatists' violation of their instructions would affect Franco-American relations.

Congressional qualms were genuine. For James Madison of Virginia the fact that the commissioners had concluded a treaty without prior consultation with the French was a direct breach of both discipline and etiquette. He and other congressmen distant from the scene interpreted their actions as inexcusable ingratitude for the enormous service France had provided America. Madison could not accept the notion that Luzerne exercised improper influence over American policy. Responding to Arthur Lee's withering attack on the peace instructions, Madison in August, 1782, had conceded that they were an offense to national dignity. "But," he explained, "it was a sacrifice of dignity to policy. The situation of affairs and circumstances at the time rendered this sacrifice necessary." Secretary Livingston, even more committed to France, had gone so far as to advise Franklin in January, 1782, to accept the French conception of a restricted western boundary.[14] When the secretary heard of the commission's deal with Britain, he confided to them, "It gives me pain that the character for candor and felicity to its engagements which should always characterize a great people should have been impeached thereby." He was particularly exercised over the secret article on the Floridas. Eventually he consoled himself, and presumably the French, with the declaration that the preliminary articles would not take effect until peace had been signed between Great Britain and France.

The commissioners took this rebuke to be a tap on the wrist, knowing well the extent of their achievements and anticipating the approval of all segments of the divided country. They did not deceive themselves. They also felt equipped to withstand any reprimand France might wish to inflict upon the erring negotiators. Leaving the phrasing to the persuasive Franklin, they confessed to being guilty of "neglecting a point of *bienséance*," as the aged diplomatist coolly described it, but found no cause to apologize. On the contrary, Franklin used the occasion of his confession to Vergennes about the preliminary treaty with Britain to ask for more financial aid. Behind the façade of a scolding Franklin earned the French Minister's admiration and a pledge for more funds. Vergennes saw compensations in the conclusion of the Angloamerican agreement. First, he could inform the stubborn Spanish with a reasonably good conscience that the American action had made the recovery of Gibraltar an impossibility. Second, whatever resentments he may have harbored against Americans had to be weighed against Franklin's warnings of Britain's plans to divide the allies.

In retrospect, the dark forebodings of John Jay and the prickly sensitivities of John Adams did indeed uncover French manoeuvers inimical to America's interests. Vergennes' plans for the disposition of fisheries directly conflicted with Adams; he contemplated appeasement of Spain in the Mississippi coun-

[14] George Dangerfield, *Chancellor Robert R. Livingston of New York* (New York, 1960), p. 158, calls this aberration "atavistic" rather than Francophilic, the instinctive recoil of the New York aristocrat from the prospect of a democratic west.

try; and he wished to confine the new republic to a state of permanent dependency on France. These charges were all true, and yet more should be said of France's position during the war. The foreign minister proved his sincerity in denying his country what she might easily have gained: return of territory lost in 1763. His concern for American independence was genuine and persistent. His patience in accepting American criticism was almost saintly in light of his full knowledge that French money paid for the war, Frenchmen and French arms fought the war, and French statecraft by entwining other European states in its coils helped to secure an American victory at the peace tables. Even if Vergennes was serving his country first, he served America well. Madison and Livingston understood this truth. So did Franklin, the most experienced and most perceptive of all American statesmen, who felt gratitude for past assistance and looked forward to continuing help from France to keep England at bay in the future.

CHAPTER VI

Diplomacy and the Confederation: Challenge and Response

☆ 1783-1788 ☆

PATRICK HENRY was among the leaders at the Virginia ratifying convention in 1788 who feared and condemned the new Constitution as insidious and needless. Why replace the old government? "The Confederation, this despised government, merits, in my opinion, the highest encomium—it carried us through a long and dangerous war; it rendered us victorious in that bloody conflict with a powerful nation; it has secured us a territory greater than any European monarch possesses—and shall a government which has been thus strong and vigorous, be accused of imbecility, and abandoned for want of energy?"

Admittedly these strong words were vented in the heat of a rearguard action by Virginia's most fiery Revolutionary orator. Nevertheless, his cry had a ring of truth to it. The governmental authority so ignominiously cast aside in 1787 was the same one that had humbled the British Empire in 1783 and then proceeded to solve the problems of imperial rule in the new western territories through the Northwest Ordinance of 1787. And if that government had been unable to secure new treaties of the magnitude of the Treaty of Paris, what alternative government would have done better? America had survived the unrest and depression that would have plagued any country moving from a wartime to a peacetime economy. The experiences of that decade were neither unique to the Articles of Confederation nor necessarily a sign of fatal disorders in the body politic. In fact, the worst problems may have been over in 1787 and 1788, as new markets in Asia opened to Americans and the most severe of the internal dislocations righted themselves.

But no matter how vigorous a case may be made for the Confederation by contemporaries or by historians of later generations, John Fiske's pejorative phrase, "the critical period," will always be identified with it.[1] Because the Articles were faithful to the ideal of a limited central authority so pervasive in the Revolution, the Congresses that grew out of them were no more powerful than the state legislatures had wanted them to be. They were the logical extensions of the Continental Congress and its painfully limited abilities to govern. So hobbled was the freedom of the Confederation that it is remarkable its governments were able to do as much as they did in their short decade of existence. The power to tax individual citizens, the power to control the issuance of currency, the power to regulate interstate trade—all of these major attributes of sovereignty—were denied to the central government under the Articles of Confederation. These deficiencies meant that the Congresses were unable to protect creditors from the ravages of inflationary currency, or to redeem securities held by investors, or even to maintain public order without funds for an army. It is not difficult to understand why men of personal property, the oligarchs of the towns, were distressed with the workings of the Confederation and prepared to support a less democratic but more orderly instrument of government.

Pressures for change, however, had a wider popular base than the aristocratic few and a wider popular appeal than the reservation of personal and real estate. The weaknesses of the Confederation as the governing instrument of a nation in a world of hostile states also attracted the attention of democrats and farmers, libertarians and westerners. The failure of the Congresses to manage a foreign policy frustrated men of varied economic and political persuasions—James Madison and John Jay at home, Thomas Jefferson and John Adams abroad. It was more than an inability of a new and sensitive nation to win instant

[1] John Fiske, *The Critical Period of American History, 1783–1789* (Boston and New York, 1888).

and automatic respect among the European powers as reflected in most-favored-nation treaties; it was the sense of frustration over impotence to pay foreign creditors their rightful debts and to squash the intrigues of Spain or England playing upon secessionist sentiments or interstate jealousies and rivalries. Loyalty to the Articles was a conditional grant at best, and on the part of the trans-Appalachian west, which felt voiceless in Philadelphia, it was frequently felt that the conditions were not being met. The conflicting interests of jealous states willing to pursue local advantage at the expense of national needs made Europe's expectation of a division of America into two or three or more units a reasonable deduction.

The more nationalist factions among the founding fathers of the Confederation were aware of the built-in centrifugal forces of the Confederation and did their best to counter them. Long before the final ratification of the Articles, conservative statesmen, as has been noted, attempted to strengthen the national character of the new government. John Dickinson, charged in 1776 with providing a basic law for the United States, did his best in the first draft to give the Articles authority over the states. He failed. Nationalists, frequently from the more conservative ranks of Revolutionary leaders, continued to work for a stronger central authority, never quite managing as much as they would have liked, but willing to build on such precedents as they could. The establishments of such executive departments as War, Finance, and Foreign Affairs provided just such opportunities for promoting centralization; and the men who occupied those offices—Benjamin Lincoln, Robert Morris, and Robert R. Livingston, respectively, in 1781—were all closely tied by economic interest and class prejudice to this conception of the national welfare.

The Articles themselves provided some of the raw materials of a stronger national sovereignty than the mood of the framers had intended, particularly where the conduct of foreign affairs was concerned. Article IX was explicit on the subject of war: "The United States in Congress assembled, shall have the sole and exclusive right and power of determining on peace and war . . . of sending and receiving ambassadors—entering into treaties and alliance. . . ." Equally explicit were the specific prohibitions in Article VI against the states sending or receiving embassies, making treaties with foreign powers or among themselves, and engaging in war without the consent of "the United States in Congress."

While these provisions may have been the product of an awareness of the realities of international life, their translation into action was made inoperable by fears of the concentration of power which inform other and more weighty portions of the Articles. How much meaning did an exclusive authority to declare war or make peace have if the means of implementing them remained a matter of the caprice of the state to fulfill? How much respect would European nations grant to the governments of the Confederation when Article II of the document made clear that "Each state retains its sovereignty, freedom, and independence, and every power, jurisdiction, and right which is not by this Confederation expressly delegated to the United States, in Congress assembled"? The answers to both these questions made changes mandatory in the eyes of almost every participant in foreign relations, whether his label was liberal or conservative.

Ironically, the Treaty of Paris, the greatest triumph of the Confederation, also was the occasion for displaying its most serious weaknesses. Each article in the final version of the peace treaty contained its own delayed-action time bomb which could blast, in the future, the hopes America had of creating a successful independent republic. The new expanded boundaries of the United States, from the Mississippi to the Atlantic, from the Great Lakes to Florida, were all subject to differing interpretations by the affected parties. The source of the Mississippi River, the northwest boundary of the country, was uncharted; the northeast boundary of Maine was uncertain; and the southern boundary with Florida was illegal, since Spain was not a party to that decision although Spain repossessed Florida as a result of the treaty. Britain's concessions on fisheries in Article III, while generous, were bound to stimulate future controversy over the distinction between "right" and "liberty" in American participation in fishing off the shores of Newfoundland. Articles V and VI promising Congressional support for the "restitution of all estates, rights and properties" taken from Loyalists and assuring the British of no future penalties against them would expose over the next years the difficulties Congress had constitutionally in making promises whose fulfillment depended wholly on the will of individual states.

The framers of the Articles had recognized the potential friction between the powers of the states and the obligations of the states in Article VI, which asserted: "No state shall lay any imposts or duties, which may interfere with any stipulations in treaties, entered into by the United States in Congress assembled, with any king, prince or state, in pursuance of any treaties already proposed by Congress, to the courts of France and Spain." Great Britain was specifically omitted in this passage, but if the Congresses would have difficulty with their commitment to friendly countries, how much more complicated was the task of convincing states to abide by the national obligations to recent enemies?

The record of the Confederation was inevitably one of failure in this critical area which in turn led to a contempt and hostility for the United States in all the courts of Europe. Notwithstanding advances in many areas of American life the continuing failure in the management of foreign relations united divergent groups behind opposition to the Articles. Even Jefferson, always sensitive to reactionary impulses in America and increasingly aware of the admiration for the American Revolution he found in influential French circles, would risk losing some liberties for the sake of national security. Repeated diplomatic impasses had led him to plead that the states must be "made one as to all foreign, and several as to all domestic matters." When this duality ultimately could not coexist under the Confederation, the reluctant Jefferson went along with a Constitution that gave the energy and cohesiveness necessary to formulate and administer a foreign policy.

There was a time, early in the 1780s, when the Confederation appeared to have fallen into the hands of nationalists who inspired visions of stability in both foreign and domestic affairs. The declining fortunes of war and the increasing dependence upon French help had sent dispirited radicals back to their states and brought to Philadelphia men who saw in the increase of strong government an advantage for their own economic and political interests.

Robert Morris, superintendent of finances from 1781 to 1783, was the driving force among this group, and he fully expected to use his wealth and influence to further his private as well as public concerns. He pointedly accepted the position on the condition that he maintain his private business operations alongside his public service. Within three days of assuming office he submitted a plan for a Bank of North America which would be both a repository for government funds and a source of loans to the government. Morris' success in securing new loans, in reducing military expenses, and generally in restoring an air of confidence in the management of public business helped to keep alive the Confederation during the difficult period of peacemaking. It should also be observed that friends of Morris shrewd enough to invest in the Bank of North America made handsome profits for themselves out of their connection with this enterprise.

In all his ventures Morris sought to emphasize central power at the expense of state authority, hoping to establish by precedence the superiority of the Confederation over its component parts. Imposition of an import duty of 5 percent was to be "an entering wedge" of a grander federal taxation that would override state claims.[2] Its attraction should have been in the specific design to repay foreign obligations, and hence to serve as an inducement for Europeans to continue the flow of loans to the American war effort. The plan failed partly because Morris presented it as a war measure at a time when the war was coming to an end. More important, the opposition forces in the states identified the move for what it was: an effort to weaken state power over taxation, with the discharge of foreign loans as a mask for establishing a permanent system of confederal taxes. By the time the Treaty of Paris was signed the nationalist-conservative tide had receded, at least for the time being. Morris retired from office in 1783.

One can speculate that if Morris' ultimate plan of funding all the debts of the confederal government had succeeded, it

[2] E. James Ferguson, *The Power of the Purse: A History of American Public Finance, 1776–1790* (Chapel Hill, 1961), p. 146.

might have won for the Articles the allegiance of those commercial classes who later supported the Constitution. Hamilton put the program into effect a decade later under the new instrument of government. Morris' failure, however, was only partial. He managed not only to keep alive the Bank of North America and stimulate the growth of similar institutions outside Pennsylvania but also kept in the forefront throughout the life of the Confederation the idea that the public debt was a national concern rather than simply the responsibility of thirteen separate states.

Whether or not funding of itself would have saved the Confederation is questionable, since the tax problem did not represent the sum of the government's difficulties with the states. Certainly the experience of Livingston, chancellor of New York, redoubtable conservative, and loyal ally of Morris, illustrated both the expectations and the limitations in the conduct of foreign policy under the Confederation. This was an exercise in the accretion of power for the central authority. Livingston's appointment as secretary for foreign affairs was itself a symbol of the victory of nationalism over particularism; his rival for the position was none other than Arthur Lee. Small wonder then that the French minister did all he could to help Livingston into office. And Luzerne's French funds did make a difference, since Lee had received more votes than Livingston in the initial count. Virginia had to be wooed away from Lee before the chancellor could take office.

There were qualities of the bookkeeper in the secretary's post which made the secretaryship far less desirable than the superintendancy of finance. Livingston was expected to keep the books of the department, receive and report all applications of foreigners, transmit communications to Congress, and correspond with ministers abroad. Initially there was sentiment in the Congress to create a commission of three to supervise the office, but the rising conservative wave of 1781 suppressed this notion. Instead of further depressing his station, the secretary secured permission to attend sessions of Congress and explain his reports. While his salary of $4,000 a year remained modest and his assistants few in number, he was able to persuade Congress to create two undersecretaries and to add the positions of translator and clerk to the staff.

Lacking the domineering personality of Morris as well as a more commanding office, Livingston never equaled the superintendent of finances in power or prestige. In his twenty months of service he did surmount both the initial dependence on France and the independence of the American envoys to Paris, and induced Congress to construe broadly the scope of his office. Although the control of the activities of the peace commission always eluded him, he was able to gain the principle from Congress that ministers abroad would report to Congress through his office. If he failed to win exclusive right to initiate diplomacy or to prevent Congress from dealing with diplomats independently of the secretary for foreign affairs, neither did the secretaries of state under the future Constitution. The power of conducting foreign affairs was always diffused, no matter how centralized executive power became. His most important service was through influence not authority; his judgment deflected Congress from appointing ministers to Lisbon or Brussels where they would have been snubbed, and his voice was prominent in the move to liquidate the embarrassing mission to Russia.

In other respects he was an ally of Congress, or at least its nationalist elements, in restraining states from interfering with foreign policy. A considerable part of his time was taken up in communicating to the states Congressional resolutions on foreign affairs, and then following these communications with admonitory notes urging compliance with national treaty obligations. The consular convention with France, for example, would have been meaningless unless the individual states passed appropriate laws to make it effective. His last Circular Letter to the states, of April 12, 1783, announcing the end of hostilities, concluded with the warning: "I need not, I am persuaded, sir, use any arguments to urge your excellency and the State over which you preside to the most scrupulous attention to the execution of every stipulation in our treaty which may depend on you or them. A national character is now to be acquired. I venture to hope it will be worthy of the struggles by which we became a nation."

An acute sensitivity to national needs characterized Livingston's service as secretary. It was the mark of the gentleman conscious of a noblesse oblige, of citizenship which embraces the nation rather than the state. This harmonious blend of service to a nation with the conservation of societal values, such as the sanctity of contract, may help explain his appreciation of the Treaty of Paris. That document may be seen as the fulfillment of an American *rentier*'s dream, an agreement that confirms a revolution without destroying the contractual basis of society. Almost as if it would atone for the chaos implicit in revolution, the treaty assured specifically and unequivocally the supremacy of private contracts. All previous debts would be honored; restitution of the rights of Loyalists would be recommended; British evacuation of troops would entail "no carrying away of any Negroes or other property of the American inhabitants." The treaty also supported commercial interests, as in Article 3 which outlined terms whereby Americans could participate in the fishing enterprises off the Banks of Newfoundland and in the Gulf of St. Lawrence; and in Article 8, in which the navigation of the Mississippi would be open to both British and American citizens. So much attention was paid to contractual obligations that Peter d'A. Jones could claim that the treaty was a reflection of the "preponderating influence of the conservative, creditor sections in the former colonies."[3]

Conspiratorial though this notion may sound the solidity inherent in the terms of the treaty was a vital factor in the support it received. Scrupulous adherence to its terms would be a bulwark against further erosion of social and economic barriers then under attack in many states. And it was more than a question of preserving for the creditor the right to collect his just debts. There were also dangers to public order which rallied to the banner of the Confederation men who felt that the radical passions of many of the states would destroy the liberties won by the Revolution. Such was the rationale of the support given to the treaty by Madison and Monroe. Northerners and southerners alike welcomed the return of Loyalists who upon accept-

[3] Peter D'A. Jones, *An Economic History of the United States since 1783* (London, 1956), p. 6.

ing republican government would be guarantors of social stability. Libertarians such as George Mason were as distressed as any Boston merchant would have been over the jest the Virginian had heard on the matter of debts after the war. It went as follows: "If we are now to pay the debts due the British merchants, what have we been fighting for all this while?"

Yet the influence of states-oriented politicians rose as a consequence of the conservative challenge. Even before the final ratification of the treaty the nationalists were leaving Philadelphia in the face of radical opposition that was strengthened by lessened need for strong central government in peacetime. Indeed, Congress itself left Philadelphia, roaming about the middle states from Maryland to New Jersey until it finally settled in New York. Unlike the war years when migration was forced upon that body from time to time to escape British capture, the movement out of Philadelphia was an effort by the newly ascendant radicals to remove Congress from the dangers and temptations of conservative Philadelphia where it could be intimidated or blandished too easily by the likes of Robert Morris and other Philadelphia financiers. Morris himself resigned in 1784 to give full time to his flourishing private affairs, but in leaving office he was unable to leave as a legacy either the impost on imports or a reputation that was untarnished. A Congressional inquiry—with Lee as one of the inquisitors—into the special favors he granted his own business interests followed him into retirement.

When Morris finally left government service in early 1784 Livingston had been gone for a year and a half. It took an even longer period for Congress to find a successor as secretary for foreign affairs. For a time Lewis Morris, of New York, one of the undersecretaries, performed the minimal duties of the office, and after he resigned Charles Thomson, secretary of the Confederation, managed the day-to-day business. The position was a logical focus for competition between the conservative nationalists and their states-rights antagonists. General Philip Schuyler was a leading contender at the end of 1782, while on the other side Arthur Lee again declared his candidacy for the secretaryship. After a host of other names, from Jefferson's to Henry Laurens', had been bruited about, Elbridge Gerry broke the impasse by putting forward John Jay, fresh from his successes in Paris.

For a man of such well-known partisan sentiments Jay was a peculiar choice for a compromise between the factions. His aristocratic origins in New York had made him an opponent of radical change early in the Revolution, and nothing occurred since that time either to deepen his affection for democracy or to make him a friend of particularism in American politics. What had changed between 1779 and 1783 was his distrust of the Bourbons that had manifested itself in his liaison with Adams against Franklin at critical moments in the course of peace negotiations. To New Englanders of the Lee persuasion, Jay now appeared to be a properly jealous and articulate watchdog of American interests against French machinations, and their idea of the French menace extended to the operations of such Francophiles as Livingston and Morris. To conservatives, however, he was still the old friend of Livingston's whose appreciation of commercial interests and of the public interest should place him in support of a stronger Confederation. Of the two expectations the latter's was the more realistic. Only in 1783 could Jay's beliefs be associated with radicalism of any kind; five years earlier or later no such confusion would have arisen.

Jay proved to be an able minister, dominating the proceedings of Congress more than any of his colleagues after the departure of Morris. He placed conditions upon his acceptance of the position beyond anything his predecessor had asked for, including an assurance that the capital of the Confederation would be in New York rather than in Trenton where Congress had been during most of 1783. Like Livingston he insisted on the right to choose his own assistants. He dispensed with a second undersecretary. Still, he chafed over the petty charges he felt Congress put upon the secretary, and aired his annoyance to the president of the Congress in 1785 in the following observation: "I have reason, sir, to apprehend that I have come into the office of Secretary for Foreign Affairs with ideas of its duties and rights somewhat different from those which seem to be entertained by Congress." While he generally received whatever he demanded, J. C. Guggenheimer points out that "as late as 1788 there were in the office, besides the Secretary and his assistants, only two clerks, or just enough . . . for one of them to be in the office while the other went to luncheon."[4]

Jay's personal command of foreign affairs was always in evidence. It explains why the Spanish minister in New York set out to woo Jay above all others in preparing for a treaty between Spain and the United States. His French counterpart flatly reported to Vergennes that Congress seemed to be "guided only by his directions." The states themselves had ample evidence of the secretary's influence in the Confederation and of his attitude toward their role in foreign relations. With all his celebrated hostility to France no official could have been more vigorous in his denunciation of those states such as Massachusetts and New Hampshire which imposed tonnage duties on French goods in violation of Article 5 of the Treaty of Amity and Commerce with France. With equal vehemence he denounced Virginia's decision to give preference to French brandies despite a most-favored-nation treaty with Holland. Congress heeded his advice with unanimous resolutions against the actions of the state legislatures.

At the end of his five years of service Jay's influence and his nationalism had increased rather than diminished. His retirement fittingly coincided with his function as a propagandist, along with Hamilton and Madison, in favor of the Constitution as it was debated by the New York Convention. The secretary drew on his own experience to urge the nation to end the chaos that had plagued the Confederation by conferring upon the new government powers to enforce respect in the states for international obligations. The resolutions by the Congress of the Confederation were unenforceable.

Jay's record in office was not without blemish; his vanity occasionally clouded his judgment. As British foreign minister Lord Grenville noticed in 1794, "Almost every man has a weak spot, and Mr. Jay's is Mr. Jay." Those who courted his self-esteem were understandably tempted to trace success in their representations to the secretary's susceptibility to flattery. He was now open to criticism for his frequently presumptuous over-

[4] Quoted in Samuel Flagg Bemis, "John Jay," in S. F. Bemis (ed.), *The American Secretaries of State and Their Diplomacy* (New York, 1958), I: 202.

riding of those who stood in the path of his own conception of the public good; he gave preferment to those groups and classes most clearly involved in international commerce. For Jay this was a matter of the national interest; for westerners in 1786 and 1787 a less favorable gloss was made of his activities. But no critic faulted his sincerity in advancing American power in international affairs. He sought as hard as any radical to press on Europe the American interpretation of neutral rights through treaties and when blocked gave impetus to the idea of mixed national commissions to resolve differences with other parties. He tried with some success to sublimate American weakness in foreign affairs through vigorous championship of international arbitration to solve international problems.

Secretary Jay needed all the native talents he could marshal to cope with the country's most troublesome problem—its relations with Great Britain. America's treatment at the hands of the former mother country dramatized as much as any other issue the difficulties of the Confederation. The history of the period might have been quite different had the hopes of the framers of the Treaty of Paris—David Hartley and Richard Oswald as well as Jay and Adams—been realized. Soured by his experiences with France, Jay in particular looked forward to a reconciliation with Britain based on mutual interests and in pursuit of mutual advantages. Shelburne's reconstructed Anglo-america, a single economic unit with separate political entities, would have changed the course of American history of the next generation as well as deflated the force of lingering Anglophobia. Instead, a vindictive policy of exclusion from the economic benefits of the British Navigation System, and fitful political intrigues among dissident groups in America, both interlaced with contempt for America's nationhood, revived the fears of Anglophobes and elevated France to an apparently permanent role as guarantor against British reconquest. Although the circumstances of the American economy permitted the British to retain as much of American trade through repression as it may have won through generosity, the political price paid for this punitive and spiteful program was high. It became even higher after Europe was engulfed by revolution.

Shelburne's plan of a grand rapprochement would have restored the benefits Americans had enjoyed under the old Navigation System, including free access of American goods to British ports and markets. Hartley went so far as to recommend a common citizenship for the two peoples. Fruition of this scheme would have denied France the diminution of British power in America for which she had gone to war even as it strengthened the ties that bound America to Britain more firmly than had been the condition prior to the Revolution. Great Britain would then have emerged from the conflict with a more prosperous empire freed from the burdens of administration. The fact that the two major competing factions in Parliament spoke of conciliation seemed to confirm American hopes of at least winning a favorable commercial treaty, if not a full share of British log-cutting privileges in Central America.

No such harmony prevailed in 1783. Even before Hartley arrived on the scene Shelburne's government had been forced to reckon with the realities of British politics. Despite his own carefully reasoned thoughts about the changing nature of the British, reinforced in later years by the new wisdom of the economist Adam Smith, Shelburne had to retreat from his stand on commercial reciprocity. His only allies were merchants whose primary investments had been in the American trade before the war and from West Indian planters who appreciated their dependence upon the United States for inexpensive and readily accessible supplies. But as Edmund Burke once put it to the great economist: "You, Dr. Smith, from your professor's chair, may send forth theories upon the freedom of commerce as if you were lecturing upon pure mathematics; but legislators must proceed by slow degrees, impeded as they are in their course by the friction of interest and the friction of prejudice." Both interest and prejudice were present in abundance as Parliament expunged the reciprocity element from the Jay-Oswald draft of the treaty in October, 1782. Shelburne himself was forced out of office for yielding too much to the Americans.

Charles James Fox, whose commitment to Angloamerica was vaguer than Shelburne's, was no more successful than the latter in appeasing the anger of such enemies of the new republic as the king who saw in every American a species of Wilkesite, or a competitor in the world market, or a pawn of hostile powers. When Hartley submitted a draft of a "temporary" commercial convention which would place American ships and goods in crown ports on the same terms that obtained before the war, Fox hesitated and equivocated. He did so even when the proposal stopped short of full reciprocity, since in the colonial times there were restrictions on American manufactures which obviously did not apply to their British counterparts. First, he backed away from direct commerce with all British dominions by denying American entry into West Indian ports for the purpose of re-exporting West Indian produce to Britain; and then, under continuing pressure in Parliament, he stopped all trade between the West Indies and Britain by American ships. It was almost full circle of retreat; the initial decision had been to repeal all wartime barriers against American trade in the West Indies.

Still, the prospect of a new era in Angloamerican commerce was not quite dead. When the Fox-North coalition collapsed in 1784, the liberal William Pitt became prime minister, the very man who in March, 1783, had sponsored a bill in the Commons that would give American shipping equal rights with the British everywhere. He too wilted before the demands of opposing groups. The alternatives to a generous settlement with America appeared too compelling to be resisted in 1783. Resentment over American behavior in the past and fears of competition in the future triumphed over voices of moderation pleading for a policy that would combine conciliation with profit.

William Eden, long familiar with American affairs, found a wide audience for his predictions of disaster for Britain should the new nation be restored to its former privileged position in the empire. Unchecked by the restraints of the old imperial system, American ships would monopolize the seas displacing British bottoms; American goods would shrivel and destroy the developing Irish provisions trade; and America would attract skilled workers from the mother country to outproduce the homeland in manufactured goods. Most of these arguments had emerged from the debate over Pitt's bill in the Commons, and were rephrased and circulated in a widely praised pamphlet, *Observations on the Commerce of the American States*, attributed to the Earl of Sheffield. This went beyond the apprehensions of Eden to outline not merely the dangers of Pitt's plan but also the virtues of a restrictive policy. Losing the war could be translated into winning the peace when it is conceived as an occasion to recapture the lost West Indian trade long dominated by colonial shipping. Ousting the Americans would leave room for cultivation of Canadian and Irish sources of provisions for the islands. As for the possible deprivation of an American market in retaliation for this decision, Sheffield asked where Americans could turn except to Britain. They had no ready substitute for British manufactures or for British credit.

These observations were institutionalized in the series of Orders in Council that made a commercial treaty impossible between the United States and Great Britain. The arguments of Burke and Pitt had no force in 1783, as the Orders systematically reduced the United States to the level of other foreign nations in the British trade. The only exception in America's behalf was the admission of enumerated articles vital to the British economy, and here the purpose was so blatant and the favor so patronizing that the effect was to degrade rather than to enhance the American relationship. Tobacco, for example, would be permitted free storage before re-exportation, but this service was acknowledged to be nothing but a means of stifling American efforts to trade directly with other European markets. The central feature of the measures was the removal of the United States from the British West Indies, and the author of this action, William Knox, a former colonial undersecretary whose post disappeared along with his plantation in Georgia in the course of the Revolution, acclaimed this as a major accomplishment. The order relating to the West Indies provided for admission of American-enumerated provisions, such as the necessary naval stores and lumber, but only in "British built ships owned by His Majesty's subjects and navigated according to law." No other products could enter the islands. Products of northern states in particular—fish, dairy products, and meats—were barred.

What permitted the British mercantilists to ignore West Indian planters worried about American reaction or opponents scoffing at the estimation of future American industrial competition was their supreme confidence that no matter how humilating their propositions, the Americans were impotent to retaliate. America needed Britain more than Britain needed America. As Sheffield observed, "At least four-fifths of the importations from Europe into the American States, were at all times made upon credit; and undoubtedly the States are in greater want of credit at this time than at former periods. It can be had only in Great Britain." So why should anyone insist on any other kind of arrangement when America would have to accept whatever was offered her?

There was one other consideration that permitted Parliament to act so boldly in American matters; and it too rested on American weakness, political as much as economic. It assumed that even if the prognosis about America's reaction should be mistaken, and that American anger would stimulate wish for revenge, the result would be the same. The United States did not really constitute a nation, for each had a set of discrete interests which would militate against their taking concerted steps in foreign relations. "We might as reasonably dread the effects of combinations among the German as among the American States," reflected Sheffield. Like the Germanies, "no treaty can be made with the American States that can be binding on the whole of them."

This was the situation Jay encountered when he assumed office in 1784. He understood clearly the British attitude, and knew that the diagnosis was basically accurate. But he also recognized that it was shortsighted and ultimately self-defeating. If Americans were to pay their debts and if they were to continue to be a part of the British economy, even in the inferior fashion anticipated by Sheffield, their prosperity should have been a matter of concern to the British. The present course of the American economy hurt both sides, something that British intelligence agents such as Sir John Temple and Edward Bancroft might have reported along with their confirmation of the decrepitude of American government. Jay wrote a note of unaccustomed despair to Benjamin Vaughan in London: "the policy of Britain respecting this country is so repugnant to common sense that I am sometimes tempted to think *it must be so*; and the old adage *quos Deus*, etc., always occurs to me when I reflect on this subject."

The secretary's former colleague in Paris, John Adams, bore the brunt of America's humiliation. As the first minister to the Court of St. James he suffered rebuffs from which he never recovered. The court took its tone from the king who never bothered to conceal his contempt for the young republic. When Adams demanded the respect due to his office, he was mocked with the suggestion that thirteen ambassadors would be necessary to represent the United States, not one. The minister consoled himself by recognizing that "This people cannot look me in the face; there is conscious guilt and shame in their countenances when they look at me. They feel they have behaved ill and that I am sensible of it." To say that he was sensible to his treatment is an understatement. Adams was willing to settle even for the ineffective Navigation Act of Massachusetts to symbolize American rejection of the inferiority assigned to the nation by Britain.

Unfortunately, while retaliation among the states was widespread it was also uneven in its scope and indiscriminate in its application. Massachusetts, more vulnerable than most states to British actions, complicated Jay's diplomacy by prohibitions for a time against all foreign shipping, including those of France and Holland. The secretary was forced to spend valuable time and energy remonstrating with Boston over damages to friends as well as to enemies. As for the varying tonnage duties imposed by many states, British merchants later admitted that the federal taxes a few years later were lower than those of individual states. But unlike a later period they were easily evaded, frequently with the connivance of rival states. Great Britain found herself in the classic position of playing one state off against another in a fashion which had been a conspicuous failure in the colonial era.

Although the overall economic mischief done by British policy can be overstated, hyperbole is impossible with respect to the fisheries or the West Indian trade. The failure of the United States to coerce the British into a more favorable posture toward American shipping meant the destruction of a segment of the economy. Newport, for example, never recovered from the loss of markets in the Caribbean.

The weaknesses in diplomacy which created these conditions did not signal the failure of the entire economy. New channels of trade opened in Asia and the Pacific which ultimately would compensate New England for their losses under the Confederation. Manufacturing everywhere expanded with independence and freedom from the restrictions of the Navigation Laws, although not to the degree feared by British competitors. The burgeoning west became the source of new markets and materials which in a generation would push the world market into the background. And even in areas proscribed by British Orders in Council, there were sufficient caveats to enable enterprising American shippers to operate with relative freedom in Caribbean ports, usually with the active collaboration of the islanders themselves. Clandestine American-West Indian connections in the 1780s were reminiscent of the relations between the Spanish West Indies and British "pirates" of the seventeenth century in which mutually profitable trade relations were conducted in the face of the express displeasure of the Spanish crown.[5]

But the triumphs of individual merchants and the durability of the economy were no tribute to the efficacy of the Confederation. They only dramatized the impotence of the secretary of foreign relations, whose own intervention seemed so futile. This was not only true in the area of commercial relations with Britain, but in almost every aspect of the treaty obligations of 1783, from contesting the St. Croix River boundary line in the northeast set in Article 2 to carrying off slaves from seaboard cities in violation of Article 7. Britain's refusal to evacuate from the military and fur posts of the Northwest constituted the most serious grievance, and this was a direct consequence of

[5] Merrill Jensen, *The New Nation: A History of the United States during the Confederation, 1781–1789* (New York, 1950), p. 199, notes that "If Horatio Nelson had not fought Trafalgar and loved Lady Hamilton, his place in history might have been recorded in nothing but a footnote about an obscure British naval officer whose best efforts in the West Indies were shattered by the ingenuity of local planters and the interloping American ship captains."

the inability of the Confederation to affect British decisions on the subject.

Initially, it was likely that the British intended to do little more than apply a loose construction to a departure marked by "all convenient speed," so that Montreal fur interests would have a chance to liquidate their investments without loss. This would be one way of realizing an objective that was not met at the negotiating tables: namely, a definite three-year stay on American soil until the fur traders had concluded their business and until their Indian allies had secured equitable treatment from Americans. The record of the colonial dealings with Indians did not breed optimism for the future. Indeed, Governor-General Sir Frederick Haldimand had been disturbed about Indian resentment over the prospect of British defeat, to the extent that he ordered officers in Northwest posts not to divulge the terms of the treaty to Indians. He feared they might turn on their former British benefactors for their betrayal. Despite this consideration Haldimand's correspondence suggested full compliance with instructions to evacuate seven forts south of the Great Lakes, much as Carleton had moved out of New York City with his troops. If his petition to stall evacuation found a ready ear in Whitehall, it was not the plight of the fur trader or Indian that moved British officials. It was an appreciation of the inability of the United States to enforce the provisions of the treaty and the sufficiency of plausible excuses to justify their course of action.

Lord Sydney, secretary of state for home affairs, set the tone of the British attitude a day before the ratification of the treaty was proclaimed by the king in a dispatch to Haldimand which observed that the United States had not complied with important parts of the treaty, notably those provisions concerning the repayment of debts to British creditors and the restitution of Loyalist rights and properties by the states. That this observation was an excuse to be seized was apparent from the fact that American compliance with Articles 5 and 6 was to follow ratification while Sydney's dispatch preceded it! This was nothing less than a brazen attempt to give some color of legality to a breach of promise, and as such was as much an insult to American intelligence as it was to American sovereignty.

Jay remonstrated vigorously against the British presence in the Northwest, without success. When none of his arguments succeeded he directed his anger against those states whose unwillingness to honor obligations continued to undercut his efforts to dislodge the British, and to the Confederation that lacked the force to command the respect of foreign countries. The bitterness of this experience deepened his own essential conservatism. Those states which respected obligations were those controlled by conservatives, and Jay was convinced of irresponsibility of those who did not look upon their inability or unwillingness to repay debts as anything but a national disgrace. Given these sentiments, his resentment of Britain's behavior was diluted almost to the point of accepting the British brief. He even let the British consul, Sir John Temple, know the contents of his report to the Congress in 1786, in which he deplored the obstinacy of the states, in advance of its official presentation; and even more surprising, he communicated to the consul an implied sympathy for Britain's position on the evacuation of the posts. This indiscretion was only partially redeemed by the fact that it made very little difference to either British or American behavior. Neither would be governed by the views of the secretary for foreign relations.

The moving force behind Jay's actions was not Anglophilia. Rather, they were the product of the depressed state of mind induced by the overwhelming inadequacies of the Confederation. From one extremity of the nation to the other he could see nothing but disaster in the incapacity of the government to cope with the diplomatic challenge. In the north, Vermont, claimed by New York and New Hampshire, could be lost to the nation as a consequence of a weak executive to solve the conflict. The Allen family, dominant in Vermont affairs, threatened to join Canada if Vermont did not receive statehood and their properties were not fully secured. How could these demands be met when the approval of all thirteen states was required before a new state could be admitted to the Union? In the meantime, Vermont acted as if it were an independent unit, and gladly accepted special commercial favors from the British government, which was quick to exploit the American dilemma.

In the west and the south the Indian problem resisted satisfactory solution. The Continental Congress as early as 1775 had attempted to provide a national Indian policy, but the states seeking advantages for themselves managed to water down the original version of Article IX of the Articles which granted the Congress "sole and exclusive right" of the regulating Indian affairs only on the condition that "the legislative right of any State within its own limits be not infringed or violated." Such a proviso rendered futile the pious hope held in the Report of the Committee on Indian Affairs in 1783, which had considered a common national policy of equitable regulation necessary for both "the honor of the federal government and the public tranquillity thereby promoted." Neither prevailed under the Confederation. New York challenged the Confederation's Treaty of Fort Stanwix with the Iroquois of western New York on the grounds that it had its own separate agreements with the Indians of that state. Similarly, Georgia undid the treaties with Cherokees, Choctaws, and Chickasaws at Hopewell in 1785 by making conflicting arrangements with an independent band of Creeks in 1786.

On paper the Indian policy of the Confederation was reminiscent of the best of Britain's management. The Ordinance for the Regulation of Indian Affairs created two departments, separated by the Ohio River. Each would be governed by a superintendent and deputies reporting to the secretary of war, who would supervise the licensing of traders and the maintenance of justice in tribal relations with the United States. In practice any state could render meaningless the authority of the Articles by imposing its own laws on Indians within the state's jurisdiction. Congress therefore was no more able to make meaningful agreements with Indians than it could with the British. Even though Indian problems were intimately linked to foreign relations, John Jay's office had no official part in their conduct.

Jay's frustrations were all the greater because the Indian question was at the heart of difficulties with Spain as well as with Great Britain. In the case of the latter, it was a minor part of a larger problem; British intrigue with Joseph Brant and the Mohawks was merely another weapon in their large arsenal of diplomatic pressures against the United States. For Spain, however, the intimate tie with Creek chieftain Alexander McGillivray, Brant's counterpart on the Spanish border, was a cornerstone of Spain's American policy, and ultimately the last desperate hope of containing the potential American tidal wave against the territories of Spain in America. In light of the essential feebleness of the Spanish crown a strong credible Indian policy on the part of Congress would have smashed Spanish machinations at their inception.

Such was not to be under the Confederation. Jay's troubles with the Spanish were to be as painful as with the British, and essentially they were more divisive. American interests in the Northwest, after all, were in their infancy, and their arrest by British activity was not vital to the economy. But Spain's decision in 1784 to end the free navigation of American boats on the Mississippi, along with the imposition of special tariffs for the deposit of goods in New Orleans, were draconian to American farmers in Kentucky and Tennessee whose channels to the outside world cut through Spanish territory. West of the Appalachians all waters flowed to the Gulf of Mexico, creating a dangerous dependence on Spanish good will for the safe conduct of products whose marketing through New Orleans meant the difference between expansion and profit, on the one hand, and withering in a subsistence economy, on the other. A satisfactory diplomatic arrangement was vital for the economic future of the west.

Many of America's troubles with Spain were of her own making, in which Spain was a relatively innocent party. The Anglo-American Treaty of Paris contained two articles, one published and the other secret, which were unacceptable to Spain. The objectionable published Article VIII had guaranteed to Britain and the United States free navigation of the Mississippi River "from its source to the ocean," even though the mouth of that river was in Spanish hands at the end of 1783. As if this were not provocation enough, the secret article allowed the boundary between the United States and Florida to be at the Yazoo River, if Britain retained Florida in the final peace settlement. If Britain returned Florida to Spain, as she did, the southern boundary of the United States would be at the 31st parallel. Spain had neither the obligation nor the intention of accepting either the American pretensions to the Mississippi or the claim to the 31st parallel. Accepting the former would not only proclaim Spain's weakness but would encourage the growth of an American population in the west that would submerge Spanish sovereignty as it moved down the river. Accepting the latter would not accord with the facts of Spain's repossession of Florida, which in her view extended to the Yazoo and beyond. There had been nothing in the Anglo-Spanish Treaty which limited the Spanish claim; British Florida had extended to the Yazoo River.

The ending of the Revolutionary War seemed only to open new conflict with Spain. The Mississippi and Florida questions were unsettled; and even more troublesome, Spain had made no formal recognition of the United States, and had no immediate intention of doing so. Reluctantly and with poor grace the King of Spain at the behest of French mediators permitted William Carmichael, chargé d'affaires in Spain, to present his credentials in the summer of 1783. The foreign minister Floridablanca had resisted this importunity in the past on the grounds that Carmichael was only a "secretary," and that by accepting him at the court a precedent might be set that would encourage other secretaries to demand treatment as ambassadors. This reasoning was never more than a pallid excuse to put out of mind and to keep as distant as possible a dangerous new neighbor. Count de Aranda, the Spanish ambassador to Paris, put the fears clearly when he noted that "This federal republic is born a pigmy. A day will come when it will be a giant, even a colossus, formidable in these countries. Liberty of conscience, the facility for establishing a new population on immense lands, as well as the advantages of the new government, will draw thither farmers and artisans from all the nations. In a few more years we shall watch with grief the tyrannical existence of this same colossus."

To put off this day as long as possible Spanish statecraft established a plan that would keep the enemy on the defensive on a number of fronts. Floridablanca began his campaign with the scheme, proposed and then abandoned during peace negotiations, of raising an Indian buffer state whose friendship to Spain and hostility to the United States would ensure security. Indian allies were not difficult to find. McGillivray induced Creeks, Chickasaws, and Choctaws to make peace among themselves and then to conclude treaties with Spain in 1784 and 1785 which would exclude all whites from their villages who lacked Spanish passports. Such materials as they would require from the outside world would be supplied through Spain. The deal was reinforced by the active partnership of McGillivray himself with the British firm of William Panton and Company, which had been licensed by the Spanish government to import British goods. Spain recognized that Spanish facilities were insufficient for this task.

The scheme worked up to a point. It had the loyal support of Indian leaders who shared a common interest in the containment of Americans. But its psychological value was impaired when Panton and his partners proved unable to compete with the enterprising Yankee rivals in supplying Indians. Nor were the chieftains able to patch up the fragmented Indian society whose inchoate organizations allowed even the inept Congressional policymakers to sign agreements with dissident leaders that served American interests. Thus the Indian buffer conception seemed unreliable to Spain, and Spain's own exhibition of fear in the face of the American challenge rendered suspect her promise of protection of the Indians in the Florida country.

Spain thereupon turned to direct diplomacy with the Confederation, sending to New York the able agent Diego de Gardoqui, to win by craft what was unobtainable by strength. Gardoqui, entitled *encargado de negocios* to discourage connotations of diplomatic recognition, approached Americans with the intention of enchanting them with his charms in such a way that their natural passions would be turned against themselves rather than against Spain. The Spanish envoy perceived sufficient schisms within the new nation to make exacerbation a relatively simple process. Spain should profit from the ensuing chaos. Hence there was guile in the generous offer of the hand of friendship to northern shippers interested in penetrating the Iberian market. It would include a reciprocal trade agreement at least as beneficial as any offered to any other sovereign power wherein Spanish ports on the mainland and in the Canary Islands would be open to American ships and goods. As an earnest of the benefits this connection would yield to America the King of Spain exercised his influence to help the United States make a favorable agreement with Morocco, one of the Barbary states that had been preying on American commerce. The price for access to the Spanish markets was to be paid by western farmers and southern expansionists who would be denied navigation rights on the Mississippi River and any boundary settlement south of the Yazoo.

Such was the nature of the gifts Gardoqui brought to America. To ensure their effect he was also empowered to provide special presents accompanied by suitable flattery and pleasantry presumably to such susceptible ministers as Secretary Jay. Gardoqui made clear his exertions and his expectations when he wrote: "Notwithstanding my age I am acting the gallant and accompanying Madame [Jay] to the official entertainments and dances, because she likes it and I will do everything which appears to me for the King's best interest." What he hoped would come out of all these efforts would be the division of America into antagonistic parts, with the west and the south reviling the commercial Northeast for selfishly sacrificing their special interests.

But even with these purposes in mind Gardoqui and particularly the Spaniards on the scene were doubtful if the results of such friction would really benefit the Spanish Empire. Could not frustrated westerners lash out at Spain as well as at New York and spill over into the Mississippi demanding on their own the reopening of the river? Gardoqui in the midst of his treaty plans saw the utility of avoiding "the vexations of such a naturally robust people, trained to war and accustomed to the last degree of greatest hardships." No amount of solicitation for Jay's vanity would manage the passions of the frontiersman. Jay himself and the Confederation he represented were unequal to that task.

Given these considerations Gardoqui was not averse to an alternative plan of inviting unhappy frontiersmen into Spanish territory with full commercial privileges, of detaching Kentucky or Tennessee and making these western territories part of the empire. In a sense, western interest in this approach was a direct by-product of the suspicions of New York raised by the fact of negotiations which westerners felt to be at their expense and without their advice. While Jay was readying treaty proposals for Congress, James Wilkinson, a general in the Revolution and still a young man of great ambitions and small scruples, entered the service of Spain, in which he was to remain for a generation as an informer and general agent. Pretending to agitate for statehood in Kentucky in 1786, Wilkinson was hopeful that Virginia's opposition would make the leadership in that territory disposed to accept Spanish protection. John Sevier and James Robertson, leaders of Tennessee communities but men of smaller ambitions and greater scruples, were also attracted for a time to the idea of a Spanish connection. To accelerate a growing disillusionment with the Confederation, Spanish authorities in New Orleans considered opening their territory to Americans who, as emigrants, would be given local autonomy as well as full privileges of trade on condition that they become formally subjects of the Spanish crown.

Inviting as these prospects were to Spain, they never amounted to more than desultory intrigue. After 1787 separatism lost its appeal even if statehood was not immediately on the horizon. Spain's hopes of detaching the outlying territories of the state ended completely with the acceptance of the Constitution and a new federal union.

But Spain's failure owed little to the counteraction of the Confederation or to the adroitness of Jay's tactics. If anything the rebuffs to Spain exposed the ineffectiveness of the Articles' diplomatic weaponry with unusual clarity and provided the setting for charges against Jay of using his office for the service of selfish sectionalism. Not that Jay was the prime mover in Spanish-American affairs. Congress controlled Indian policy through other agents independent of the secretary's authority; and Spain's dallying with western accomplices was obviously managed outside conventional lines of communication. But in the area of Jay's operation as a diplomatist the results were almost calamitous. Instructed expressly to negotiate a treaty which assured the navigation of the Mississippi and maintained the American claim to the 31st parallel, Jay *in camera* did precisely the opposite. He negotiated a treaty of commerce and alliance wherein Spain granted the many concessions in the Spanish mainland ports that Gardoqui had brought with him to America along with a proposal of a formal alliance. The latter would promise intervention in America's behalf for the return of the Northwest posts "by force of arms if it otherwise cannot be promptly secured." In return for these extensive services the United States would relinquish her claims to navigate the Mississippi for a period of twenty to thirty years, depending on the life of the treaty.

Jay knew the risks he ran in appearing to sacrifice the vital interests of the south and the west. His actions would seem to confirm the bias of such as Rufus King who frankly opposed the expansion of the west for fear of losing citizens whose presence was needed in the east. Nature having separated the sections by mountains would intervene to make a separate nation from the mass of western settlers. To avert suspicion that he was pandering to this kind of thinking the secretary asked Congress for the establishment of a select committee to advise and direct his activities so that he could engage in secret talks with the Spanish without inviting excessive criticism in the event he had to deviate from his instructions. James Monroe of Virginia, a vigorous opponent of the proposed treaty, admitted that Jay had spoken freely to him as early as December, 1785, on the need to "forbear from the use of the river for twenty-five to thirty years." Jay had obviously given serious attention to the momentous step he made in 1786, and had done it with candor and with a sense of proprieties. But he did not succeed in winning the appointment of an advisory committee to bestow its blessing on his negotiations.

On one issue he won a point which revealed to the Spanish that he had lost the case. By a vote of seven to six Congress changed his instructions. He could continue to talk freely with Gardoqui, although to knowledgeable observers of the New York scene—and Gardoqui was one of the most knowledgeable—the fact that southern opposition to the whole proceedings gained six votes doomed any results that might have followed from the conversations. Nine states would have been the minimal number to approve a treaty with Spain. Recognizing his Pyhrric victory for what it was, Jay wisely declined to pursue the matter further, and looked for the forthcoming Constitutional Convention to manage this and every other problem of foreign affairs. But his prudence did not disarm his opponents; Monroe among other southern *enragés* never abandoned his conviction that the cloture of the Mississippi was part of a massive betrayal of the south and the west in behalf of Jay's class and section. Formally, the Jay-Gardoqui negotiations ended shortly before the demise of the Confederation when a Congressional resolution took the matter out of Jay's hands.

In retrospect, Jay's behavior was hardly as monstrous as his critics have claimed. Posterity has judged him to have been an honest man. He also had an honest case to present to the country. The specific material benefits to the tobacco trade, for example, should have been seen as a national, not just a sectional, asset. More groups than shipping magnates of New England or grain producers from Pennsylvania would profit from the new Spanish markets. Special payments for American products would enter the fractured economy as a life-giving elixir at a time when the nation was being buried in state-issued paper money. On the political level Spain would be an instrument to pry Britain loose from its obstreperous positions. At one stroke Spain would do what France had conspicuously been unable to do: namely, give America strength to push the British from the west. And finally, if the Mississippi issue were separated from the Florida boundary question, the Spanish would probably yield to the American claim for the 31st parallel.

Such were the attractions that he could present to the country. What was even more persuasive was the absense of genuine alternatives in dealing with the Spanish problem. How else could the weak instrument of government survive the challenge in which Spain, like Great Britain, emerged more as a voracious shark than as the huge helpless whale of Henry Adams' imagery?[6] Why not make a virtue out of a necessity? If

[6] Arthur P. Whitaker, *The Spanish-American Frontier, 1783–1795: The Westward Movement and the Spanish Retreat in the Mississippi Valley* (Boston and New York, 1927), pp. 15–16, points out that "In 1783 the realities of either the Americans' hope or the Spaniards' fear seemed remote, and to American eyes the Spanish whale looked very like a shark."

Spain would not yield on the navigation issue, then let the United States forbear, not surrender, the claim to use the Mississippi for a generation, and raise the claim later when it could be enforced. "As that navigation is not *at present* important, nor will probably become much more so in less than twenty five or thirty years, a forbearance to use it while we do not *want it*, is no great sacrifice." So spoke the secretary for foreign relations in 1786.

In declaring flatly the absolute lack of choice for American policy, Jay was the supreme pessimist, whose professional misanthropy grew out of the frustrations of the office. He was mistaken certainly in his timetable of the growth of American power; and he was mistaken also in his overestimation of European superiority. He was probably the victim of his own prejudices as well, valuing too highly the commercial privileges and too lightly the southern and western conceptions of their own interests and the passions that would be aroused from neglecting them. A basic problem was that Kentucky needed a Mississippi outlet in 1786, as well as in the near future. Whether Jay was carried away either by the prospect of an easy escape from his immediate preoccupations or whether he was myopically absorbed with the fortunes of his own section of the country remains open for debate. That he misjudged the mood of the nation is less debatable.

The behavior of France during the agonizing confrontations with Britain and Spain gave a special poignancy to Jay's sense of America's isolation in a hostile world. The ally gave the secretary no comfort, although it is likely that he never expected to find any from that quarter. When Jefferson reported in his capacity as minister to France that Vergennes did not place the American right of navigation "within their guarantee" under the terms of the alliance or of the peace treaty, Jay instantly concluded that the minister referred to navigation rights on the Mississippi. Actually Jefferson was referring to the French guarantee of America's boundary, and most specifically the Northwest boundary with Great Britain. Jay's construction of this letter to apply to navigation was as much a reflection of his attitude toward France as it was of his compulsion to justify his treaty plans with Spain.[7]

The secretary was probably not seeking to deceive the Congress, nor was he deceiving himself in his suspicions about the French ally. The reports of Jefferson as minister to France through much of Jay's tenure reveal clearly how unstable a support the French would be to America's foreign policy. For the optimistic Jefferson this insight took time to assimilate. He had left for France in 1784 to join Adams and Franklin in treaty-making with European powers with high hopes of French cooperation in these efforts. His appreciation for the French had quickened during the war years when he felt himself a beneficiary of French assistance in the war with Britain, and they persisted into the postwar period when he realized how valuable the ally could be in countering continuing British malevolence toward the United States. His initial triumphant reception in Paris as the successor of Franklin convinced him at least of the benevolence of the French intelligentsia. And in the next five years he could, and occasionally did, take pride in the treaty he signed with Prussia in 1785 as well as in the work of Adams in the treaties with the Netherlands, and of Franklin with Sweden, in 1782 and 1783 respectively. Above all, Jefferson had the right to bask in some self-congratulations over the influence he exerted among friends who were to lead a revolution in the year of his departure from France, 1789.

All these small triumphs while gratifying to the ego did not conceal from the minister the essential failure of the United States to win over France and Europe to the new liberal conception of international economy that he had envisaged at the end of the Revolutionary War. Jefferson had undertaken initially "nothing less than a diplomatic mission to convert all Europe to the commercial principles of the American Revolu-

[7] Arthur B. Darling, *Our Rising Empire, 1763–1803* (New Haven, 1940), pp. 107–108, observes that "Jay construed this episode to mean that France would uphold Spain's argument against the United States on the Mississippi as her ministers had supported Aranda in regard to the boundary of the Southwest."

tion," in the words of Merrill Peterson.[8] This was not to be. Favorable treaties with Sweden and Prussia, countries with few prospects of serious trade with the United States, were not the answer to America's difficulties. What was needed was a massive breakdown of the mercantilist thinking and practices of the Old World to permit the new nation to redirect its commerce away from British channels. The goal was not merely the securing of greater economic benefits for Americans; it was essential to the ending of British domination of all American affairs, economic and political. Nothing that Jay in New York or Adams in London informed him about British attitudes after 1783 gave him any reason to doubt the peril facing the United States if she failed to meet this challenge.

If Europe disappointed, at least France should have responded to America's need. To this end Jefferson employed all his many charms to move such men as Lafayette and DuPont and such groups as the physiocrats, with their concern for free trade, to change French economic policy toward the United States. France must extend the few concessions made to American economic interests and capture for herself the lucrative commerce Britain had enjoyed for over a century. To do this new laws had to be enacted. The links implied in the mutual acceptance of a liberal doctrine of neutral rights and most-favored-nation treatment must include, according to the reasoning of the American minister, the free entry of American products into the French market in exchange for French supplies and manufactures.

Jefferson had no chance for permanent success on the eve of the collapse of the *ancien régime*. Hapless France could not help herself, let alone a distant and uncertain ally. Even when a ministry—finance or foreign—was willing to yield to America's importunities, as in the case of the decree of 1784 which would permit American ships legal entry to the West Indies, it would retreat under pressure of angry French merchants fearful of American competition. During the short time it lasted the decree was a daring departure from the French past, involving

[8] Merrill D. Peterson, "Thomas Jefferson and Commercial Policy, 1783–1793," *William and Mary Quarterly*, Third Series, XXII (October, 1965): 592.

as it did the opening of seven ports for ships under 60 tons which brought in lumber, pelts, and tar in return for molasses and rum. Vergennes, ever the realist, recognized that the islands needed the supplies, and if they did not get them in this fashion, they would secure them by smuggling. But the break with custom was beyond France's capacity to absorb. The same fate met Jefferson's efforts to serve New England's whale oil, South Carolina's rice, and Virginia's tobacco. Although he was able to secure some reduction in whale-oil duties and some promises of rice imports, not even with Lafayette at his side could he undercut the combination of Robert Morris and the French tobacco monopolists who determined the quantities of French purchases of American tobacco. The most Jefferson could manage in this situation was to induce the Farmers General to buy a stipulated amount of tobacco outside of Morris' private contract which would be carried either in French or in American ships.

Tobacco was at the heart of Jefferson's problem. For Jefferson to reorder the American economy the abolition of tobacco and other monopolies was a prerequisite. Otherwise, American merchants would remain captive to the British system with its manipulation of credit and its long familiarity with the habits of American clients. France must be able to see her own advantage in the winning of political power as well as financial profit through generous terms to American shippers. Alternatively, "our merchants," Jefferson lamented, "must abandon the French markets, if they are not permitted to sell the productions they bring, on such terms as will enable them to purchase reasonable terms in the manufactures of France." Vergennes was in substantive agreement with almost all of Jefferson's arguments, but there was little he or any other minister could do to effect a remedy. Such concessions as America did win turned out to be inadequate palliatives, and no one recognized this problem more clearly than Jefferson himself.

Jefferson's wide-ranging intellect responded to these frustrations according to the mood of the moment. On occasion he would write friends that the only hope for survival was the abandonment of international commerce, so that the United States might "stand, with respect to Europe, precisely on the footing of China." But he accompanied this notion with the confession that he was speculating with "a theory which the servants of America are not at liberty to follow. Our people have a decided taste for navigation and commerce . . . and their servants are in duty bound to calculate all their measures on this datum." On other occasions, particularly after his perception of the inadequacy of the French counterweight to British power, he appealed to Americans to develop a mercantilist economic policy that would extract the compliance of Europe to American needs. In this spirit he breathed an air of nationalism headier than Jay himself could take. Unlike the secretary for foreign relations, Jefferson urged the building of a navy to challenge the Algerian pirates rather than pay ransom to rescue American prisoners. For the minister in France the Algerian problem was another face of Great Britain's hostility. Protected by a great navy, the British could look complacently on the damage done to the merchant marines of smaller nations. Jefferson subscribed fully to the accuracy of the sentiments Benjamin Franklin claimed to have heard in London in 1783: namely, "that if *there were no Algiers, it would be worth England's while to build one.*" While the British enemy continued to feed and prosper on American impotence, Jefferson found no redress from either the underdeveloped nationalism of America or the decadent nationalism of Europe.

Despite his disappointments he valued the fact of a French ally against the enemy, if only because there was no one else to help; and he worked to ingratiate himself with the French court down to the end of his stay in Paris. Embarrassed by the unpaid debt to France, he urged Congress to retain the good will of the French by accepting the proposal of Calonne, the finance minister, to transfer the American debt to a consortium of Dutch bankers for collection. In such a circumstance the obligation to France would be eliminated, and in the event of American defaulting on the debt the consequences would be less serious if the creditor was a group of private businessmen rather than the French government. In assuming the debt at a probable discount the presumption was that the Dutch financiers knew the risks they were taking. Congress rejected the idea on the grounds, publicly at least, that such a deal would be an implicit indictment of the good faith of the United States. *Sotto voce,* however, Congress admitted an apprehension that Dutch bankers might be more difficult to deal with as creditors than the more obliging and less efficient French officials.

Jefferson's attitude on the subject of financial obligation was an uneasy mixture of gratitude for France's willingness to bend the terms of repayment with resentment over the probable reasons for the tolerance. What did France want in exchange for America's postponement of payments? Jefferson was not sure, and yet he was suspicious that France might demand in the future an active American participation in a West Indian war as compensation for her benevolence. For this reason he was inhibited in complaining too vigorously against French hedging on its promises in the West Indies. A specific commitment to France would be too high a price to pay for open access to American ships in those ports.

Jefferson's growing reservations about the ties with France led him into a close communion with Jay on French affairs, and contributed to the one major accomplishment of American diplomacy with France under the Confederation, the conclusion of a mutually satisfactory consular convention. Both men had been disturbed by the element of extraterritoriality implicit in the convention Franklin had signed in 1782, and felt that its wording put the United States in the place of a protégé or client of France. Consuls and vice-consuls could present their credentials to the states where they resided rather than to the government of the Confederation. More serious was the provision that permitted consuls to appoint agents with consular privileges of their own who would operate in distant parts of the country. The most distressing of all to Jay and Jefferson was the right of a consul to arrest and sequester ships of French subjects and return them and their passengers to France, a right which smacked of inordinate control over French emigration to the United States. The new convention of 1788 removed these and other obnoxious articles. Signed by Jefferson, it was the first convention ratified by the new federal Senate.

Jefferson's harmony with the Constitution-makers spread to issues broader than consular conventions. All his experiences in France confirmed the importance of a vigorous central authority in the United States if the respect of Europe and the proper behavior of Great Britain were to be secured. Debts had to be paid, reciprocal agreements had to be met, navigation laws had to be enforced. Could the Confederation manage these tasks? It might have been Jay or Adams writing when Jefferson claimed in 1785: "You see that my primary object in the formation of treaties is to take the commerce of the states out of the hands of the states, and to place it under the superintendence of Congress, so far as the imperfect provisions of our constitution will admit, and until the states by new compact make them more perfect." By 1787 he was even more sensitive to the incapacity of the Confederation to control the actions of the states and to the effect that incapacity had upon the conduct of foreign policy. Although his correspondence during the debates over the Constitution reveal serious doubts the new instrument, "he never doubted," as Dumas Malone has observed, "the wisdom of putting diplomacy in federal hands."[9]

Jay's endemic suspicion of France and Jefferson's newly acquired caution were understandable in light of their experiences as diplomatists in the new nation. But neither of them ever penetrated the extent of France's unreliability. It is unlikely that even the watchful secretary had anticipated the cold-blooded projection by Louis-Guillaume Otto, chargé d'affaires in Philadelphia in 1787, of a nation rent by dissension to the point that he could advise his government to include in contingency plans the seizure of New York or Newport lest the British occupy them first. Nor was he aware of a report from the eccentric and inept French minister, the Comte de Moustier, contemplating the reoccupation of the Mississippi valley. But he did perceive clearly that France not only was unable to serve the United States, but could look with some complacency upon the consequences of her inability to help.

When the totality of the Confederation's problems in foreign affairs come under review, France's contribution to them was relatively minor. Vergennes and his successor Montmorin may have been anxious to maintain the United States in the position of a dependent client; but France was not an enemy. As all the diplomatists of the new nation recognized, America's great-

[9] Dumas Malone, "Jefferson and His Time," II: *Jefferson and the Rights of Man* (Boston, 1951), p. 174.

est perils in the 1780s came from fundamental internal flaws rather than from specific external challenges. If the former were remedied, the latter would be soluble. Whatever the differences prevailing among the founding fathers, the Constitutional Convention of 1787 was the repository of the faith of anyone burdened with responsibilities in foreign affairs.

CHAPTER VII

Diplomacy Under the Constitution· The First Years

☆ 1788-1793 ☆

THE DRAMATIC, even melodramatic, confrontations of the personalities of Thomas Jefferson and Alexander Hamilton have attracted so much attention in their time and afterward that observers of the first generation of the Federal Union frequently reduce the diplomacy of the Washington administration to the level of a duel between the two great cabinet members. The nature of their antagonism lends itself to a Manichaean contrast between good and evil. Depending upon the angle of observation, Jefferson or Hamilton was the wise defender of American interests against the cunning servant of a foreign power, either France or England. Thus, the Hamilton-Jefferson duel has its counterpart in Anglophilism and Francophilism, and the control of American foreign policy was made the object of their activity. Victory for Hamilton meant the triumph of an Anglophile, aristocratic, mercantile elite; victory for Jefferson meant the ascendancy of Francophile democratic, agrarian masses. The polarity is conveniently absolute.

Historians have contributed to the sharp division between the two men not because of particular partisan bias—although this is occasionally present—but frequently because of the enormous difficulty in providing independent judgments of the actors in this period. No matter what the intentions of the scholar may be, his search for objectivity becomes entangled in the web of traditional evaluations. When Paul Varg determined that Hamilton was "above all a realist who fatalistically accepted the existing framework, and dedicated himself to obtaining the best bargain possible," he automatically placed himself in the Hamiltonian camp. If Hamilton was the realist, then, as Varg concluded a paragraph later, Madison was the "idealist in foreign policy," a pejorative description of a man who "never felt it necessary to balance goals with the power available."[1] By contrast, Albert Bowman and Cecilia Kenyon identified Hamilton as the idealist who, according to the latter, required a patriotism from the people he did not expect from the advantaged classes, and, according to the former, formulated his foreign policy not on conditions as they actually were but on what he wanted them to be.[2] Realism in these views was on the Jeffersonian side. Both men, as Bowman saw them, "recognized the value of neutrality, but Hamilton would have surrendered it to Britain's demand . . . while Jefferson would have used it as a diplomatic weapon against all Europe."[3]

The temptation to categorize is irresistible; the historians themselves are prisoners of the past. Even when scholars attempt, as the foregoing have, to strip the situation of its emotional undertones, the language of the familiar controversy seems to impose itself upon the writers. This is not always the case; other writers flaunt their biases in a way that presents no difficulty to the reader. When Henry Cabot Lodge claimed that Hamilton's thoughts were "unbiased by sentiment for or against any other nation," or when Julian Boyd entitled a book *Number 7: Alexander Hamilton's Secret Attempts to Control American Foreign Policy*, the reader has no difficulty in identifying the authors with the main stream of the hagiographical tradition in the study of American foreign policy.[4]

[1] Paul A. Varg, *Foreign Policies of the Founding Fathers* (Lansing, 1963), p. 72.

[2] Cecilia Kenyon, "Alexander Hamilton: Rousseau of the Right," *Political Science Quarterly*, LXXIII (June, 1958): 171–178; Albert H. Bowman "Jefferson, Hamilton and American Foreign Policy," *ibid.*, LXXI, (March, 1956): 18–41.

[3] Bowman, *op. cit.*, pp. 21–22.

[4] Henry Cabot Lodge, *Alexander Hamilton* (Boston and New York, 1882), p. 160. Julian P. Boyd, *Number 7: Alexander Hamilton's Secret Attempts to Control American Foreign Policy* (Princeton, 1964).

What is missing in many of the analyses of the conflict within Washington's cabinet are not only the nuances vital in the understanding of the conduct of foreign policy but also important *dramatis personae* whose roles are either given perfunctory mention or who are wholly submerged in the rivalry between the secretary of state and the secretary of the treasury. John Jay, Gouverneur Morris, and Washington himself appear too frequently as pawns of Hamilton; while Madison, Monroe, and William Short emerge as extensions of Jefferson's personality. John Adams in the beginning of the Federalist period at least behaves as some species of sport or crank except when he is clearly on the outer edge of the Hamilton circle. To assert that these influential and complicated personalities have been slighted is not to deny that scholars have attempted to give them consideration in their writings. Dumas Malone, the most authoritative of Jefferson's biographers, scoffed at the notion that Madison and Hamilton parted ideological company only upon the return of Jefferson to America.[5] John C. Miller, a leading student of Hamilton, made clear the legitimate claim of Washington as a prime mover in foreign policy, rather than as a befuddled conservative led docilely to his positions by the dominant Hamilton.[6] But despite impressive disclaimers, the other statesmen of the period, even when the stamp of their personality is felt, are placed on a Jeffersonian or a Hamiltonian field rather than accorded separate ground of their own.

Another approach to foreign policy might subsume the differences among cabinet members under a substantial consensus broad enough to encompass all the members of the Washington administration and most of the Congress as well. Irrespective of personality conflicts and future ideological affiliations the leaders of the government agreed that the Confederation had failed to support a viable American foreign policy. They all looked upon the reconstituted Union as an opportunity to extract vital concessions from Europe which had been unattain-

[5] Dumas Malone, "Jefferson, Hamilton, and the Constitution," in W. H. Nelson, (ed.), *Theory and Practice in American Politics* (Chicago, 1964), p. 14.

[6] John C. Miller, *The Federalist Era, 1789–1801* (New York, 1960), pp. 12–13.

able in the past, from the relocating of boundary lines to the expansion of trade.

In this light Washington was the spokesman for a nation. Those factions for whom he did not speak had retired in confusion from the national scene. The Jeffersonians were not drawn from those groups. The sheer extent of agreement in Philadelphia rendered the President unprepared for the fierce differences over the national mandate which developed in subsequent years. His mind, never quick at its best, could neither comprehend fully the protean nature of the cabinet struggle nor accept its implications for American politics. Unwittingly, Washington contributed to Jefferson's problems by virtue of his own bent for foreign and military affairs. Hamilton, on the other hand, owed much of his freedom of operation to the president's lack of expertise in financial matters. Moreover, the vast areas of Hamilton's activities, including consular affairs, provided the secretary of the treasury with a measure of influence with the president and the Congress that would have aroused the resentment of any secretary of state, let alone a man who had been his senior in age, distinction, and service to his country. The absentee Virginian, fresh from his laurels in France, had reasons other than ideological to build an opposition to Hamilton. Jefferson was jealous of the younger man's prestige and power in the new government.

The transfer of a personal distaste for each other's manners and mannerisms to ideas and policies was neither automatic nor immediate. The forces that brought Hamilton and Jefferson together under Washington were strong enough to keep them together despite a variety of misgivings on the part of each man. Each had his reservations about the Constitution which in other circumstances could have separated them from the outset. To Hamilton the document was insufficiently responsive to the need for a secure governing body and hence excessively susceptible to the ravages of democracy. To Jefferson, viewing the Constitution through the eyes of Madison and Monroe, the document encouraged incipient monarchism by presidential reelection and implicitly threatened civil liberties by its silence on a bill of rights.

Although hindsight reveals wide philosophical gaps from the

outset, it often overlooks their agreement to act in concert under an imperfect Constitution which they both recognized to be the best possible instrument of government available in 1789. There is no serious states-rights element in Jefferson's *arrières-pensées* of that year; Hamilton's proposal for the restoration of the national credit was no less welcome than Madison's plans for a navigation system. Both were expressions of a growing American nationalism. Both suggest an independence of British and French influences, and the cultivation of an independent policy designed to win both security and prosperity. If the common ground on which Hamilton and Jefferson stood in 1789 collapsed under them by 1793, the course of European events more than incompatible philosophies accounts for the breakdown.

The French Revolution fashioned new meanings for France and England in the minds of the two secretaries, indeed in the minds of a considerable part of the country. Hamilton increasingly found in Great Britain the model of the good society, the font of America's commercial growth, and the protector against French imperialism. His Anglophilic tendencies had been evident in the 1780s, but they were to be deepened and widened by the European changes. For Jefferson, France was to become even more definitely than before the counterweight to British commercial power as she added the new function of bellwether of republicanism in a hostile monarchical world. The Anglo-French war of 1793 pushed the country and the two men into actions that had not been anticipated five years earlier. Given the joining of Hamiltonianism and Jeffersonianism into an American system of political economy a generation later, the observer may claim that Anglophilism and Francophilism were the sources of the devisive passions that marked the 1790s rather than agrarianism and mercantilism. A foreign policy still tied to the fortunes of Europe, which neither statesman had desired in 1789, dictated the direction of American politics.

The place of foreign policy and the management of diplomacy were important issues to the framers of the Constitution, even if they were not central to the worries of the nation at large. The proper conduct of foreign relations lay implicit in the elaborate distribution of powers among the three branches of government. Each could check the other two, but all of them contained ingredients which reinforced a national authority over foreign affairs of an order so conspicuously absent under the Confederation.

In clear, if negative, terms Section 10 of Article I of the Constitution denied to the states the power to enter "into any treaty, alliance, or confederation," or to "lay any imposts or duties on imports or exports," or to "enter into any agreement or compact with another state, or a foreign power, or engage in war, unless actually invaded, or in such imminent danger as will not admit of delay." Some of these inhibitions were drawn directly from the Articles of Confederation, but unlike the latter the new basic law specified measures of their enforcement to end once and for all the dangers inherent in thirteen sovereign states. To administer foreign policy an equally clear mandate went to the president in Section 2 of Article II. As head of the executive branch of government he could make treaties and nominate and appoint ambassadors and consuls "by and with the advice and consent of the Senate." The most explicit of all the powers given to the judiciary concerned foreign affairs. Section 2 of Article III extended to the judicial power "treaties made, or which shall be made," and to all cases affecting ambassadors or consuls. Finally, Article VI announced to the world that "all debts contracted and engagements entered into, before the adoption of this Constitution, shall be valid against the United States under this Constitution, as under the Confederation," and that the Constitution, including treaties made in its name, "shall be the supreme law of the land."

Small wonder that every statesman with experience in foreign affairs rallied to the support of this document. It addressed itself precisely to those troubles which had exposed the impotence of America under the Confederation. Its allure was powerful enough to quiet the suspicions of southern politicians who had been aroused over Jay's treatment of the Mississippi valley. When Patrick Henry invoked Jefferson's reservations about the Constitution to support his case that central power would be inimical to southern liberties, Madison quickly countered by pointing out to the Virginia ratifying convention that Jefferson's objections did not involve rejection of the Constitution; he had merely wanted improvements. Besides, as Madison emphasized, Jefferson's backing and filling over the document never applied to foreign affairs. Jefferson in August, 1787, had made clear: "I wish to see our states made one as to all foreign, and several as to all domestic matters." A few months later he expressed his appreciation to Madison for the tax powers that would be given to the federal legislature to free it from the interference of state assemblies.

The American minister to Great Britain was even more fervent in his blessing of a stronger central government. Adams' experiences in London had been more painful and humiliating than anything Jefferson had suffered in Paris. It was in London after all that the principle of the *alternat*—the custom of having each contracting party be first-named in its own copy of the treaty—was officially excluded from the American treaty. Under strict instructions from Whitehall, David Hartley had signed his name first on both copies of the Treaty of Paris, while the American followed in alphabetical order.[7] Here was a supreme symbol of American inferiority which John Adams was not likely to forget or forgive. The Constitution, however, could help to reduce its significance.

John Jay, one of the signers of that treaty, was also one of the three propagandists of the *Federalist Papers*, working for the passage of the Constitution through the New York ratifying convention. While his specific contributions were few quantitatively, all of them reflected the expertise he had acquired as the Confederation's foreign minister. He wrote only five of the eighty-five essays, but after Hamilton's introductory paper the next four were Jay's handiwork and all of them related to the necessity of frustrating Europe's ability to divide the Union against itself. The fact that this theme is established so early in the presentation suggested the priority Hamilton, Madison, and Jay gave to the problem. Jay advised in Federalist Paper Number 4 that if Europeans "see that our national government is efficient and well administered, our trade prudently regulated, our militia properly organized and disciplined, our resources

[7] Robert R. Davis, "The Foundations of American Diplomatic Treaty Etiquette," *Foreign Service Journal* (March, 1968): 21–22.

and finances discreetly managed, our credit re-established, our people free, contented, and united, they will be much more disposed to cultivate our friendship than provoke our resentment." But if they see America weak and fragmented, the nation would be exposed "not only to their contempt, but to their outrage."

The new secretary of state, successor to the secretary of foreign relations, would not only subscribe to the foregoing sentiments, but he would agree as well to the benefits of union outlined by the secretary of the treasury that would confound "all the combinations of European jealousy to restrain our growth." Hamilton's paradigm of a hostile Europe competing with the United States in commerce of every kind and envious of America's potential strength, expressed in Federalist Paper No. 11, was close to Jefferson's perception of Europe in 1789. Particularly apposite is Hamilton's resentment of Europe's pretensions of superiority over America, expressed almost in the same language Jefferson used to rebuff the ideas of Buffon and Raynal when he was in France: "Men, admired as profound philosophers, have, in direct terms, attributed to her inhabitants a physical superiority and have gravely asserted that all animals, and with them the human species, degenerate in America—that even dogs cease to bark after having breathed awhile in our atmosphere. Facts have too long supported these arrogant pretensions of the Europeans. It belongs to us to vindicate the honor of the human race, and to teach that assuming brother, moderation. Union will enable us to do it."

If Jefferson and Hamilton shared anger over the pseudo-scientific slanders of some French philosophes, they shared as fully in the initial building of a fabric of government sturdy enough to implement the promise of the Constitution. The two men had not met until Jefferson returned to the United States early in 1790 to assume his office, but the absence of immediate friction was due more to a common outlook on national problems than to Jefferson's notorious reluctance to involve himself openly in any feud. The secretary of state could even accept Treasury's personnel force of some seventy men, with functions in consular affairs intruding into his department, in contrast to his small staff of five, with limited duties, as long as he could accept Washington's assurance that his office was the more important and the more distinguished.

Jefferson appeared as ready as Hamilton to act on the principle that the executive branch should have maximal independence, at least in foreign affairs. And his blessing was not merely by indirection. In April, 1790, shortly after taking up his duties he presented a memorandum on the powers of the Senate over diplomatic appointments. His theme was that such a transaction was altogether executive and almost exclusively so, "except as to such portions of it as are specially submitted to the Senate. Exceptions are to be construed strictly." As for the president's question on the propriety of consulting the Senate on which countries should be approached about diplomatic exchanges, Jefferson asserted that there was no constitutional requirement for soliciting such advice. He felt it impolitic to set a precedent. The Senate's powers extended no further than the approval or disapproval of the person nominated by the president. In displaying this loose construction of presidential authority, the secretary of state put himself in a position indistinguishable from that of his conservative predecessor, now Chief Justice Jay, whom Washington had consulted on the same issue.

Given this attitude Jefferson and Madison were not hostile to the Hamiltonian program as they first understood it. The raising of revenue through a tariff, the repaying of obligations through federal assumption of the debts of the previous governments, and the creation of a navigation system to promote American shipping were not objectionable to the secretary of state. The liquidation of the foreign debt was welcomed by Madison. Even Jefferson's negative views on the federal assumption of state debts, in exchange for a federal capital on the Potomac River, were visible only after the event; he was the broker to the arrangement initially.[8] Jefferson in 1790 may have had doubts about the implications of many of Hamilton's positions, but he was able to concede that whatever differences prevailed then,

[8] Jacob E. Cooke, "The Compromise of 1790," *William and Mary Quarterly*, Third Series, XXVII (October, 1970): 524, challenges Jefferson's "exaggerated claim that [the bargain] was responsible for the passage of the residence and assumption measures."

his opponents were nonetheless "good men and bold men, and sensible men."

It may be claimed that before the end of 1790 Jefferson and Madison, each working on the other's fears, discovered in Hamilton's program a divergence from the common good and in his person an arrogance that annoyed them at every turn. Funding of debts appeared to be a device to enrich speculators at the expense of the original creditors; the assumption of state debts appeared to be aimed blatantly at subsidizing the commercial north at the expense of the agrarian south; and the blunting of Madison's efforts to construct a navigation system appeared to be the product of a dangerous attraction to monarchical Britain. Yet it is questionable if the conclusions of conspiracy suggested above were fully articulated, even though the foundations for them were being laid. It was not just the intellectual opacity of President Washington that made him fail to perceive irreconcilable differences in the cabinet. If they existed at all they related to means, not to objectives. For the president in his first two years in office the consensus of 1789 over America's relations with the outside world persisted. And most of the evidence that suggested otherwise belongs to a later stage of the Hamilton-Jefferson rivalry.

Washington's conception of foreign policy and the means to effect it was relatively simple to define. It proceeded from the assumption, shared by his cabinet, that a weak Confederation had denied to the United States her proper acceptance in the world; that the desirability of alliances to effect acceptance was severely qualified; and that an independent policy in the hands of a stronger government would secure independence without placing the country under obligation to any foreign country. The federal government therefore assigned for itself the tasks of repaying debts to ally and former enemy alike in order to win favorable trading relations with all of Europe, push the British out of the Northwest posts, and coerce the Spanish into opening the Mississippi River to American commerce. To put these plans into motion the president looked primarily for assistance from the Department of State, which made that office a vital creation of the First Congress, even if the duties of the secretary judged by the modest size of his office appeared to be light in the early days of the new Federal Union.

Washington's most pressing burden was what Samuel Flagg Bemis called the "sinister symmetry" between British and Spanish policies in America.[9] Both powers posed severe threats to American sovereignty by their arousal of Indian hostility within American borders, and both encouraged separatist movements in their respective areas of influence in Vermont and in Kentucky. They refused to budge from their fixed positions or even to pay attention to American interpretations of the treaty obligations of 1783. In 1789 the British continued to occupy the fur posts of the Northwest and showed no inclination to change the commercial relations with the United States that had grown out of their contempt for American power of retaliation. Similarly Spanish authorities kept the Mississippi closed to American shipping and insisted on the Yazoo as the boundary line between Florida and the United States, two points on which they permitted no flexibility at the end of the decade.

From France there was no reason to expect more assistance than the Confederation had received in applying pressure on Britain or Spain. The French, as Jefferson knew, always had some sympathy for the American objectives but lacked in 1790 to an even greater extent than before the capacity and the will to intervene on behalf of the United States. The new secretary of state had enough suspicion of Montmorin's renewed interest in a French colony in Louisiana to question the nature of French assistance in this matter. Besides, there were other considerations that diminished France's utility as an ally. The possibility of a new European war entangling the United States in defense of the French West Indies would be too high a price to pay for French help, especially if the value from such aid continued to decrease with the spread of a debilitating revolution in France.

A survey of the world in the beginning of the Washington administration made it clear that such ventures in foreign policy that the United States might undertake would have to be done alone and with faith in her own resources. The president's first

[9] Samuel Flagg Bemis, "Thomas Jefferson," in *American Secretaries of State and Their Diplomacy*, II: 16.

step was to commission Gouverneur Morris, his former aide-de-camp, as a special agent to Great Britain to examine British intentions toward America's new government. Perhaps a recognition on the part of the British that the deficiencies of the past governments had been corrected might induce the Foreign Ministry to re-evaluate its early practices. If Morris should elicit a suitable response in London, the Spanish, always insecure in imperial issues and sensitive to the shifting tides of power, might be intimidated into making concessions in the west. An accommodation with Britain could be the shortest path to the opening of the Mississippi and to the guarantee of the loyalty of the west. Washington may even have looked on Jefferson to be Jay's successor because of the Virginian's favorable reputation among impetuous westerners.[10] Nor did the president exclude France from a role in these proceedings. As long as his protégé Lafayette exercised influence in the liberalized monarchy, French power might be available at a critical moment. Washington never held an intrinsic objection to Jefferson's conception of France as a counterweight to Britain in the balance of power.

The step beyond the dispatch of a mission was more difficult. What was Morris going to use as his weapons to effect change in British thinking toward the United States? Two major responses proved to be antithetical to each other and the source of so much internal division that neither had a chance to be properly tested. The more important—because the more successful—approach to Britain involved Hamilton's plan of assuming the debts of the earlier governments to win the favor of domestic as well as of foreign creditors. The secretary's program was comprehensive and sophisticated. To succeed in restructuring the American economy along commercial and ultimately manufacturing channels he felt the United States required the close cooperation of that paragon of sound economy and expanding credit, Great Britain. That nation would buy American raw materials, extend loans to promising American business ventures, and by the volume of Angloamerican commerce promote the fortunes of shippers. In the long run, America would create

[10] Darling, *Our Rising Empire*, p. 134, implies that Jefferson's reputation in Kentucky was a major factor in his selection as Jay's successor.

an economic base which would outbid British competitors in manufacture; but in the short run, British good will was paramount as a prerequisite for the building of American power. By deferring to the British economy and accepting the unequal treatment of American commerce the British would be inclined to relinquish the posts in the Northwest and to arrange a more equitable commercial agreement with the United States. Repayment of debts would symbolize America's good faith as well as Hamilton's vision of America's national interest.

Madison's understanding of the nation's needs impelled him toward a sharply different course of economic behavior which collided with Hamilton's. The uneasiness that Madison and Jefferson had felt over the special favors conferred upon speculators in the funding program was intensified by the hand Hamilton had in defeating Madison's tariff and tonnage proposals in the House of Representatives in 1789. As early as April of that year Madison had presented a list of tonnage duties for the promotion of American commerce, which presumably the secretary of the treasury subscribed to, much as the House leader had concurred with the principle of funding. But Madison's method of influencing British economic policy toward America was essentially to adopt immediately a variation of Britain's Navigation System. By imposing higher duties on British than on other foreign commerce there might be a reconsideration of the discriminatory provisions of the Orders in Council of 1783. Nine-tenths of American imports came from Great Britain, and over half of them in British ships. By penalizing Britain the Congress would not only foster the increase in American shipping but also provide an opportunity for the French ally, which had relaxed some of her monopolistic restrictions on American commerce, to be rewarded for her service.

The Madison device was simple to execute. The Congress would place a high tax on the products of those countries without treaties with the United States and heavier tonnage duties on foreign ships than on American ships. Thus six cents a ton would be charged for ships of United States registry, thirty cents for ships with commercial treaties, and fifty cents for ships without such agreements. There would be no tariff discrimination except for a 10 percent discount on imports of all goods carried in American bottoms. Within the confines of a single act the national revenue would be increased, American ships favored, friends rewarded, and enemies punished.

The tariff and tonnage bill passed the House but failed in the Senate where Hamilton's influence prevailed. Madison's proposals were watered down to the point where there was discrimination in favor of American shipping but no special discrimination among foreign shippers.

While Hamilton's defense of British interests was to grow with the years and to assume an ideological and personal bias, his reasons for subverting Madison's navigation bill were tactical rather than Anglophile. Like Madison he wanted a strong and independent American economy. The route to this objective divided over England and France. At another time, only a few years before under the Confederation, shippers would have welcomed the Virginian's scheme, just as Madison himself had toyed with the desirability of the central government accepting assumption of state debts. As John Miller points out, northern businessmen would have hailed Madison as benefactor and looked upon his measures as a useful restraint upon British cupidity.[11] But not in 1790. Prosperity had returned, and with it an awareness that commercial profits grew out of a close and undisturbed relationship with Great Britain. They had little confidence in the ability of France to perform the vital functions served by British merchants in supplying goods to America and an entrepot for American products. The success of Madison's system ultimately depended upon France's ability to replace Britain, even if this was not explicitly written into his Navigation bill. It is worth wondering if a successful trade act under the Confederation, improbable as it may have been, would not have foundered on the same inhibitions about French commerce.

Hamilton's fears in 1790 went beyond the question of a French alternative. He foresaw a drastic cutback in British imports if the duties were sustained and consequently a dangerous reduction in revenues at a time when his entire program

[11] Miller, *The Federalist Era*, p. 18.

rested upon a few well-oiled channels of funds. Without British imports who would pay import duties? Not the few French shippers who showed no signs of increasing their supplies or the American revenues. Furthermore, Hamilton was convinced that foreign capital was fundamental to the flourishing of his commercial system, and this could only be tapped in Britain. For an underdeveloped country, "every farthing of foreign capital . . . is a precious acquisition." And farthings were to be found only in British currency.

Neither Hamilton nor Madison divulged fully the positions England and France would have to play in the unfolding of their programs. The relationships were not fully formed in either case, although of the two Hamilton's links to England were more advanced than Madison's with France. Julian Boyd has demonstrated that Hamilton's personal ties with Major George Beckwith, Lord Dorchester's aide in New York in 1789 and 1790, were closer than one might expect between cabinet officer and an unofficial foreign diplomatic agent; they resembled that of a secret agent and his contact.[12]

Beckwith had no formal or even informal authority. Neither Washington nor Jefferson knew of the nature of his assignment and would not have been aware of any significance in his visit to New York in the summer of 1790 had not questions arisen over his diplomatic status during the Anglo-Spanish crisis over Nootka Sound. Beckwith had brought along and communicated privately to Hamilton a warning from British Foreign Minister Grenville that if discrimination against British ships and goods should materialize in a navigation act, the British government would counteract vigorously. The "continuance of the indulgencies shown to your shipping in our ports in Europe, depends upon your own conduct." To Hamilton this note meant that Britain could destroy at any moment of her choosing the basis of America's existing prosperity. He was intimidated, and responded undiplomatically, to say the least. Beckwith was able to report by means of his illicit information from the secretary of the treasury that the United States would frustrate the Madison bill. For the next three years the British government through

[12] Boyd, *Number 7*, pp. 12–13.

Beckwith, and later through official minister George Hammond, was able to maintain a repressive policy toward the United States secure in the knowledge that Hamilton would neutralize attempts at retribution.

What the secretary anticipated in return for his personal exertions on Britain's behalf was a generous commercial treaty that would open more privileges to American trade with Britain and to American ships in the British West Indies. To achieve this end he was willing to interfere recklessly with the plans of the president and the secretary of state. Whitehall's foreknowledge of America's anxiety for accommodation closed the options Gouverneur Morris in London may have had to bend British policies. Even when Grenville's information was erroneous or distorted—since Hamilton frequently attributed to the president views he did not have—the effect was the same. Great Britain was encouraged in its obstinacy by the advice of this highly placed official.

Morris, a tart-tongued conservative, was no kept man of the British aristocracy, and in fact incurred British displeasure by the company he kept with the French ambassador to Great Britain, his old friend Luzerne, to whom he indiscreetly disclosed the terms of his instructions. But he did know the president's mind and occasionally used ambiguously threatening language to make his point in a manner Washington or Jefferson would approve. Failing to make headway on the matter of a commercial treaty, beyond the courteous evasions of the foreign secretary, he turned to an area that should have alarmed the British: pressures on the Northwest posts. "We do not think it worthwhile to go to war with you for these posts; but *we know our rights, and will avail ourselves of them when time and circumstances may suit.*" None of this veiled intimidation penetrated British sang-froid because Hamilton had already informed Beckwith that the expeditionary force sent against the Indians in the spring of 1790 was not intended for action against the British posts. Hamilton had ensured the failure of the Morris mission by his intervention, and it is doubtful that the consequences advanced his hopes for a treaty with the British.

Nowhere was the secretary of the treasury's presence in foreign affairs felt with more telling effect than in the short-lived but lively Nootka Sound crisis of 1790. British traders had established a base in Spanish waters of the Pacific northwest; and when Spanish officials captured British merchant ships, imprisoned British nationals, and destroyed illegal British bases an apparent *casus belli* was at hand. Here was an opportunity for American statecraft to press its advantage. With Britain at war with Spain there would be competition for the good will of the United States, and Morris in London was immediately aware of a change in atmosphere. War or preace in Europe was the key to British feelings toward the envoy. "When, therefore, they came a little forward," he reported to Washington, "it proved to me their apprehension of a rupture." Now the time had come to break British and Spanish obduracy over evacuation of the Northwest posts and the opening of the Mississippi to American flatboats.

Morris was correct in his assessment of the British temper. The Foreign Ministry was in a quandary over the direction relations with the United States should take. American aggressiveness at this juncture could damage the credibility of the ultimatum Britain had issued to Spain demanding redress for British prisoners and restoration of the British posts in the Pacific. Spain might be encouraged to resist on the strength of American hostility to her enemy. As a consequence Whitehall vacillated between encouraging the United States to engage jointly in a war with Spain by yielding to American importunity and encouraging instead western separatists to immobilize America and thereby nullify the American factor in the balance of power. The Foreign Ministry finally decided to test cautiously both causes. Morris was received with greater cordiality than before as conversations with him began to introduce the possibilities of a British minister going to Philadelphia and a commercial treaty following from that step. At the same time Levi Allen, whose family had sought a British link under the Confederation, was led to believe the British were genuinely interested in returning Vermont to the British Empire.

Beckwith's dispatch of April 7, 1790, containing Hamilton's information, steadied British nerve in dealing with Morris and permitted a return to normal truculence in dealing with America generally. Hamilton's assurance was evidence enough that the United States was not bent on an Indian war that would affect the British position and was not interested in a renewed French association that would ally the Americans with Spain in a crisis. Hamilton had unwittingly affected British planning at a moment when conciliation was in the air, and thereby helped by his intrusion to postpone the very kind of commercial agreement which his friendship with Beckwith was supposed to effect.

Secretary of State Jefferson would have agreed with Hamilton's views on cautious Indian and French policies had he known of the conversations with Beckwith, although he would have disapproved vehemently of the conversations themselves. Jefferson immediately had seen in the Nootka Sound crisis an opportunity to win concessions from Britain which would never have been offered under normal circumstances. In response to the president's question about the answer he would give the British in the event they should request permission to pass through American territory enroute to the Mississippi, Jefferson advised submission to the hypothetical British request only after a price had been extracted for compliance. The secretary made clear to Morris that the American wish was for neutrality, which Britain could have if she did not move into Louisiana or the Floridas in the course of a Spanish war. To Washington he counseled evasiveness and the avoidance of any commitment for as long as possible.

Spain presumably would have the same right to cross American territory if she asked for it, but only after the Spanish had been reminded of America's deep interest in the navigation of the Mississippi and of the friendship both countries would enjoy if Spanish territory east of the Mississippi were in exchange for an American guarantee of the inviolability of territories west of that river. The terms for Spain were obviously stiffer than for Britain. Jefferson was not worried over any offense to France in a neutral stance; indeed, he hinted to the French that it would be in their interest to lessen the number of Spain's enemies by using the Franco-Spanish alliance to plead America's territorial cause.

This flurry of diplomatic recommendations bore no results, save to earn as an occasion for Hamilton to charge Jefferson with weakness and timidity. The response of the secretary of the treasury to the president's question was predictable. In a rambling document that cited international law to justify a positive or a negative answer to the British, he came down finally for consent to the hypothetical British request, just as Jefferson had done. The air of judicial deliberateness may have been just for cabinet consumption, since in private Hamilton had committed himself to the British side. Yet the secretary had no sense of impropriety in his dealings with Beckwith. The traditions of the Confederation included private communications with foreign agents, and his advice to the British included a stern warning against such ambitions as they may have entertained about New Orleans. At the same time Hamilton rendered futile Jefferson's attempts in the arts of diplomacy with the British. A favorable bargaining position had been undermined.

The immediate effects of American cabinet ministers operating at cross-purposes were not significant. Spain's increasing discomfort with the radicalized Bourbon partner and increasing awareness of military shortcomings led to submission to British demands. The Nootka Sound imbroglio ended abruptly in the fall of 1790. And with its passing British interest in a change in relations with America passed too. Whether or not it had access to privy counsels of Washington's administration, the British Foreign Ministry would have continued its hostile attention to American commercial and territorial interests.

Ever since Jefferson had returned to the United States his reservations about American expectations from the outside world became more pronounced. Particularly his experience with Great Britain left him no grounds for optimism before 1790, and nothing occurred in 1790 to make him revise his impressions. Without knowing the details of Hamilton's ties to Beckwith he suspected no good for American foreign policy would come out of that association. Jefferson could find neither virtue nor sense in the Hamiltonian logic behind deferring to Britain's imperial interests in return for British amelioration of the Angloamerican economy. Before the end of 1790 the British coloration of Hamilton's funding and banking plans began to assume a more important place in Madison's and Jefferson's thinking than the services those plans were to provide for the proper exercise of efficient governance.

There was a temptation for Jefferson to turn more fully than he might have otherwise to France for a counterbalance. France was, after all, a country whose people and culture he enjoyed, and from which he derived hopes for the future development of the American economy. The continuing French Revolution promising regimes closer in spirit to America's increased both his affections and expectations. France could correct the fatal dependence upon Britain by opening her ports to American shipping along the lines implied in the Treaty of Commerce in 1778 and by supplying the manufactures and credit facilities with which the British, in his judgment, had enslaved America in the past.

Such may have been the secretary's impulse but it was not his immediate response to Hamilton's challenge. His conception of France was too coldblooded to make this kind of reaction plausible in 1790. Jefferson's approach to French assistance was more exploitive than Hamilton's view of England. His warnings to France were far more menacing at the time of the Nootka Sound crisis than were Hamilton's elliptical admonitions to Britain; the latter were buried under a mound of assurances of American respect for British interests. By contrast the secretary of state showed scant sympathy for the diplomatic gaffes of the French minister to Philadelphia, Comte de Moustier, and expressed hostility to proposals the minister had for possible French recovery of Louisiana. Moustier's successor, Jean Baptiste Ternant, was to find the secretary of state as prickly a man to deal with as any of the Hamiltonians he encountered.

In some ways Jefferson was more impatient with the government of the National Assembly than he had been with the *ancien régime.* The former should have been more attuned to the potentialities inherent in the Franco-American liaison, and should have taken steps to free West Indian colonies from the restrictions that had bound the pre-Revolutionary statesmen. The political as well as the economic benefits of an American economic entanglement with French commerce were just what his French friends now in power had desired when they described their dreams to Jefferson during his ministry in France. But these changes were slow in coming, and the American secretary of state was pointed in expressing his displeasure. When the French consul in New York demanded that two American consuls appointed by Congress to the French West Indies be recalled on the grounds that the appointments contradicted French commercial regulations, the secretary rejected the complaints out of hand. In fact, he had encouraged Congress to make those appointments in the first place to focus French attention upon the American ally. Jefferson ultimately won this argument under color of the consular convention of 1788, although to preserve form the consuls went under the label of "commercial agents." It was a Pyhrric victory if such concessions which should have been freely offered by the Revolutionary ally had to be extracted so painfully.

What Jefferson was unwilling to confront, although he had sensed the problem immediately, was that the new France as a reformed monarchy or later as a republic was no more anxious than the old France had been to declare a common market for both countries to share. The genuine concession which Minister Jefferson had won in the 1780s did not lead to a widespread transfer of American commerce to French markets. American profits from French sources frequently wound up in the coffers of Britain as British merchants continued to supply American importers with products France should have provided. French manufacturers lacked both the quantity and the variety of goods as well as the expertise to compete with the experienced British traders. Consequently French ardor for the American market cooled quickly for lack of reciprocation.

Jefferson displayed his understanding of this problem when he urged Frenchmen to reduce their investments in brandies and silks, and to challenge British control of the markets in areas outside luxury items; but his knowledge of obstacles did not make him less annoyed with French behavior toward the United States. Hence he had no emotional qualms about turning aside French objections to the tonnage duties of 1789 even though he shared from the very beginning Madison's objectives in discriminating through those duties in favor of French shipping. The duties, he assured French critics, did not violate the Treaty of 1778, since all ships were required to make the payment much as American ships did in French ports. As long as the United States did not deprive France of a most-favored-nation status, she was not deviating from the terms of the treaty. That Jefferson should have been so scrupulous about defending Hamilton's mangling of Madison's program in which the British were given equality with the French mystified friends of France such as Senator William Maclay, who wondered why "Jefferson should seem to countenance this." The answer lay in the secretary's awareness of France's own lapses from the spirit of alliance. He saw no advantage from a unilateral confession of error.

His cognizance of the impropriety of the law with its undertones of undue tenderness to Britain was apparent from his interest in giving France some earnest of America's special friendship. He did not see the gesture as a matter of treaty obligation but as a response to France's concessions on behalf of American whale oil. Jefferson recommended in a report issued early in 1791 that the United States relax her tonnage requirements for France, with the express requirement that no other country be so favored unless it reciprocated in kind. While he avoided a wrangle over the construction of the treaty he invited one with Congress, since legislative approval was necessary to put his idea into effect. A number of routes were open to the desired end. The administration, for example, could deny the French insistence upon special treatment in tonnage on the grounds that they misread the treaty, and at the same time ask that the law be modified to exempt them from payments as a free gesture. Or, Congress could follow his preference and make changes in the law in a spirit of friendship without reference to the treaty but with expectation of compensatory treatment from the French. Neither of these paths was followed. The most Jefferson could evoke from the Hamiltonian Senate was a negative action of rebuffing the French construction of the treaty of 1778.

Although he failed to win his point in this report, he still felt that the publication of two other reports he had prepared by the winter of 1791 deepened America's relationship with France. His ultimate objective was the recasting of the treaty arrangements.

The other reports allusively emphasized the virtues of a French connection by contrasting it with a stark portrayal of Britain's arrogant exploitation of America's economy in the first two years of the federal government's life. An elaborate explication of the state of the whale-oil and codfish industries unfolded the unfair commercial competition between the United States and Great Britain in which the fisheries provided only one major example. The British, according to the findings of the secretary of state, were "mounting their navigation on the ruin of ours." To redress the imbalance created by British practices either bounties must be provided or relief from duties secured not only for the welfare of American fishermen but also for the ultimate independence of American commerce. He made it clear that an American navigation system in which bounties might be included was the only appropriate solution to this problem.

Even more inflammatory than the tale above was Jefferson's accounting of the Morris mission to London. This report had actually been prepared two months before the others but Hamilton's objections to its tone of vigorous reproach to Britain helped to delay its delivery, with the unintended result of firing Congressional emotions against British behavior in a manner the other reports could not achieve. Fed the information by Beckwith, the secretary of the treasury did his best to defuse the issue by discrediting Morris, claiming that his failure was largely the result of his undiplomatic and provocative consorting with the French ambassador and of his use of indiscreet language in his communications with the Foreign Ministry. The president, however, shared Jefferson's view that the fault was Britain's. Hence the release of a report which indicted British policy in the guise of a description of Morris' problems in England. From the correspondence with the special emissary, Jefferson concluded that Britain had no intention of surrendering the Northwest posts, let alone of compensating Americans for the deportation of slaves, which had been the ostensible occasion for Morris' visit. The British would come to terms only if "we would agree to make it a treaty of *alliance* as well as *commerce* so as to undermine our obligations with France." Under no circumstances, the secretary reported, would the British yield their present commercial advantages. It was even unlikely that they would send a minister.

The cumulative effect of these three papers upon the Congress in 1791 fanned the Anglophobia which Hamilton was so anxious to dampen. And his behavior helped to open opportunities for Jefferson to exploit. As Julian Boyd puts it, "In their anxiety to shape foreign policy Hamilton, Schuyler and Johnson had damaged their cause by placing themselves and their nation not in the posture of negotiators but in that of petitioners. . . ."[13] Their meddling might have led Congress to adopt a policy of economic retaliation which Madison and Jefferson had been unable to win the year before.

Jefferson's hopes for a change were high enough to permit him to instruct ministers abroad on the usefulness of Madison's navigation proposals as a model for other nations to adopt. They should emphasize reciprocity in their talks, a principle which the British refused to accept out of their arrogance and out of their overweening power. Should all the commercial nations in the world band together, they could force Britain to grant equity to every state. "This act is perfectly innocent as to other nations," he assured them, "is strictly just as to the English, cannot be parried by them, and if adopted by other nations would inevitably defeat their navigation act and reduce their power on the sea within safer limits." In effect, the secretary of state was asking for a peacetime equivalent of the League of Armed Neutrals in conformity with the spirit of the Plan of 1776. Yet the idea was neither utopian nor altruistic. It seemed to Jefferson to be the quickest way to free America from British domination. It was also one more invitation to France to move into the vacuum that would be left by the removal of the British commercial predominance in American life.

France offered no help to Jefferson's plan. The liberal monarchy and the National Assembly continued to be unresponsive to the American market in 1791. They were not satisfied with Jefferson's rationalizations for the tonnage laws, and were conscious of the Hamiltonian influences which served Britain. Foreseeing few opportunities in the American market, the mer-

[13] *Ibid.*, p. 31.

cantilists who controlled the National Assembly managed to force the government to revoke those privileges granted before Jefferson left France. As Madison and Jefferson worked against Hamiltonian opposition to reorient the American economy the French government moved steadily away from free trade.

The pro-British Hamiltonian forces in Congress seemed to have triumphed despite all his efforts to awaken friends and allies to the virtues of a navigation program. The new navigation bill of 1791 suffered the fate of the old. Even though Madison was a member of the committee which composed it, the omens were unfavorable. It passed the House by a majority of one, and ultimately was transformed into a harmless instruction to the secretary of state to report to Congress at the next session on the conditions of foreign commerce in the United States along with measures to improve them. Jefferson interpreted these instructions to be a sentence of execution for the retaliatory program against Britain, and commented accordingly: "The measures therein spoken of as in contemplation for the purpose of bringing Gt. Brit. to reason, vanished in reference of the subject to me to report of our commerce and navigation, generally in the next session of Congress. I have little hope that the result will be any thing more than to turn the left cheek to him who has smitten the right."

By the time Jefferson had written these words to his friend John Rutledge, the division in the cabinet had become irreconcilable. A Jeffersonian faction became visible in 1791 as well as self-conscious in the course of Jefferson's and Madison's botanical and political visitation to New York and New England. Philip Freneau, poet and liberal journalist, received a position in the Department of State which facilitated his editorship of a new journal, the *National Gazette*, devoted to rebutting the monarchical and Anglophilic elements in the cabinet and Congress. The secretary of state tried to keep aloof from the heat of the battle, unlike his opponent Hamilton who took up his pen with spirit to charge the Jeffersonians with corruption and Francophilism.

Despite Jefferson's instinctive reluctance to indulge personally in debate, he was caught up in the passions of the literary war. The occasion was not planned and the opponent was a former friend. Indeed, this unhappy and unexpected clash appeared to be with the wrong opponent. As the polarization of the Washington administration widened, Vice President John Adams became alarmed over the course of the French Revolution and its influence on the outside world. Consequently, when Jefferson spoke of political "heresies" in connection with criticism of Paine's pamphlet on the *Rights of Man*, his target could have been Adams whom friends of France had labeled as a bearer of heretical views. Jefferson's comments evoked sharp rebuttal from "Publicola," Adams' precocious son John Quincy, which marked a major breach in the relations between the two veteran diplomatists. Their separation at this time was all the more unfortunate because of the mutual reluctance of the men to turn their back on the past. Adams had no Hamiltonian attachment to Great Britain. The contretemps, then, symbolized the breakdown in communications within Washington's government.

The course of events in the latter part of the Federalist decade make reasonable the temptation of scholars to see inevitable failure in all of Jefferson's struggles in the cabinet, to be redeemed only after he became president himself. Hamilton's ascendancy seemed all-pervasive long before Washington's first term ended. It was not just that Jefferson or Madison were frustrated over funding, over the Bank of the United States, or over tonnage and tariff programs. The secretary of the treasury moved steadily and with increasing assurance into foreign affairs, with notable influence on diplomatic appointments. To France went Gouverneur Morris, who may have kindled Hamilton's annoyance during his London mission, but was still a "high flying monarchy-man" to Jefferson. Morris' links to France had been with the aristocracy and he had acute distaste for the Revolution and revolutionaries, which both cabinet members were aware of. Morris went to France without the blessing of the secretary of state and with the belief that the secretary of the treasury had been responsible for the appointment. To England went Thomas Pinckney, a Charleston aristocrat whom Jefferson had never met and of whose appointment he had no prior notice. If one were to categorize men according to an Anglophile and Francophile or a Hamiltonian and Jeffersonian frame, there should be no hesitation about the proper placement of the ministers to Great Britain and to France in 1791.

Much the same may be said for the British and French representatives in America at this time. One important by-product of the threat of a navigation system was the dispatch of a minister to Philadelphia from London, George Hammond, who immediately took up the same comfortable and confidential relationship with the secretary of the treasury that his unofficial predecessor Beckwith had enjoyed. The news of this appointment had been Hamilton's ace in the sleeve which he was able to use in combatting the retaliatory plans of Madison in the spring of 1791. Presumably rumors about the impending decision stayed the hand of the House of Representatives, or at least mollified enough Congressmen to take the steam out of Madison's campaigning against Britain. Actually the British decision had antedated Jefferson's Anglophobic reports. The most that can be legitimately claimed is that American Congressional unrest advanced Hammond's travel schedule; the original decision to send an envoy reflected the fears of the Nootka Sound period.

The important element in the Hammond mission was not British fear of Republican reaction so much as it was the influence of Hamilton's advice upon the instructions of the minister. Whitehall responded in a manner that would have chagrined the secretary of the treasury. Hammond's instructions allowed no treaty to be contracted, merely dalliance with American politicians. He had no authority to make any settlements with respect to the Northwest posts or commerce. The views he could and did express were largely concerned with a utopian Indian barrier state similar in language and spirit to the British and Spanish schemes of the 1780s. Even Hamilton reacted negatively to this approach.

Hamilton bore a responsibility for the patronizing tone this twenty-seven-year-old diplomat adopted in dealing with the seasoned secretary of state. Jefferson quickly took his measure in forcing him to reveal he had no powers to negotiate a treaty, and then concisely demolished the tired old British arguments which Britain used to justify her violations of the Treaty of Paris. Samuel Flagg Bemis calls Jefferson's response to Hammond's lengthy and tendentious charges against American handling of debts and Loyalists the "greatest diplomatic note, indeed one of the cleverest arguments in the history of American diplomacy."[14] Hammond's one consolation from the rejoinder was Hamilton's assurance that the "intemperate violence" of Jefferson's language did not represent the sentiment of the nation or the views of President Washington. Thus coached by his American friends, Hammond stayed away from the secretary of state in the future, dismissing him in much the same way Hamiltonians were doing in 1792. The British minister was reported to have said: "The Secretary of the Treasury is more a man of the world than Jefferson and I like his manners better, and can speak more freely to him. Jefferson is in the Virginia interest and that of the French."

The French minister, Ternant, who arrived a few months before Hammond, shared some of the British minister's feelings about Jefferson. The Frenchman also noticed the chilled, sharp tones of the secretary's pen, and observed that Jefferson preferred to deal with him by correspondence than by personal conversation. In contrast the secretary of the treasury took a warm interest in the minister's person and in his views on a prospective new Franco-American treaty. Ternant had the misfortune of discovering in Hamilton the first American who—for reasons of his own—broached the subject with him. Aside from the impropriety of the secretary of the treasury interfering in a matter of foreign affairs, it is obvious that Hamilton and Ternant parted friends, while Ternant left an audience with Jefferson convinced that the secretary of state was cold and aloof. There was a reasonable explanation for the difficulties between the two men, and most of it centered on Hamilton. Jefferson suspected that the outburst of Hamiltonian charm was intended to create precedents for an Anglo-American commercial treaty, and Franco-American conversations along this line would be a useful beginning. He preferred to omit any new agreement

[14] Bemis, "Thomas Jefferson," p. 32; Malone, *Jefferson and the Rights of Man*, p. 412, agrees with Bemis. A. L. Burt, *The United States, Great Britain, and British North America* (New Haven, 1940), p. 121, disagrees, considering Hammond to be sensitive to American feelings at this time. See discussion in Malone, pp. 412–413.

with France rather than allow it to be a vehicle for a dangerous commercial treaty with the British.

Given the variety and complexity of his frustrations as chief officer in charge of American foreign relations, Jefferson's willingness to stay in office beyond Washington's first administration is a matter worthy of consideration. The major answer may well lie in the role Washington himself played in Jefferson's contest with Hamilton and in Jefferson's expectations about America's future foreign policies. It was not until the summer of 1792 that the president became aware of the depth of the personal friction between the two men, and it is doubtful that he ever grasped fully the philosophical differences separating them. The impending presidential election forced the president to consider his cabinet problems. The result was his decision to retain the cabinet intact, at least for the immediate future. Washington's reasoning, colored by his refusal to recognize factional government, was clear. But what of Jefferson's? Did he believe after Hamilton's successes of 1791 and 1792 that his views would prevail in 1793 with Washington? Or did he hope that another year in Philadelphia could bring a new turn in fortune that would change American policies? Or did he understand that the president was not a committed Anglophile, monarchist, or Hamiltonian, and hence open to Jeffersonian persuasion?

If Jefferson responded positively to the latter question, his reaction was not a measure of his naïveté. Prior to the wars of the French Revolution, the French upheaval evoked considerable sympathy from Washington, if only because his disciple Lafayette was one of its leaders. When the president did follow Hamilton's guidance, it was often for the very reasons that moved Jefferson in his early days as secretary of state: the New Yorker's policies offered solutions to pressing financial claims, promoted the conception of executive authority, and promised strong stable government capable of winning Europe's respect. There was no conscious Anglophilism in this posture. Washington's temper would not have tolerated the trespasses of Grenville, Dorchester, Beckwith, or Hammond had he known of the illicit connections they made with their American confidants.

The president's appointment of Thomas Pinckney to the

Court of St. James was an expression of his preference for men of his own cast of character rather than a sign of Anglophile sympathies or a concession to gratify Hamilton's importunings. Not surprisingly, the men of his own persuasion would be inclined toward Britain rather than toward France even if no revolution had intervened to intensify emotions. It is worth noting that once Pinckney reached England and was caught up in the defense of American neutral rights stemming from the Anglo-French war of 1793, his behavior hardly accorded with that of a British sympathizer or Hamiltonian agent. Nor was Morris in France Washington's or Hamilton's instrument to undermine the Franco-American alliance. Morris, like Hamilton, was one of the president's former aides-de-camp in the Revolution, that corps of young officers for whom Washington acquired a permanent affection and to whom he permitted special indulgences. While the minister's reputation as an indiscreet bon vivant continued to give the president some qualms, his misconduct was strikingly similar to his recent experience in London. A penchant for intrigue led him to consort with the British ambassador in Paris, in much the same spirit that he had joined the company of the French ambassador in London two years before. Although Jefferson may have become increasingly disenchanted with Morris, and obviously would have been happier with his former secretary and present chargé d'affaires, William Short, in the office, he did not oppose the choice of Gouverneur Morris publicly; in fact, he recognized that Short's experience and age were too junior to warrant the promotion. More important, Jefferson in 1792 gave no indication that Washington's selection of Morris was in any way part of Hamilton's subversive schemes.

In sum, the president's choice of men naturally ran to conservatism. There was no necessary equation between conservatism and Hamiltonism in the first administration, even though the secretary of state may have judged Hamilton's almost familial ties with Washington as potentially destructive. Jefferson's major objectives, moreover, which included the settlement of American border controversies with Britain and Spain, the negotiation of a new commercial treaty with France, and the maintenance of the French alliance, were all programs to which the president subscribed. While the subtleties of Jefferson's vision of America may have escaped the president, the latter's reaction to British impudence was not lost on the secretary of state. Despite Hamilton's assurances to Hammond, Washington had seen and had endorsed Jefferson's sharp rebuttal to Hammond's indictment of American policy.

The initial stages of the French Revolution did nothing to shake Jefferson's confidence in his fellow Virginian. Lafayette after all was figuratively a classmate of Hamilton and Morris in their relations with Washington; Washington took a vicarious pride in his achievements under the liberalized French monarchy. In view of these perceptions Jefferson's appeal to the president to stand for re-election was a signal of his genuine concern that only Washington could save the nation from its internal enemies. They also explain why Jefferson responded favorably to Washington's plea that he remain in the cabinet and support him in his continuing service to the nation.

Both men were undoubtedly sincere in their mutual professions of dependence, and both were basically mistaken in their prognosis of the immediate future. The spread of the European war in the next year to engulf both Britain and France pushed Washington into an increasingly Anglophobic position and pushed Jefferson out of the cabinet. The president was a Hamiltonian in his second administration. That the secretary of state remained in the cabinet for even one year was testimony to his faith in the ability of a basically pro-French public opinion to tip the balance of power in Congress and in his own ability to convince the president to follow his advices.

Events abroad would also have their place in countering British influence, and in the succeeding years Jefferson found in Europe's convulsions the key to America's salvation even as he looked at those convulsions with foreboding and anxiety. He had good reason for concern. Spain certainly offered few prospects for assistance in budging Britain as long as her estrangement from France continued. For a brief moment in 1791, when Britain's appointment of a minister plenipotentiary to the United States seemed to confirm their recurrent fears of a joint Anglo-American assault against their lands, the Spanish were tempted to negotiate in Madrid to resolve their differences with the United States. If someone other than the sick and indolent William Carmichael had been in charge of American affairs there, something might have developed from Spain's new mood. Jefferson did what he could to take advantage of it by sending Short to Madrid from his newly appointed post in the Hague. But by the time Short arrived, Spanish incentive for cooperation had evaporated. Having joined Britain in a grand coalition against the new French republic, the government no longer feared American collusion with the British. Consequently the two Spanish commissioners in Philadelphia, Josef de Viar and Josef de Jaudenes, displayed an arrogant unwillingness to restrain their Creek clients in the southwest while Britain tightened her hold on the northwest. As Jefferson summed up the problem in 1793: "There is too at this time a lowering disposition perceivable both in England and Spain. The former keeps herself aloof and in a state of incommunication with us except in way of demand. The latter has not begun auspiciously with C. and S. at Madrid, and has lately sent 1,500 men to New Orleans, and greatly strengthened her upper posts on the Mississippi."

Jefferson derived little more satisfaction from his relations with France in 1792 and early 1793. He was doubtful of Ternant's friendship, and saw no sign of reciprocity in France's domestic legislation. In April, 1792, the secretary had presented once again his plan of offering to citizens of each country the privileges of natives in the ports of the other, which would open France's West Indian trade to the United States and give to the French a status above that of Britain's. The last monarchical government of France was interested but too feeble to advance the plan. Morris had suggested that Jefferson not press the case at this "unpropitious moment," the summer of 1792. Before the year was out a new republican government was willing to consider the idea, if only as a military measure; but the circumstances of the following year would make it irrelevant for both countries.

Surprisingly Morris provided the secretary with sound and accurate reports in this period of rapid change. Not that his personal tastes or behavior had undergone violent change; it was the Morris of old who participated in a plot to smuggle

Louis XVI out of republican France. But over matters of policy, such as the American debt to France, he and Short shared doubts about the wisdom of suspending debt payments to the new republic or about giving payments only to the king. The secretary of state himself and the Dutch bankers had raised the questions; and to his credit, although never really acknowledged by Jefferson, the American minister to France, insisted that the debts be paid as planned before the upheaval. The creditor was the nation, not the crown, Morris claimed. He persisted and won. His peccadillos and aristocratic biases notwithstanding, Gouverneur Morris revealed himself in his communications to be more flexible and less censorious than the former chargé d'affaires and minister to Holland, Short, in evaluating the shortcomings and errors of republican France. Short was candid in his dispatches and reserved in his private relations, while Morris wrote cautiously but frequently behaved impulsively and occasionally with abandon.

While Morris from Paris and Short from the Hague wrestled with their respective perceptions of the meaning of the French Revolution, their chief in Philadelphia was undergoing a serious change in perspective on American foreign relations as Washington began his second administration. The role of France had assumed a new meaning for the secretary of state, and his attitude changed accordingly. The impatience and harshness he had displayed toward France on such matters as mercantilism disappeared along with the French monarchy to be replaced by a respect for the French Revolution which he had never articulated while minister to France in the previous decade and had not indicated to Ternant the previous year. It is tempting to explain his shift in terms of intensified partisan conflict at home in which the presumed Francophilism of the majority of Americans, particularly after France had adopted a republican form of government, could be a useful weapon to turn upon his enemies. But there is little new here; France was always a center of his calculations for lifting the British burden from America. The new element in 1793 was his recognition of the implications of the expanded war of the French Revolution. To him it was now a war of the repressive society of autocracy and monarchy against an embattled French Republic fighting for the survival of republican government everywhere. Its failure would doom America to the rule of Britain and monarchy.

Such was the spirit of Jefferson's correspondence with Lafayette and Barlow, and other French and American friends in France after Britain joined the coalition against France. France as instrument of American policy was converted into a France that was a cause in herself. Herein is the explanation for Jefferson's rebukes to his disciple Short for his now petty complaints against French statecraft and his wavering faith in revolution at a time when "The liberty of the whole earth was depending on the issue of the contest between monarchism and republicanism." An apparent insensitivity to the fate of French friends at the hands of the shifting revolutionary forces, including the flight of Lafayette himself into exile and prison and an equally apparent indifference to stirrings of French imperial ambitions in America under republican auspices, underscored the overwhelming power of his new perceptions. At earlier and later times he was and would be alive to the injustices to his friends and threats to his country. Only the passions of the moment could account for satisfaction in the image of half the world made desolate by war if the other half could be rescued from monarchy.

This was Jefferson's mood at a moment when these same events turned the president violently against France. Within the cabinet the battle between Britain and France had extended the boundaries of the older conflict, since Hamilton's concern for Britain's victory was as deep as Jefferson's for France. And as the shadow of that war crossed the Atlantic it appeared to cloud the previously shared assumptions about America's future that had united the two men under the president. By the end of 1793 the nation was as divided as the cabinet. Jefferson resigned on the last day of that year.

CHAPTER VIII

The Hamiltonian Apex

☆ 1793-1796 ☆

FROM THE Neutrality Proclamation of 1793 to the Farewell Address of 1796, Alexander Hamilton's mind and pen were everywhere in evidence, although not always in open view. Thomas Jefferson wrote off the president as the alter ego of the secretary of the treasury. As a result of his continuing faith in republicanism and admiration for France, the secretary of state, in his own eyes, was first a casualty of Washington's evolving political position and ultimately an enemy of the president. When Jefferson referred in 1796 to "Samsons in the field & Solomons in the Council but who have had their heads shorn by the harlot England," his target was obvious. This language of abuse indulged in by both sides was a token of the bitterness that separated the Washington administration from its opposition in the middle of the decade. It was also a reflection of the Hamiltonian ascendancy.

In the setting of the election of 1796, Washington's assertion to Jefferson that he himself "was no party man" sounded pathetic if not mendacious. Yet only a few years before, on the eve of France's declaration of war against Great Britain, Washington believed himself to be a friend of France—a troubled friend, perhaps, after Lafayette's flight and the king's execution, but one who was aware of France's services to America in the past. At least his ideas about war and peace for the United

States were satisfactory to the secretary of state, sufficient for him to write in 1793 that "a fair neutrality will prove a disagreeable pill to our friends, though necessary to keep us out of the calamities of war."

None of the principals involved in the shaping of American foreign policy wanted involvement in the European war. The sympathies of the president and the secretary of state, different though they were in many respects, were in full agreement on denying military assistance to the French ally. The secretary of the treasury would not only avoid war but would use the occasion to break the alliance and remove the United States from any obligation to France. His grounds were political and philosophical and deeply emotional. France was an enemy of civilization as long as revolution gripped the nation, while England was the one nation in the world that could protect the world from the French terror as well as the only government that could advance the American political economy.

While Washington was never to grasp fully the nuances of the Hamiltonian order for America, his biases against the chaos implicit in revolutionary disorder rendered him susceptible to the ministrations of Anglophiles and Francophobes. They were assisted by hyperbolic and often slanderous attacks of Republican newspapers and pamphlets, which were as effective as any Hamiltonian wile in prejudicing the president against France and Jefferson's advice. But Hamilton's strongest ally in the long run was the behavior of the French governments and their emissaries and friends in the United States in provoking a fracture in the alliance after the election of 1796 that ultimately proved irreparable. The baldness of France's contempt for American sensibilities at critical moments of Franco-American relations in Washington's second administration facilitated the Hamiltonian program of supporting the British war effort in exchange for a more intimate and more profitable role for America in the British economy.

Hamilton's ambitions should have run afoul of the emotions generated in America by a basically anti-British population, sympathetic to the French Revolution and resentful of the obnoxious British war measures. The British government seized American ships and goods on the high seas in defiance of the

American interpretation of neutral rights, encouraged the Indian allies to resist American advances in the west by retaining the Northwest posts, and struck at the roots of American sovereignty by impressing sailors from American merchant ships. Hamilton's genius allowed him to convert his vulnerability into a strength. The ancient ties of kinship and custom served his cause, but so did his own vigorous efforts to demonstrate to America the many benefits of a British connection. By 1796 he could claim the allegiance not only of New England merchants and Philadelphia bankers, but also of western farmers who sought opportunities along the Mississippi and potential settlers of the northwest who would give credit to Federalists for clearing the Indians and the British out of those territories.

The impressive demonstrations of affection for France, which occasionally awed Jefferson and his friends with their vigor and vehemence, had essentially a shallow base. Gratitude for past services and admiration for the pluck of a sister republic in the face of a united monarchical Europe were sentiments easily blown away by the force of passing events. Such electoral power as Jefferson was able to muster in 1796 emerged far less from a visceral Francophilism inherent in American republicanism than in the serious frictions within the Federalist opposition that created disaffection for its presidential candidate for reasons only distantly connected with foreign policy. France in fact alienated a good part of American public opinion in the election of 1796 by her heavy-handed propaganda on behalf of Jefferson and by her concurrent threats of punishment in the event of his defeat. This misjudgment of American attitudes repeatedly allowed the administration to divert attention from British provocations. The behavior of the French ministers from Genet to Adet made credible what would not have been accepted under other circumstances: a farewell address from President Washington directed against French dangers to American sovereignty. In the face of France's diplomatic blunders Anglophobia lost much of its force.

A case may be made in this period that Hamilton had become far more dependent upon his British polity than Jefferson ever was in his views of and dealings with France as secretary of state or as squire in Monticello from 1794 to 1796. Despite his periodic outbursts of fealty to the Revolution and his allusive but persistent support of economic connection with France and his more covert, occasionally indiscreet, assistance to Genet's or Michaux's imperial interests, Jefferson was more exploitive in his use of France for the advancement of American welfare than Hamilton was of Britain. After Jefferson's defeat in the presidential campaign of 1796, Adet asserted with considerable justice that "Jefferson I say is American and as such, he cannot be sincerely our friend. An American is the born enemy of all the European peoples." Given the imperial objectives of revolutionary France it was just as well that Jefferson's Francophilism had important reservations. Counterpart reservations were far fewer with respect to Hamilton's Anglophilism. Washington's success in holding France at bay was at the price of a neocolonial status in the British Empire. But it was a status that Hamilton considered vital to America's political and economic survival. Whether or not the Farewell Address was wholly his creation, its message marked the apex of his influence.

News of France's declaration of war against Great Britain fired the country with enthusiasm for the French cause in the spring of 1793. Popular societies sprang up overnight in apparent imitation of the Jacobin clubs of France to provide a loud claque for the actions of the French Republic in democratizing French society and in challenging the supremacy of Great Britain on the world scene. To conservatives in Philadelphia and elsewhere these societies were as frightening as the Jacobins themselves, even if they did belong, as Eugene Link judges, to the tradition of the Sons of Liberty or to contemporary British radical clubs.[1] The most powerful of all the societies, the Philadelphia Democratic-Republican Society, claimed such luminaries as David Rittenhouse, Alexander Dallas, and George Logan as members. They gave heart to Jefferson's resistance to Hamilton's influence.

If Jefferson was correct in his estimate that ninety-nine out of one hundred Americans cheered the Revolution in January of that year, Hamilton's sharp challenge to the legitimacy of the

[1] Eugene P. Link, *Democratic-Republican Societies, 1790–1800* (New York, 1942), p. 20.

French Republic was all the more galling to bear. The first reaction of the president to the news of the extended European war and to the death of the king was to submit questions to Hamilton and Jefferson about the proper course for the administration to follow. The secretary of state was at once suspicious of Hamilton's hand in the formulation of the questions; he and Attorney General Edmund Randolph had doubts even about the propriety of questions on neutrality, although neither officer had any wish to involve the United States in the hostilities. What distressed Jefferson in particular were the insinuations implied in the wording of the questions.

Of the three major queries, two were gratuitous and opened opportunities for the kinds of mischief Jefferson had foreseen in Hamilton's answers. Why should the treaties of 1778, the major question raised, be in jeopardy at this time? The secretary of state's official views on this subject had been embodied a month before in his instructions to Gouverneur Morris to recognize the legality of the National Assembly. Its legitimacy was no problem for Jefferson: "We surely cannot deny to any nation that right whereon our own government is founded, that everyone may govern itself according to whatever form it pleases. . . . The will of the nation is the only thing essential to be regarded."

The secretary of the treasury was not only ready but anxious to deny precisely this right when he claimed that the original contracts were made with Louis XVI and not with the usurpers who had murdered their sovereign and temporarily ruled France.[2] The treaties, Hamilton advised, should be suspended until the air was cleared and the legitimate authorities were restored to power. It was unfair to disinherit Louis' heirs. How would the royal government react subsequently toward the American ally if it defeated the revolutionaries? The act of war itself was sufficient to absolve the United States from its obligations under the alliance, since that treaty stipulated assistance

[2] Gilbert L. Lycan, *Alexander Hamilton and American Foreign Policy, A Design for Greatness* (Norman, 1970), p. 155, vigorously denies that Hamilton intended to denounce the principle that treaties bind nations as well as governments. Historians, he claims, have been guilty of giving Hamilton a "bad press" on this issue.

only in a defensive not an offensive war. Hence, concluded the secretary of the treasury, the administration should refuse to receive Edmond Genet, the minister of the republican government, and await the results of the war in Europe.

The secretary of state responded vehemently to the Hamiltonian logic that linked the abrogation of treaties with the rejection of the French envoy. He ridiculed the notion that the end of the monarchy meant the end of the alliance and its responsibilities. Rhetorically he asked, "Who is the American who can say with truth that he would not have allied himself to France if she had been a republic?" French assistance in 1778 would have been welcomed whatever the government had been at the time.

Much of Jefferson's spleen may have been misdirected at this point. It was unlikely that Hamilton had any serious expectation that his argument would break up the alliance. After all, the president, with the concurrence of the cabinet, had agreed earlier to accept a republican successor to Ternant. Nor could the explicit instructions to Morris of the previous month be easily countermanded. What Hamilton may have sought was just to put the secretary of state on the defensive, and to make eventually an ostensible concession on the matter of recognition in order to extract an advantage in another area of Franco-American polity. At any event, the president agreed to Jefferson's insistence upon the continuing validity of the alliance and upon the propriety of receiving Edmond Genet, the republican envoy.

In the perspective of later American diplomatic history, Jefferson's stand on the recognition of foreign powers had become identified with American respect for the sanctity of treaties, the acceptance as binding of an obligation made to another country irrespective of the government in power as long as the latter fulfills its responsibilities toward the United States. If such a precedent in foreign policy was begun in 1793 it was neither by forethought nor by express intention.[3] The secretary of state was

[3] Alexander DeConde, *Entangling Alliance: Politics and Diplomacy under George Washington* (Durham, N.C., 1958), notes that "Washington set another foreign-policy precedent—American adherence to and respect for the sanctity of treaties."

making his own partisan case for France against the forces of France's enemies and of his own.

The heart of the controversy lay in the form American neutrality would take. This was the third and crucial question raised by the president. Hamilton desired a neutrality that would minimize the aid the United States was supposed to offer an ally and hence lessen the impact of the alliance upon Great Britain. If it also offended the French, so much the better. Hamilton won on both counts. As with the other two questions, the president had tipped his hand before he had raised the issues. Six days before he had presented the list to the cabinet he had written to both men of the need for a "stict neutrality" that would keep the United States out of the agonies of a foreign war. Jefferson did not disagree; he never allowed his enthusiasm for France to carry himself away to the point of active involvement in France's Continental war effort. He was equally averse to responding to any French call for help in the West Indies that might lead to war with Great Britain. Such an event could bring financial disaster and internal chaos or even a British occupation that would hurt both France and the United States. Hamilton's bargaining strength on this question fed on Jefferson's admission that neutrality must be asserted, even at the risk of France's displeasure.

Where the two statesmen parted company openly was over the expression of this neutrality. Should it be couched gently and elliptically, as Jefferson wished, so that the ally and friend would see an advantage in America's neutrality; or should it be issued brusquely in a fashion that would imply disregard for treaty obligations and submission to the British criterion of the proper role of a nonbelligerent? Hamilton urged on the president a proclamation of neutrality which would tell the world that the United States intended to pursue "a conduct friendly and impartial towards the belligerent powers," and would prohibit American citizens from helping either belligerent by unneutral acts.

Jefferson hoped to counter the idea of a proclamation by recommending that the Europeans bid for such terms of neutrality that may be earned from their behavior toward the

United States. Why discard an opportunity to win economic and other benefits from the belligerent nations, he asked, by advertising in advance a service to one and a provocation to another? As in the Nootka Sound crisis, the secretary of state noted possibilities of coercing Britain to yield to this lever. Threats of navigation laws had failed in the past to pry them loose. Fears of the Franco-American alliance might accomplish the objectives which had not been reached by other measures. Since the discomfiture of Britain, let alone punishment, was precisely what the secretary of the treasury would never permit, this line of reasoning against promulgation of neutrality met a hostile response. Jefferson, with the strong support of Madison, then turned to a constitutional objection to proclaiming neutrality. An executive proclamation without the approval of Congress would infringe upon the constitutional power of the legislative branch to declare war. Against this construction of the Constitution, Hamilton in his anonymous *Pacificus Papers* replied that the president could make such a proclamation by virtue of his powers as commander-in-chief when Congress was not in session.

Hamilton triumphed. The most Jefferson could extract from the victor was the deletion of the term, "neutrality" from the document that Attorney General Edmund Randolph drafted on April 20. The secretary of state was still uneasy with the results and very sensitive to the bitter commentary of Madison, who condemned the proclamation as a shabby denunciation of America's psychic debt to France and a dangerous accretion of executive authority. Aroused by fears of creating "an English neutrality" and angered by Hamilton's anonymous blasts in print, he urged Madison to take up his pen and "cut him to pieces in the face of the public." Under the name of Helvidius the Congressional leader proceeded to follow Jefferson's advice. It was gratuitous, though, in the summer of 1793. The matter of Congressional control was essentially irrelevant. The proclamation was already in effect, and it was bound to antagonize the French.

In a sense Jefferson had compromised his opposition to announcing neutrality by his underlying preference for the advantages of abstaining from war. He was deluding himself in believing that he could advance a conception of neutral rights in this conflict that would serve the French cause. The opportunities for manipulating "neutrality" were all on Hamilton's side. The very use of the term itself in all but the official declaration was a source of comfort to Britain and of disturbance to France. And Jefferson knew this when he used the metaphor, "disagreeable pill" to describe it. When he urged Morris to point out to the French that "we shall be more useful as neutrals than as parties by the protection which our flag will give to supplies of provision," he was applying sugar coating to the pill as well as expressing his own hopes for the future. The pill itself, neutrality, was not just the result of Hamiltonian machinations; the secretary of state himself would have administered it without the prodding of a hostile colleague.

Jefferson's genuine distress over the effects of neutrality grew out of its practice in the late spring and summer of 1793. In April, however, the arrival of an attractive new minister, Genet, who appeared to offer everything—including a new liberalized commercial treaty—and ask for nothing, portended success for his expectations of managing a friendly neutrality with France. The secretary could discount the warnings about him from Morris as he observed the triumphal march of the young Frenchman from Charleston to Philadelphia. Opportunist and impetuous Genet may have been, but Jefferson saw in him a man who asked neither for American entry into the war nor for American defense of the French West Indies. After his first conference he wrote to Madison: "It is impossible for anything to be more affectionate, more magnanimous than the purport of his mission." In his relief over France's graciousness in overlooking the sinister side of neutrality, Jefferson was willing at first to overlook in turn the vanity, impetuosity, and extravagance of Genet's behavior. Indeed he contributed to the Frenchman's general euphoria by making derogatory comments in private about Federalists. Genet later claimed that Jefferson's information about the president's arrogation of power inspired his own fatal attacks on Washington. But this contretemps came in the summer; earlier the two men and the two countries appeared to be happily coexisting with the Neutrality Proclamation.

France's unruffled reaction to the proclamation had sound foundations. American neutrality was certainly preferable to American participation in the war. The record in the Revolutionary War would not of itself stir sentiment in France for demanding the mobilization of an American army. A neutral America fulfilling the promises of the commercial treaty of 1778 would be of much more use than a belligerent America whose ships would be subject to British seizure and whose armies would probably require French subvention and rescue. What Genet's instructions called for were accelerated payments on old debts, increased foodstuffs for the French West Indies, provisions for the homeland on American carriers, and—not least—a base for military operations against Spanish Louisiana at a time when Spain was an ally of Great Britain.

The last objective, while insignificant in the short run, was the most dangerous in the long run. It exposed France's imperial visions that would have brought the two allies into collision had they been realized. Jefferson never comprehended the extent of French imperialism under the Girondists, France's masters in 1793, in the way he recognized Napoleon's at a later date. He even contributed his mite to France's ambitions by supplying André Michaux, a distinguished French botanist, with a letter of introduction to Governor Isaac C. Shelby of Kentucky. Even though the scientist had a bona fide assignment from the American Philosophical Society to engage in research on trans-Mississippi flora, Michaux's primary mission was political. The secretary of state was abetting a plan for an independent state west of the Mississippi under French protection, which was a potential danger to American security. He knew that Michaux intended to commission Americans for an expedition against Spanish Louisiana. Although he warned against any enlistment of Americans within United States borders, he confided to Genet that he did not "care what insurrections should be excited in Louisiana," beyond America's sovereignty. Jefferson displayed his basic lack of care in the absence of any warning to the Kentuckians about Michaux's purposes. He should have cared. Genet claimed he had read his instructions to the secretary of state, so the purposes of the Michaux botanical expedition were no mystery to him. But its implications were. Had Jefferson realized their extent, his reservations about Genet and French policy would have been deeper and have come sooner.

The western operation was only one of many among Genet's assignments that created difficulties for the secretary of state. The minister's most flamboyant manoeuver was his deliberate refusal to accept the American interpretation of the treaty of 1778 on the matters of commissioning and equipping privateers in American ports, of recruiting American seamen for French service on American soil, and of utilizing French consulates as admiralty prize courts for disposing of British merchantmen. Genet ultimately commissioned twelve privateers which later captured more than eighty enemy vessels that were tried, condemned, and sold by French consuls in the United States. All of these actions were done under color of the Franco-American treaty, as interpreted by the French minister. Similarly he used the bonds of alliance to condemn American sluggishness in responding to British seizures of American vessels carrying French goods. To him this was betrayal of the principles for which Jefferson was supposedly a champion. "A true neutrality," he pointed out to the secretary of state, "does not consist in the cowardly abandonment of their friends in the moment when danger menaces them."

Jefferson concurred in this particular sentiment, and made every effort at cabinet meetings to press the case for a "fair neutrality" that would allow American ships to carry French goods according to the American interpretation of international law. In most instances, however, he could barely win "even a sneaking neutrality" for France. But despite occasional indiscretions in his initial encounters with Genet, Jefferson's basic position was closer to Hamilton's than he would be willing to admit on more issues than he could have anticipated. For example, there was no difference between the two cabinet members in their reaction to French minister's attempts to secure advance payments from the Treasury on American Revolutionary debts. Such payments had been made to Ternant for relief of French refugees from Santo Domingo. Genet now wanted the balance to be spent on provisions and naval stores in the United States. There should have been nothing in this arrangement to invite charges of compromising American neutrality, even though an unstated purpose of the monies would probably be the financing of privateers. Yet Hamilton's opposition to the discharge of the debt in this way met with surprisingly little demurral from Jefferson, whose single remonstrance was to ask that the denial be couched in friendly terms. Jefferson's concern was with the tone not the substance of the denial.

Even the tone changed as Genet, emboldened by popular acclaim, challenged Washington's authority. The minister's assertion that the treaty conferred on France the right to arm privateers in American ports or to commission officers in the United States was no part of Jefferson's understanding of the Treaty of Amity and Commerce. Article 22 obligated the United States to close her ports to British prizes and to the servicing of British privateers in wartime, but it did not extend to France by implication the privileges it denied to France's enemies. All the treaty allowed was the opening of American ports to French ships and their prizes, a conventional permission that was to be found in the Anglo-French Treaty of 1786. Fitting out privateers or setting up prize courts was of a different order, and Jefferson made clear to Genet his own views on this matter so directly that Genet later mused that the secretary of state's communications needed only Hammond's signature to identify them as British documents. Thus Jefferson's sensitivity to French trespassing on treaty privileges and his distaste for entanglement quickly soured the optimism he initially expressed over the possibilities of a new treaty with France. As much as any mistakes of Genet, the secretary's insistence upon a course of independence from France's policies opened the way for Hamilton's Anglophile program. "In the very last resort, therefore," observes Arthur Darling, "Jefferson would prefer as did Hamilton to risk a war with France than have it with Britain."[4]

Genet eased Hamilton's way by the suicidal folly of his brash assault on the president. Of all the cases in which the French minister challenged the administration, the example of the *Little Democrat* was the most serious. Knowing and discounting the prohibitions of the Neutrality Proclamation, Genet per-

[4] Darling, *Our Rising Empire*, p. 151.

mitted the prize ship, *Little Democrat* (formerly *Little Sarah*) to be outfitted in Philadelphia as a privateer in July, 1793. Asked by Governor Thomas Mifflin to keep the vessel in port, he not only refused to comply with the request but, according to Pennsylvania's Secretary of State Alexander Dallas, he then denounced Washington and threatened to plead for public support over the president's head. Jefferson and Washington, recognizing the dangers of British reprisals, tried to temporize and failed. The ship departed unhindered. Britain glowered, Jefferson lost face, and Hamilton increased his personal influence. In new rules governing activities of belligerents in America, the Neutrality Proclamation was defined more carefully and its enforcement turned over to the secretary of the treasury's customs officers.

Such Francophile biases as Jefferson might have held in other circumstances were fully dissipated in his relations with Genet. No one exceeded the secretary of state in the vigor of his denunciation of the French minister or subscribed more wholeheartedly to the cry for his recall. "Never in my opinion, was so calamitous an appointment made, as that of the present Minister of F. here. Hot headed, all imagination, no judgment, passionate, disrespectful & even indecent toward the P. in his written as well as verbal communications. . . . He renders my position immensely difficult." Hamilton of course did not make it any easier for him when he spread Mifflin's story about Genet's threats against Washington. The result was a serious weakening of both the French alliance and the Republican opposition.

Genet's verbal attacks against Washington continued until the new Committee of Public Safety, the Jacobin successor of the Girondists, issued an order for his recall and arrest. The Girondist Genet, for all his impulsiveness, had sufficient sobriety to stay in the United States instead of returning to France to explain the failure of his mission. He never paid attention to the primary function of an ambassador: namely, as his superiors pointed out, that he was appointed to "treat with the Government of the United States, not with a portion of the people; to be an organ of the French Republic near Congress, and not the head of an American party." The committee's anger with its agent was probably severe enough to doom him to the guillotine had he returned home. At the same time the Jacobins did not forget that Genet's counterpart in France, Gouverneur Morris, had been equally indiscreet, and they asked for his dismissal.

Genet was a calamity for his cause and for those Jeffersonians who had looked to France for aid in resisting Hamiltonian government. Still, his behavior owed something to the crowds that came out to idolize him on his arrival in the United States. Among those carried away by the reception accorded him was the secretary of state himself. Whether or not Genet would have listened to sober advice from anyone is questionable, but Jefferson bore a responsibility for failing to anticipate the troubles Genet brought upon himself and by extension upon the Jeffersonians.

Jefferson resigned at the end of the year with a sense of failure. The arrogance of France and the attacks on the person of the president had offended most of the country, promoting the fortunes of the Hamiltonians and leaving their enemies in disarray. But it is important to observe that Jefferson's cold assessment of the balance of power in 1793 would have prevented any policy of his from satisfying the French under any circumstances. What the French wanted—American assistance for a revived empire and for fighting the British in the guise of neutrality—Jefferson no more than Hamilton was prepared to offer.

Dispirited though Jefferson was in his last months in office, he still had grounds for being optimistic about the future of American foreign relations. Monarchism had not yet triumphed in the United States, and Great Britain had not yet recolonized America. In fact, Anglophobia did not decline substantially during the course of the Genet affair. And for good reason. Great Britain's conduct in the war threatened America's sovereignty even more than in the past, since it now included seizure of American nationals and property from American ships under the sponsorship of new and provocative Orders in Council. Instead of showing appreciation for Hamilton's commercial policies, the British plunged ahead with war measures that seemed myopic to their friends in America. As John Miller phrases it, they "planted dragon teeth in the United States, but they never ceased to be surprised that a crop of Anglophobes sprang up."[5]

Two Orders in Council canceled the effect of much of the anger that had been rising against France as a consequence of Genet's activities. The first, in June, 1793, declared a blockade against France with the intention of diverting all French-bound provisions to Britain. While the British would pay for the flour they took, Jefferson complained that the Order violated the nation's neutrality by compelling the United States to serve the British cause. France, as the secretary of state anticipated, was all the more aggrieved because she had provided economic assistance of this very sort at critical moments in the American war of independence. Retaliation was swift as the Girondists applied an embargo on American ships carrying grain to England in the summer of 1793.

Hamilton countered Jefferson's protests by observing that authorities on international law had concluded that provisions were a form of contraband. Besides, the British did pay for the cargoes they seized. But the secretary of the treasury had no plausible responses to the second Order in Council, in November, 1793, which was issued to implement the British swoop upon the French West Indies. In aid of this operation British warships were to seize all ships carrying goods of all sorts into the French islands or transporting them from the islands to the mainland. And to make the catch more impressive no warning was to be given to unsuspecting American carriers. News of the Order was suppressed to the end of the year. As a result more than two hundred and fifty American ships were captured and condemned in British West Indian admiralty courts. Early in 1794 the severity of the Order was mitigated by subjecting to capture only those vessels laden with French West Indian goods bound for European ports. It was not enough to calm the storm that the initial actions had aroused any more than the Rule of 1756 could meet the American understanding of international law. Many of the ports which Americans frequented had been open to their ships before the beginning of the war.

The Federalists appreciated the dimensions of the problems

[5] Miller, *The Federalist Era*, p. 141.

British maritime behavior had given them. Hamilton's exegesis on the provisions orders lacked his customary assurance; his private complaints to Hammond labeling the laws as harsh and unprecedented had more conviction. When the secretary of state directed Pinckney to make a stiff protest to Whitehall, Jefferson met no resistance from his rival. Despite Hamilton's backstage efforts to influence British measures, Grenville did nothing but respond to the criticism with his habitual courtesy on the assumption that the United States would not go beyond a verbal protest.

The foreign secretary was mistaken. The rising American temper over British depredations against shipping and over the impressment of seamen permitted Jefferson to use his departure from Philadelphia in December as an occasion for a full-scale condemnation of British policy, and by extension, of Federalist policy. If his final year in office had been a trial to him, the new year offered opportunities to redress the failures of the past. Federalist measures could still be undone and their purposes unmasked. More important, Washington's identification with Federalists at the end of 1793 had to be reckoned something less than total if his secretary of state could frame a report to Congress which rationalized a critically anti-Federalist program that portended a much harsher line toward England.

In reviewing American relations with Britain and France Jefferson made a point of exposing Genet's errors in full, but at the same time he arraigned Great Britain, with apparent presidential blessing, for far more serious crimes. Drawing on materials gathered over three years in office and working on a theme dating back to his French years, the secretary of state regaled Congress with a thorough listing of British economic sins against America. Speaking of maritime commerce as if he were a New England shipper, he provided statistical evidence of persistent British discrimination against American shipping since the Revolution. By contrast France was a model of benevolence. From Great Britain the United States imported over seven times the value of goods that she took from France, and over fourteen times as much as Holland supplied. Yet American ships carried only 43,000 tons from the British Isles as opposed to 116,000 tons from French ports. To make matters worse, the British re-exported most of their American imports, drawing thereby additional and gratuitous profits as middlemen which under proper circumstances would have gone to Americans through direct trade with the ultimate consumer.

This valedictory report, a veritable "farewell address" as Merrill Peterson identifies it,[6] which restated the need for redirecting American economy away from Britain and toward France, went back to the Continental Congress for its origins and reasons. It led directly to Madison's last great attempt to punish Britain through punitive legislation and to relieve America from dependence upon the British commerce through an American version of the British Navigation System. Although Madison had failed in 1789 and 1791, a particular conjunction of events in 1793 with attending increase in Anglophobia could give him victory in 1794. The resolutions he offered the House of Representatives in January were those of 1791, with the extra sting of an additional tariff designed to settle losses suffered by American citizens at the hands of the odious Orders in Council.

Against this pressure Federalists fought what seemed for a time to be a rearguard action. W. S. Smith of South Carolina, speaking from Hamilton's script, mustered a strong counterattack. After asserting the ritual claim that France's hostility was greater than Britain's, he pointed out that hostile or not the French were impotent to help or to hurt the United States. Failure to accept the British version of international law, on the other hand, could lead to war and disgrace. As for British terms of trade, Smith noted that no country was altruistic in its economic policies. Britain's practices were not different from those of other countries. If that nation dominated American commerce it was a consequence of natural causes: the tradition of easy credit terms, familiarity with each other's customs, and the availability of a rich market.

Unstated but equally valid in rebuttal were political as well as economic reasons for Anglophilia, notably Hamilton's concern for the survival of Great Britain in the face of the French Revolution's anarchy and atheism. In Federalist eyes these were not vague ideological nightmares but genuine products of

[6] Peterson, "Thomas Jefferson and Commercial Policy," p. 609.

Jacobin outrages witnessed in the streets of America, all by-products of French ideas. A victory for France over England would give heart to French partisans in America and increase the vigor of their attacks upon society. The emotions that inspired Hamilton's compliance with British needs made a mockery of his reputation as a mercantilist.[7] Jefferson's and Madison's ideas fit the description far more readily than Hamilton's at this point, as they shifted from free trade to a navigation system that beckoned Federalist merchants to open their markets and seek new channels of trade rather than remain tied to the former mother country. In this light the Hamilton program emerges as one of subservience to a British master for reasons of state rather than of economy.

Whether New England shipping magnates or Philadelphia bankers responded equally to the ideological note is not quantifiable and always speculative. What was clear in 1794 was their unwillingness to respond to the appeal of Madison for reasons of fiscal prudence. On one level, they recognized the damage the British navy could do to their investments with its superiority on the seas. It seemed reasonable to settle for what the British were willing to concede as long as they could still extract profit from the trade and still expect compensation for losses at the hands of British privateers. If an economic war had followed from the passage of Madison's resolutions, all chances of compensation would disappear.

The old Republican dream of replacing Britain with France as the trading partner was unrealistic. The shippers knew what Jefferson himself had perceived years before: namely, that the French lacked the expertise, the experience, and the will to perform services which Great Britain had given for generations. And this cold balancing of values was certainly evident in Hamilton's thinking when he contemplated the havoc war with England would inflict on the American economy: ". . . it deprives us of a supply for which no substitute can be found

[7] W. A. Williams, "The Age of Mercantilism: An Interpretation of the American Political Economy, 1763–1828," *William and Mary Quarterly*, Third Series, XV (October, 1958): 431–432, elaborates on this point. He suggests that "Perhaps the most to be said of Hamilton's mercantilism is that it was latent and limited, for his actions belied his rhetoric."

elsewhere—a supply, necessary to us in peace, and more necessary to us if we are to go to war. It gives a sudden and violent blow to our revenue, which cannot easily, if at all, be repaired from other sources. It will be so great an interruption to commerce as may very possibly interfere with the payment of duties which have hitherto accrued, and bring the Treasury to an absolute stoppage of payment—an event which would cut up credit by the roots."

The imperatives of economic necessity could have been swept away in the popular outburst of anger over British actions in the winter of 1794. Smith's speech failed to stem the resentment already stirred by Jefferson's report and Madison's proposals. It rose higher when news of the Order in Council of November, accompanied as it was by stories of the capture of scores of American ships in the West Indies, reached Philadelphia. Hardly had the meaning of this outrage been assimilated when the United States learned of a treaty between Portugal and Algiers ending hostilities between the two countries in 1793. As long as hostilities had lasted the Barbary pirates had been sealed off from the Atlantic and from depredations against American shipping. If the two countries were now at peace the Algerians would move out into the Atlantic to prey upon American commerce. Here was another example of British malevolence, since Portugal was a client state of Britain. As Monroe looked upon the scene, from the Caribbean to the Mediterranean American ships were "kicked, cuffed and plundered" by British inspiration if not always by British arms.

As if these provocations were not enough, the running sore of Britain's occupation of the Northwest posts became reinfected in the midst of the new tensions over British maritime policies. Governor John Simcoe of Lower Canada, mistakenly believing General Anthony Wayne's army in Ohio had intended to attack British posts, sent a detachment of troops sixty miles beyond Detroit to the rapids of the Maumee River. This belligerent gesture had its counterpart in the speech of his superior, Lord Dorchester, before an Indian delegation in which he hinted at an imminent war between the United States and Great Britain that would permit the Indians to recover their lost lands of the northwest. The speech was delivered on February 10, during the Congressional debates over Madison's bill. Its contents filtered back to Philadelphia late the following month in time to destroy Federalist plans for modifying Republican punitive legislation against Britain.

Ironically, the inflammatory Dorchester speech triggered a reaction in America that overshot the mark as far as Madison was concerned. So angry was the Congress over its implications that the House leader's proposals seemed too mild. The national mood demanded something more. The fact that Jonathan Dayton, a New Jersey Federalist, could propose seriously the sequestration of all debts owed to British creditors with the provision that they be converted into compensation to those Americans who suffered from the Orders in Council suggested a Federalist impatience with Great Britain resembling that of the Republicans with Genet's France six months before.

It was unlikely, however, that most Federalists intended war to be the appropriate response, or even a release from financial obligation. They talked the language of arms; Theodore Sedgwick, an orthodox Massachusetts Federalist, proposed an army of 150,000 men with 80,000 in reserve from the states, all to be paid out of new taxes. But suspicious Republicans looked upon this recommendation as a Federalist ruse to sidetrack Madison's commercial resolutions by action that seemed more drastic but in reality would do nothing more than strengthen the central government to a dangerous degree. The troops so raised could be used against the states or against Democrats rather than against the British. As Madison observed to Jefferson, "You understand the game behind the curtain too well not to perceive the old trick of turning every contingency into a resource for accumulating force in the government."

Six frigates emerged from this crisis in addition to a two-month embargo that shut off food supplies to the British West Indies. War might have resulted from the mounting passions; but it did not. While Hamilton's spokesman, W. S. Smith, spoke of "aggression, heaped upon us with tenfold aggression," the secretary of the treasury himself successfully offered a diplomatic solution that removed both war and Madison's proposals from immediate consideration: namely, a special mission to London.

Not long after the Jay Treaty had been signed, Jefferson referred to his former colleague with grudging admiration as a "colossus to the anti-republican party" and "an host within himself." These were fair descriptions of Hamilton's massive presence at all stages of the Anglo-American rapprochement of 1794 and 1795. Nowhere was his mastery of men and events more prominent than in the machinery which set in motion the negotiations with Great Britain. The initial idea for a special presidential mission to London came from Hamilton's friends—Rufus King, George Cabot, Oliver Ellsworth, and Caleb Strong—but it was Hamilton's advice to Washington that made up the president's mind. Indeed, he advanced the project by wisely withdrawing himself as candidate and recommending in his place Chief Justice John Jay. Despite some criticism of Jay's Anglophilism he was confirmed by the Federalist-dominated Senate and left for England on May 12, 1794.

Hamilton's invocation of a familiar American device blocked Madison's navigation system as well as the seemingly more radical proposals for retribution against Britain. Madison's proposals still under debate could be set aside as potentially embarrassing to the negotiations in London. The navigation bill passed the House but was defeated in the Senate by the interposition of Adams' vice presidential vote. So high were American emotions that even Hamilton's genius barely suppressed Congressional action. Whatever the margin, he won.

The British played their part in the easing of tensions by their warm reception of Jay. They had begun to retreat from their more provocative stances as early as January when the November Order in Council was modified and Pinckney was assured by the foreign minister of Britain's innocent intentions in her advocacy of the Portuguese-Algerian truce. Hammond in Philadelphia contributed to the spirit of pacification by declaring his belief that Dorchester's sentiments were not those of the Foreign Office. He was correct. Grenville at last recognized the possibilities of war with the United States adding to his Continental burdens and was prepared to evacuate the posts without demanding an Indian barrier state as a condition precedent. The subsequent rebuke to Dorchester and the governor general's resignation from office were important marks of Britain's receptivity to conciliation with America.[8]

How far Great Britain was willing to bend to protect her sources of supply, her expanding markets in America, and her thin defenses in Upper Canada was never adequately tested because of the excessive submissiveness of Anglophiles in America to the British position.[9] Jay's instructions were stern and clear, but they were diluted by Hamilton's persistent indulgence of Britain's positions. The secretary of the treasury was prepared to accept in advance the British gloss on provisions as contraband, on the validity of the Rule of 1756 with respect to American use of French West Indian ports, and on the inapplicability of the Franco-American agreement on "free ships goods" to British maritime practice in wartime. Hammond communicated these sentiments to Grenville, who profited from them at every turn in his dealings with Jay.

In the planning of the special mission, the new secretary of state, Edmund Randolph, found himself on the periphery. Mistrusted by the Federalists as a Virginian with agrarian proclivities and with French sympathies, he had little rapport with Jefferson who had frequently dismissed the former attorney general as a fence-sitter in cabinet debates trimming his views according to the pressures from the Treasury Department. Randolph was a lonely figure in Washington's administration before and after Jefferson's departure. Although Monroe reported that the idea of Jay's mission had emanated from Randolph, there is an element of pathos in the secretary of state's letter to the president, of April 6, 1794, in which he asserted that he "was among the first, if not the first, who suggested this

[8] Reginald Horsman, "British Indian Department and the Resistance to General Anthony Wayne, 1793–1795," *Mississippi Valley Historical Review*, XLIX (September, 1962): 272 ff., observes the devastating effects of British behavior upon their Indian allies. After being fired up by Dorchester's speech they felt that Whitehall's disavowal was an act of betrayal.

[9] Albert H. Bowman, "The Struggle for Neutrality: A History of the Diplomatic Relations between the United States and France, 1793–1801," unpublished Ph.D. thesis, Columbia University, 1954, p. 202, claims: "Historians have generally accepted uncritically Federalist propaganda to the effect that a disastrous war with Britain was the only alternative to accepting the treaty."

mission to your consideration." Randolph was making a brave show of being in command of his office. It was not credible.

A better index to his influence on the Jay mission was the brusque way in which his uneasiness about reconciling Jay's position as chief justice with his service in the executive branch was brushed aside by the administration. While he did draw up the official instructions, he had little control over their implementation. Jay was given leeway to operate as he saw fit, for his only explicit instructions were to enter into no engagement contrary to the obligations under the Treaty of 1778 and to accept no commercial treaty that failed to open the West Indies to American commerce. Beyond these were only recommendations. First, he was to seek compensation for damages and injuries inflicted by British ships operating under the provision order. Second, he was to settle the disputes that had arisen from the Treaty of Paris, with special attention to continued British occupation of the Northwest posts. Third, depending on the results of the first two points, he was to make a treaty of commerce that would allow Americans entry into the East and West Indies, win acceptance of the principle of free ships, free goods, and limit the scope of contraband articles. The philosophy of the Madison navigation proposals underlay the stipulation that no commercial treaty would be signed which did not grant admission to American ships in the West Indies on the same terms enjoyed by British ships sailing between the United States and the Caribbean ports.

Much of the language of the instructions was as strong as any Jeffersonian would wish. Jay's mission had among its many objects that of keeping "alive in the mind of the British minister the opinion which the solemnity of a special mission must naturally inspire, of the strong agitations excited in the people of the United States, by the disturbed condition of things between them and Great Britain; to repel war, for which we are not disposed, and into which the necessity of vindicating our honor and our property may, but can alone, drive us. . . ." And to drive this point home Jay had the special weapon in the fifth article of his instructions, the exploitation of a new Armed Neutrality composed of Russia, Denmark, and Sweden, whose ministers in London he could sound out concerning the United States membership.

The combination of British nervousness over the effects of Jefferson's valedictory report and the exigencies of a war that depended on American supplies might have forced Whitehall to yield to Jay's instructions. Jay's inability to make the most of his possibilities in London must be blamed in large measure upon the limits of the British willingness to concede, particularly their obsession with a maritime posture which required the maintenance at almost all costs of a rigid interpretation of neutral rights. But their rigidity owed much to Hamilton's interposition in the negotiations that made the final treaty signed on November 19, 1794, his own more than it was Jay's. "More aptly," concludes Samuel Flagg Bemis," the treaty might be called Hamilton's Treaty."[10]

The secretary of the treasury had worked on both Jay and Hammond with equal success. To the former he urged a relaxed and loose construction of indemnification, to the point of suggesting that the United States compensate its own injured citizens, and recognize the British Rule of 1756 as valid international law. To the latter he assured that "it was the settled policy of this Government in every contingency, even in that of an open contest with Great Britain, to avoid entangling itself with European connexions." So Hammond reported to Grenville in a letter that arrived in time to allow the foreign minister to believe that there was no danger of an American link with a new Armed Neutrality.

Jay's Treaty did secure for the United States what Hamilton had felt were the minimal conditions for a rapprochement with Great Britain: the evacuation of British posts in the Northwest, and indemnification for spoliations committed beyond the authority of the Order in Council of June 8, 1793. Jay himself took satisfaction from other concessions inserted into the treaty. Some of them were comparatively insignificant, such as the

[10] Samuel Flagg Bemis, *Jay's Treaty: A Study in Commerce and Diplomacy*, (New Haven, 1962), p. 373. But Jerold A. Combs, *The Jay Treaty Political Battleground of the Founding Fathers* (Berkeley and Los Angeles, 1970), p. 157, observes, however, that "It is unlikely that Hamilton's injudicious revelation to Hammond about America's intentions toward the Armed Neutrality had much effect on the negotiations."

granting of reciprocal trading privileges to all Indians in Canada except for those within the jurisdiction of the Hudson's Bay Company. Others, such as the legalization of the American trade with the British East Indies, had important implications for the future. To the jurist Jay, the treaty satisfied his long-standing interest in peaceful negotiations as solutions to international problems by establishing mixed commissions to determine boundary lines and settle debts. Here was a clearcut victory of the principle of arbitration over the Old World principle of violence.

The American envoy found these victories all the sweeter because he had to fight for them against the malevolence of such powerful British ministers as Lord Hawkesbury, chairman of the Board of Trade and Grenville's principal adviser on American affairs, who was convinced that the foreign minister had made too many concessions. Only Jay's adamancy about ceding any American territory prevented a new boundary from being drawn in the Northwest. If British creditors had had their way a lump-sum payment rather than arbitral commissions would have been the answer to their claims. Grenville as well as Jay displayed firmness in resisting pressures from British merchants in the Canadian trade to postpone delivery of the western posts for three years. Although the social success Jay enjoyed in London raised suspicions about his adversaries playing upon that worthy's well-known vanity, the close personal bonds formed between Grenville and Jay in the course of the negotiations appear genuine. A. L. Burt was sufficiently impressed by their mutual efforts in fashioning a treaty to observe that "for its successful conclusion both the United States and the British Empire owe them a great debt of gratitude."[11]

Given these reasons for satisfaction, Jay had little presentiment of the reception his treaty would meet in America. The

[11] A. L. Burt, *The United States, Great Britain, and British North America*, p. 156. Miller, *The Federalist Era*, p. 178, compares it favorably with the Treaty of Ghent. For a more sober estimate see Bemis, *Jay's Treaty*, p. 370. DeConde, *Entangling Alliance*, emphasizes the treaty's blighting effect on the French alliance. To Bowman, "Struggle for Neutrality," p. 202, the treaty "meant that the United States accepted absorption into the British economic power sphere and the role of at least a passive ally of Britain in her life or death struggle with France."

Jeffersonian newspaper *Aurora* must have been fantasying when it noted on February 7, 1795, that when Jay left for Bath after completing his labors in London, it was "no wonder he should be short breathed, and have such palpitations as to need the Bath waters to restore him, after subscribing to so dishonourable a treaty as that said to have been concluded." The details of the treaty were not known in the United States. Nor were the details of Jay's social life. The evidence of that winter showed that he was basking in the limelight of a popularity that the regularly accredited envoy Thomas Pinckney had never enjoyed. If he was short of breath on occasion his palpitations were probably the result of rushing from one state dinner to another in the company of such dignitaries as the Lord Mayor of London, the Archbishop of Canterbury, and William Pitt. His treatment, like the treaty itself, may have been as Bradford Perkins believes "the first proof that independent America was important enough to secure any concessions from a major power. . . ."[12]

Jay never wavered in his conviction that he not only did his duty as special envoy but did it well, even after the storm burst over him. In a letter written in the summer of 1795 he could still write: "The treaty is as it is; and the time will certainly come when it will very universally receive exactly the degree of commendation or censure, which, to candid and enlightened minds, it shall appear to deserve." That time may have seemed distant that summer. Most of the country, including the Federalist managers of the treaty in the Senate, had recognized the dangers to the administration and to the whole fabric of America's relationship to Great Britain which the treaty had created.

When Jay was dispatched to London, his major mission was to end British depredations on the high seas. The treaty he signed not only had nothing to say on this subject but also appeared to accept the British definitions of neutral rights and freedom of the seas. British interpretations of international law

[12] Bradford Perkins, *The First Rapprochement: England and the United States, 1795–1805* (Berkeley and Los Angeles, 1967), p. 5. Charles R. Ritcheson, *Aftermath of Revolution: British Policy toward the United States, 1783–1795* (Dallas, 1969), p. 351, goes even further in his favorable view of the treaty by relating it to the "final passage into oblivion of British bitterness at the American War."

were written into the treaty. Nor did Jay secure the commercial treaty Hamilton had wanted or the privileges such a treaty would have accorded American commerce, with the exception of a limited entry into the West Indies which was so inadequate that Article XII, in which it was embodied, was deleted by the Senate. Conspicuous by its silence in the treaty was the flaming issue of impressment which had been a major preoccupation of Pinckney before Jay's arrival on the London scene. Westerners were upset over Jay's failure to gain a British commitment against interference in Indian affairs in the Northwest, while southerners were angry over his failure to provide compensation for loss of slave property carried away by the British army during the war. And the Jeffersonians in particular were incensed, even before they knew the specific terms of the treaty, over the strains the treaty would make in America's ties with France.

For all of the foregoing reasons the administration did not make public the contents of the treaty when it finally reached Philadelphia on March 7, 1795. In fact, the public was not to know those details until they were leaked by the Republican press in early July. The cabinet had no reason to be surprised at the direction the treaty was taking; Hamilton after all had been the major manipulator. Having resigned from the cabinet at the end of 1794 he was a private citizen in New York and was now apparently critical of Jay's handiwork. Before his resignation he had expressed reservations about Grenville's draft, particularly about Article XII, which linked limited admission of American ships to the West Indies with full British privileges in American ports. In light of his own interference with Jay's negotiations, his complaints were not convincing, and his commentary on Jay's handiwork as an "old woman's treaty" smacked of humbug. What distressed Hamilton was its obvious vulnerability. He wished to dissociate himself from the inevitable charges that would arise from it.

Secretary of State Randolph, always an outsider in Federalist councils, was also critical. But there was a touch of irrelevancy about his commentaries. His emphasis was on the British position with respect to Negro slavery, although he shared the general revulsion toward Article XII. His discomfort was more genuine than Hamilton's, but it lacked meaning. His stand on the slave issue reflected a Virginian bias, and his other objections reflected his ignorance of what was going on about him in the Hamiltonian cabinet.

Despite the absence of strong executive leadership, the Senate, meeting behind closed doors and pledged to secrecy, passed the treaty by the barest required two-thirds margin of 20 to 10. Secrecy alone accounted for its passage, although the Federalist majority salved their consciences by deleting Article XII from the text. The treaty passed conditionally on June 24, 1795, over two weeks after the president had reluctantly submitted it.

Less than a week later the Republican paper *Aurora* printed the text, and with this act unleashed the pent-up fury of Democrats, Jeffersonians, anti-Federalists, Francophiles, and nationalists of every description upon the Washington administration. No major city, not even Boston, was spared violent demonstrations against Jay, Hamilton, and even the president himself. It was fortunate for Jay that he had been elected governor of New York just before the text of the treaty was available to the press. As it was, the walls of the house of a prominent Boston Federalist held this message for Jay and his friends: "Damn John Jay! Damn everyone that won't damn John Jay!! Damn everyone that won't put lights in his windows and sit up all night damning John Jay!!!" Hamilton, attempting to debate opponents on the subject in New York, drew shouts and stones. One of the latter struck him on the forehead. In withdrawing, he was said to have replied: "If you use such striking arguments, I must retire."

It was a cool and very temporary retirement from the heat of passions, for Hamilton proceeded to publish over the next six months the influential Camillus Papers, with contributions from fellow New Yorkers Jay and Rufus King. Repeatedly his theme underscored America's need for peace with the country whose trade and mercantile capital was responsible for the revenues of the government and the prosperity of the soceity. With all its faults then, Jay's Treaty blunted those areas of friction—through Britain's evacuation of the Northwest posts and partial compensation for damages committed by British seapower—which could lead to war. Ultimately, and perhaps inevitably in light of the symbiotic nature of Hamilton's ties with Washington, the arguments of the Camillus Papers persuaded the president to look upon the treaty as a vital cement in the Anglo-American relationship.

But neither the artifice of Hamilton nor the power of political or economic logic were the final factors in convincing a reluctant president to sign the treaty. His initial doubts about its wisdom were deepseated, and his presentation of the treaty to the Senate had been made without a recommendation for its passage. While some of his doubts may have been reinforced by the predictable vehemence of popular resentment—at least until he was aware that he was one of its targets—part of his reservations stemmed from apprehension over the potential effects the treaty would have upon the French alliance. In this his mood appeared closer to that of his disciple, Randolph, who had welcomed Jay home with the suggestion that his own "*private judgment*" was opposed to ratification. Such a result would have minimized the embarrassment the secretary of state had already suffered in assuring Monroe, the American minister in Paris, and Joseph Fauchet, the retiring French minister in Philadelphia, that French interests would not be adversely affected by the treaty. When Pierre Adet, Fauchet's successor, arrived on June 30, a most inappropriate time, and raised the expected questions about the treaty, Randolph resorted to the clause in Article XXV with which he tried to satisfy himself and the president, if not the French envoy, of the compatibility of Jay's work with the Franco-American alliance: "Nothing in this treaty contained shall be construed or operate contrary to former and existing public treaties with other sovereign States." A presidential veto would have relieved the secretary of state of facing the consequences of this misleading assurance.

Another check to Washington's signature was the alarming news that Great Britain had reintroduced the provisions orders three days after the Senate had passed the treaty. It was as if the British had stifled their hostility to the United States while the Senate debated, only to return to their old ways once the result was clear. Although the intensification of the war rather than cynical or unthinking insensitivity to American feelings may explain British behavior,[13] the apparent betrayal of America's trust increased Washington's hesitations about putting his imprimatur upon the Senate's decision. The president, even more than his secretary of state, would suspend an executive decision until the provisions order had been clarified.

At this critical moment a stroke of good fortune for the Federalists, mixed with some guile and malice, abruptly ended Randolph's career and determined Washington's course of action on Jay's Treaty. Randolph, the lone southerner in the cabinet and a man of ability but with no reputation for fixity of purpose or of loyalty, found himself confronted with the charge of collaboration with the former French minister, Joseph Fauchet, in the service of France. One of the Frenchman's dispatches had fallen into British hands on the high seas and from there went to Hammond with instructions to use it either to tone down Randolph's hostility to Britain or to remove him from the cabinet. Randolph's two colleagues, Secretary of the Treasury Oliver Wolcott to whom Hammond had given the original document and Secretary of War Timothy Pickering who read and translated it, showed the dispatch to Washington immediately upon his return to the capital on August 11. Without any warning in advance the president promptly presented the compromising document to the secretary of state and demanded an explanation. Randolph, accusing his colleague of combining an insult with conspiracy, immediately resigned from his post. He subsequently submitted an explanation for his conduct in a long and occasionally incoherent apologia which excoriated Washington for his shabby treatment of an old and devoted friend.

In retrospect the intercepted letter was a sampling of the web of self-delusions that Fauchet wove for himself during his short stay in America. He had come to Philadelphia as a young man of the Jacobin persuasion with no knowledge of English and little experience in diplomacy in order to observe and influence the American government, much in the spirit of every French embassy back to Gérard's time. While he did come empowered

[13] Josiah Newcomb, "New Light on Jay's Treaty," *American Journal of International Law*, XXVIII (October, 1934): 687, points out that the provisions order of 1795 had a substantially different legal base from that of 1793.

to disavow Genet's conduct, to disarm the privateers illegally commissioned, to dismiss those consuls who participated in condemning prizes, and to restrain the Louisiana adventure, he was also expected to achieve many of those objectives by other means. Above all else, he had to secure for France a favorable interpretation of neutral rights. In the course of his labors he saw a good deal of the secretary of state and made a number of generalizations about him, which included characterizations as a man of weak character and a partisan of France. In the dispatch seized by the British, Fauchet claimed that Randolph had given him "*précieuses confessions*" about friendly political figures and about democratic societies anxious to combat British influences. With the Whiskey Rebellion a live issue in western Pennsylvania, Randolph apparently approached Fauchet for money to be distributed among flour contractors who would spy on Hammond's agents.

The details of the scheme were murky, the translation faulty, and the judgment of the cabinet that of a kangaroo court. Fauchet had been embellishing his accounts of his activities to impress his superiors. Indeed, when bearded by Randolph at Newport on the eve of his departure, he recanted and formally rejected the notion that Randolph had been involved in either intrigue or bribery. It was too late. Fauchet's retraction and Randolph's *Vindication*, later published, could not remove the impression that the secretary of state had been trying to raise money from French connections for himself and for his political friends in Pennsylvania. While recent scholarship has made a convincing case for Randolph's innocence of the original charges, his conduct was indiscreet if not scandalous.[14] He permitted his enemies to elevate indiscretion to treason in order to serve the political purpose of saving the Jay Treaty.

Randolph's fall from grace allowed the president to see new and sinister reasons for Randolph's opposition to the treaty, although in reality the former secretary's doubts were no stronger than his own and did not have their source in French gold. Washington signed the treaty the day before the intercepted dispatch was sprung on Randolph without waiting for the Brit-

[14] See, in particular, Irving Brant, "Edmund Randolph, Not Guilty!" *William and Mary Quarterly*, VII (April, 1950): 180–198.

ish to remove their new provisions orders. Here was victory for the Federalists, plucking success from what might have been disaster.

The Randolph scandal also set the course for Washington's behavior in his final year of office. He now turned his back on the stance of impartiality he had worked so hard to keep in the past. Republicans were now his and his country's sworn enemies. The betrayal of Randolph recast the opposition, and Washington's treatment of the disgraced official revealed its harshness: the peremptory charge, absence of a hearing, and the cold acceptance of his resignation. No longer would the president appoint a man "whose official tenets are adverse to the measures which the general government are pursuing; for this, in my opinion would be a sort of political suicide." Not that he would have appointed such a figure in the past; it was simply that the range of enemies had widened so considerably. French influence, as Washington saw it in 1796, had reached to the highest levels of government and was inextricably associated with his personal enemies.

The hostile reaction of France to Jay's Treaty dominated the last year and a half of the president's tenure in office. And France had a powerful case for her hostility. Fighting for the life of her evolving revolution, the new republic had anticipated the nonbelligerent support of her ally. Instead the Federalist administration offered the hand of friendship to Great Britain in the form of a de facto alliance. By accepting the British construction of neutral rights the United States acquiesced in Britain's war of attrition against France. Especially galling was the refusal of the Francophobic new secretary of state Pickering to allow French ships to be outfitted in American ports and then denying the right of the French to sell British prizes in the United States on the grounds that such action would violate Article XXIV of the Anglo-American Treaty of 1794. When Pickering protested the Directory's decree of July 2, 1796, whereby neutral vessels would be treated in the same manner as the British treated them, he had the further gall to claim that France had violated her treaty obligations by not distinguishing the United States from other neutrals. Thus France should be bound by the free ships, free goods agreement while Britain was free to do as she chose. France was not to be assuaged by the fine point that legally Pickering was correct in observing that France was bound by treaty to respect America's neutral rights while Great Britain was not so bound.

France's exasperation found an audience in the United States among those who cherished the French struggle for liberty and feared Britain's reconquest of America if France should fail. They felt that the spirit at least of Article XXII of the Franco-American treaty, which specifically denied to foreign privateers belonging to enemies of either nation the right to fit their ships or to sell their prizes in the countries of the allies, was flagrantly contradicted by the terms of the Jay Treaty. It was understandable if Frenchmen such as Genet could even have concluded that this article granted those rights implicitly to the allies which it explicitly denied to their enemies.

While Jefferson should have laid that question to rest when he denounced Genet two years before, the aura of special favor surrounding the Jay Treaty rekindled French resentment. James Monroe, as minister to France since May, 1794, played his part in exacerbating it. Whether Monroe sinned more than he was sinned against was immaterial; there was more than enough blame for both sides to share in the handling of French relations. The administration obviously chose Monroe in the first place because of his ties to Virginia Republicans and because of his friendship for France. Since his instructions had been to calm the French while the Jay negotiations were underway, the Federalists had counted on his special sympathies to placate the worried ally. There were enough earmarks in this appointment to raise the specter of a Federalist plot which hid from both the French and Monroe the true state of affairs in the Anglo-American relationship.

The equivocal responses of Randolph and Jay to Monroe's queries about the latter's mission raised the suspicion that Monroe was to be a decoy, to divert French suspicions until the treaty had been completed. Yet Washington's choice of Monroe was in keeping with the same sense of fitness that led to his sending Jay to London: namely, that a *persona grata* can accomplish more than a *persona non grata*. A replica of Gouverneur Morris would have been an insult as well as an error, and Monroe was a more reasonable envoy to Paris than Pinckney—who had been considered for the post—would have been.

Innocent or not, the Monroe mission worked well at first. The minister was feted in Paris and shown marks of favor in the lifting of some of the retaliatory restrictions which had been placed on American shipping. The Jacobins were all the more prepared to greet Monroe warmly, since he was the only diplomatist remaining in Paris during the Terror.

From the Federalist point of view Monroe overplayed his role. So enthusiastic was his pleasure over the accolade accorded him by the Convention that Jay came to be concerned over the "disagreeable sensation" which the American minister's fervor for the French cause created in London. Randolph, against his better judgment, was forced to reprove Monroe for his extravagant praise of the French Republic. In light of these circumstances, added to the long-standing enmity between the two men, Jay's reluctance to give Monroe details of the treaty he was shaping was hardly surprising. Jay even refused to let Monroe have a copy, claiming the treaty must be kept confidential until ratified. He was willing only to offer assurances that nothing offensive to France was contained in it, and ultimately to reveal the provisions orally by special courier if necessary.

The truths that Monroe did not know—and indeed refused to know, since he turned down Jay's offer of confidential information—he suspected. So did the French. Monroe's discomfort with the negotiations in England was aggravated by an indiscreet promise he had made to reveal to the French government the provisions of the treaty as soon as he had learned of them himself. He thereby compromised his mission by an act no minister had a right to commit, as Jay pointed out to him after Monroe had confessed his commitment to France: "It does not belong to ministers who negotiate treaties to publish them even when perfected, much less treaties not yet completed, and remaining open to alteration, or rejection." From the standpoint of Monroe's enemies the Virginian stood charged with misdemeanors of all kinds. He had befriended Paine after the latter's insults to the president, he had allowed the Directory to see a personal letter from Washington to Morris which hinted at

American subservience to Britain, he had mismanaged government funds and speculated in French-confiscated estates, and he had misled the French into believing that the country disapproved as he did himself the shocking Jay Treaty.

In this mixture of fact and rumor it was the last charge that deserved reproof, and received it in full measure from the biting pen of Secretary of State Pickering. Monroe's reaction was one of outrage over the Federalist conspiracy which enveloped him in its coils. He returned home firm in the belief that the French had been betrayed by the treaty and that only the election of a new and better government in 1796 could save America. But before he left France, he advised the French to distinguish between the government and the people, and to remember that "the number of your friends is considerable, and that number is daily increasing." His implication was that the new office-holders would be pro-French after the expiration of Washington's term of office. By impressing the new French Directory with the wisdom of this counsel, he averted a crisis and warded off the Directory's plan of breaking the alliance with the United States. At the same time he exaggerated the Francophile sentiments of the public and tempted French agents to interfere in the new presidential election in support of Republican candidates.

The temptation to intervene became irresistible to the French minister Adet as the fevers of campaign oratory rose in the summer of 1796 and after the last hope of defeating the effects of Jay's Treaty died with the House of Representatives' appropiations for its implementation. On the eve of the election Adet proclaimed the Directory's decree of July 2, 1796, that France would treat American vessels exactly as the British did; then proceeded to charge that the Jay Treaty had made a treaty of alliance with England by accepting the treaty's dictation of policy on the sale of British prizes in American ports. Finally, he asserted that the virtual nullification of the Franco-American alliance required the suspension of his functions as minister to the United States. This uncertain state of Franco-American relations would "last until the Government of the United States returns to sentiments, and to measures, more conformable to the interests of the alliance, and the sworn friendship between the two nations." A copy of this note went to the *Aurora* as a manifesto with a summary of its contents published before the State Department had completed its own translation. Here was the climax of France's involvement in the American election.

The victory of Federalist candidate John Adams was more a rebuke to France than it was a testament of Hamiltonian politics. The Federalists divided in the campaign over the choice of Adams, a doubtful Anglophile, and Thomas Pinckney, a redoubtable Hamiltonian, with damaging results the party would later pay for with defeat. French attempts to intimidate the electors into supporting putative "French" candidate Jefferson obscured this internal quarrel. Yet the meaning of that election cannot be found simply in a rejection of foreign interference. In the abstract at least it cannot be said with assurance that the majority of Americans did not sympathize with the French shouts of outrage. What the election results more definitely told was the success of the retiring president in pointing to the accomplishments of his administration in fashioning a government strong enough to protect the borders from Spanish, British, and Indian threats and to ensure prosperity for an economy dependent upon European markets. The Federalist record was worthy of electoral appreciation, even if it included the price of a British control of the terms of international trade. This record as much as the open participation in American politics by the French government undid Jeffersonians. That John Adams won the election in the face of the divisive Hamiltonian presence in the party was a tribute to the authority of President Washington.

Westerners from the Great Lakes to the Florida border had reason in 1796 to credit the actions of the central government for security from Indian attacks in the Treaty of Greenville, for the removal of the British from their posts in the Jay Treaty, and for the opening of the Mississippi and the advantageous marking of the Florida boundary in Pinckney's Treaty with Spain. An unexpected bonus for Federalist diplomacy had been the amelioration of most of the issues which had bedeviled Spanish-American relations since the Revolution.

Fearful for her American possessions Spain had directed her diplomatic efforts toward encouraging Indians to create a buffer state that would withstand American pressures and toward enticing western leaders to detach their territories from the United States or to emigrate with their followers to Louisiana. The cloture of the Mississippi was the instrument that gave strength to Spanish negotiations with westerners and the United States government alike, as the abortive Gardoqui dealings with John Jay under the Confederation had revealed. Spanish stubbornness softened only if war clouds appeared on the horizon or if an Anglo-American rapprochement was in the offing. When Hammond arrived in Philadelphia as the first British minister in 1791 the long-standing phobia about a combined British and American attack against Spanish America led Spain to accept William Short, the dynamic young chargé d'affaires in France, as Carmichael's partner in diversionary talks. But when the danger of an Anglo-American accord receded and when Spain joined Britain in the war against France, negotiations withered. Jefferson left office two years later feeling that the two Spanish agents in Philadelphia, Josef de Jaudenes and Josef de Viar, had no intention of conceding any Spanish claims in America. Although Spain raised the possibility of an alliance with the United States, it would have entailed a guarantee of all Spanish possessions, raising suspicions that this was simply another ploy in Spain's game with the United States.

There would have been no resolution of the impasse as long as the Spanish had hopes for their intrigues with the Indians or with the westerners or had expected continued American weakness in the face of British and French challenges. Such was the situation when Manuel de Godoy, the Spanish foreign minister, undercut the Short-Carmichael delegation by insisting upon a personage of higher rank to represent the United States in Madrid. At the same time the new minister kept alive the idea of an alliance which would be developed by the two junior Spanish emissaries in Philadelphia. All the while Spaniards on both sides of the Atlantic were encouraging American separatism as vigorously as in the past. Indeed, each of these programs contradicted the others. Jaudenes complicated negotiations in the capital by concealing from Washington and Randolph the details of the Spanish overture for alliance in order to further his western designs.

The changing pattern of European relations which coincided

with the conclusion of Jay's Treaty suddenly put an end to Spanish dallying with America. First, Spain's ardor for a connection with Britain had cooled. An uncomfortably powerful British navy using the French Revolution as an occasion to destroy French naval power provided a lesson for the Spanish; namely, that the new ally was more interested in destroying France—republican or monarchical—than in restoring the Bourbons. Spain's turn could be next. While they worried about British naval power, they were forced to take into account France's successes on land, particularly the invasion of Iberia itself at the end of 1794. William Short, then languishing in Madrid, recognized the unnatural cast of the Anglo-Spanish alliance and offered to intervene in Spain's behalf with the French government. Though nothing came of this suggestion, the fact that Godoy and Gardoqui gave it respectful attention was a signal of new American opportunities. Thus when Spain and France did make peace, Americans could make the most out of Spain's fears of British reprisals for deserting the alliance, since an obvious place of retribution would be in America, rendered with the help of the United States. Jay's negotiations in London, coming to their conclusion just as Spanish fears were rising, assumed a frightening significance to Spanish ministers. Spain was now ready for detente with the United States.

Had Thomas Pinckney, Washington's choice to fill the role of distinguished American in Madrid, proceeded promptly from London to Madrid before the Jay Treaty had been ratified, Spanish concessions might have been fully commensurate with their fears. But Jay and Pinckney both thought that news of its ratification would help America's case, and so the latter was in no hurry to reach Madrid. Short, the man on the scene, disagreed, but Short lacked power to do anything about it, doomed as he seemed to be to perpetual disappointment in all his assignments—France, now Spain, and later in Russia.

Whether Pinckney's leisurely journey to Spain made a difference is speculative. A matter of record, however, was the remarkable pliability of the Spanish when he did arrive. Not that he achieved all that he wanted. The special emissary may have been needlessly disturbed about the new Franco-Spanish Treaty of Basel, which he felt would free Spain for a more single-minded pursuit of American ambitions. Spain did not grant the right of deposit at New Orleans or open ports to American commerce in the spirit of the Plan of 1776, or even of the Franco-American commercial treaty of 1778. But Pinckney was shrewd enough in his dealings to resist Godoy's insistence upon a Spanish-American alliance, or a triple alliance that would embrace France as well. The American claimed that Jaudenes in Philadelphia had never raised the issue with the State Department. By ignoring his instructions in favor of his own favorite western adventures, the Spanish envoy provided an excuse which Pinckney ably exploited. He succeeded in winning a qualified privilege of deposit at New Orleans for a three-year period. No such limitation marred the acquisition of the 31st parallel as the new Florida boundary line.

The Spanish ministers had yielded not to the weight of American military power but to the specter of the future west, embodied in ambitious Americans who would not restrain themselves for long before crossing the Mississippi River. They were also victimized by the vagaries of the shifting European balance of power, which left them in 1795 fearful that the Jay Treaty may have presaged an Anglo-American alliance. Pinckney's accomplishment at San Lorenzo was in making a "frontier treaty" in which the voice of the frontiersman was heard; but it also was the work of statecraft that capitalized on Spanish misjudgments of the meaning of Jay's Treaty.[15] President Washington was justified by the record to go before the country confident in the service his foreign policies had given to the United States.

While 1796 should have been a year of satisfaction if not of triumph, in fact it was a year of agony for the president. Attacks against his administration and against his person were more vigorous and more extravagant than ever before. Almost as hard for him to bear was the steady battering of the office of the

[15] Whitaker, *Spanish-American Frontier*, p. 217, uses "frontier treaty" to underscore the Spanish fear of the frontiersman as the operative factor in Godoy's concessions. Samuel Flagg Bemis, *Pinckney's Treaty: America's Advantage from Europe's Distress* (New Haven, 1960), places primary credit for the treaty upon diplomatic issues; Godoy's uncertainty about the terms of Jay's Treaty and the possibility in it of an Anglo-American entente explains his concessions.

president. The funding of debts, the establishment of a National Bank, the suppression of the Whiskey Rebellion in Pennsylvania, and the mobilization of executive resources in favor of Great Britain all represented accretions of power to the central government which in turn stimulated increasingly desperate counterthrusts by the Republican opposition. The personal insults suffered by Washington were partly a result of the Republican conviction that he was a prisoner of Federalism.

In the power of the purse the Republican-controlled House of Representatives had one last resource in 1796 to direct a constitutional challenge to their enemies. By demanding that the president submit papers relating to Jay's Treaty before providing funds for its implementation, the House asserted its own role in the making of foreign policy and at the same time hoped to use this assertion to arouse once again public opinion against the treaty. The latter may have been signed and ratified, but Congressional control over the regulation of commerce required the approval of both branches of the legislature. When the president refused to lay before the House the details of the negotiations, a House resolution then formally placed on record its authority over any treaty that needed legislation to put it into effect. Thus, over presidential objection, the treaty returned to the fore in an election year as a subject of passions and occasion to remind the electorate of its sinister purposes. The tide of Republican reaction against Federalist foreign policy in many ways reached its peak over the House actions against the treaty in the spring of 1796.

Then the tide receded. The reasons for the recession defy simple explanations. France's counterattack came too late to have an effect upon this spring debate. Nor were the initial Federalist rebuttals effective. Robert Harper's attempts to tie all appropriations into one packet—Jay's, along with Pinckney's, the Algerian, and the Indian—failed. Perhaps the advice of Hamilton guiding Federalist action from his perch on the sidelines had its usual beneficial effects; petitions and letters from Federalist leaders and prominent men of affairs throughout the country were brought to bear against Congressmen standing in the way of the treaty. They warned of the prospect of a war with Britain following upon a House repudiation of the treaty as well as a breakdown of the American economy that would affect every part of the country. These pressures had their effect upon waverers.[16] So did the condemnation of President Washington, who termed the Republican tactic "a dangerous precedent." Madison, surveying the wreckage of his plans in a letter to Monroe, felt that presidential disapproval: "Besides the alarm of war, in the smaller states a great excitement was produced by the appeal of the President in his message, to their particular interest in the powers of the Senate."

While business interests naturally applied the greatest pressures against the House, what depressed Republicans particularly was the appeal the Federalists suddenly enjoyed in the west. This was best expressed by that most eastern of men, Fisher Ames of Massachusetts, when he warned in unaccustomedly emotional language of the consequences of sabotaging the treaty. He invoked the Indian menace, reminding his rapt audience of sensations he had never experienced personally: "the yells of savage vengeance, and the shrieks of torture. Already they seem to sigh in the West wind; already they mingle with every echo from the mountain." Joseph Priestley, who had been exposed to the rhetoric of Pitt and Burke, called the speech "the most bewitching piece of parliamentary oratory he had listened to." Enough Republicans capitulated to secure a one-vote majority for the treaty. What Ames had managed was to summon to the administration's side the achievements of Washington's second term, many of them directly serving the democratic west.

This critical decision in the House of Representatives offers a clue to the success of Washington's Farewell Address in influencing the election of 1796 that is often overlooked because of the attention given to French intervention. The guileful hand of Hamilton may have been behind Washington's pen, but the excitement and alarm over French intrigue no matter how skillfully manipulated by the former secretary of the treasury were

[16] See Stephen Kurtz, *The Presidency of John Adams: The Collapse of Federalism, 1795–1800* (Philadelphia, 1957), pp. 57 and 72, sees the House challenge to Jay's Treaty overwhelmed by the weight of public opinion. Combs, *The Jay Treaty*, pp. 185–186, disputes this point, asserting that the Republicans never surrendered their principles, but were defeated by errors in their parliamentary tactics.

not sufficient by themselves to account for the popular success of Federalism in a country populated by an overwhelming Republican majority. Certainly the cleverness of a partisan document in which a different standard was applied to British behavior as opposed to French was a triumph for Hamilton. In the guise of wisdom offered from above the battle, an embattled and angered Washington presented the nation a self-serving summation of Federalist foreign policy that appeared as a campaign document for an election in which foreign policy was a primary issue. But the Farewell Address was something more than a political statement.[17] Washington's concern about foreign entanglements, and in this case the French alliance, was not just the inspiration of a puppet-master. The intrigues against which he had warned could come at another time from British or Spanish sources—as indeed they had in the past. In this recognition Washington and his successor, John Adams, differed from Hamilton.

Washington's admonition against the French meddling could not have been better timed. France always pursued a foreign policy that postulated a role for the United States which was anything but fraternal. This policy would have been pursued irrespective of American behavior in the 1790s. France's vision of empire, particularly the reconstruction of Louisiana, would have the United States as a satellite. As Stephen Kurtz observes, "The French government had come to understand the psychology of fear by 1796, and by embroidering its policy of imperialism with the ideals of liberty and fraternity France had succeeded in becoming the greatest military power of the revolutionary era."[18] The Directory listened to General Victor Collot speaking in geopolitical terms of France's future in America: "When two nations possess, one the coast and the other the

[17] Arthur A. Markovitz, "Washington's Farewell Address and the Historian: A Critical Review," *Pennsylvania Magazine of History and Biography*, XLIV (April, 1970): 173–191, has a full discussion of the varieties of interpretations of the meaning and the authorship, ranging from Binney to Bemis and to Williams. His own view appears closest to that of Alexander DeConde. "Washington's Farewell, the French Alliance, and the Election of 1796," *Mississippi Valley Historical Review*, XLIII (March, 1957): 641–658, namely, that the Address was essentially a warning to the Jeffersonians.

[18] Kurtz, *The Presidency of John Adams*, p. 126.

plains, the former must inevitably embrace or submit. From thence I conclude the western stages of the North American republic must unite themselves with Louisiana and form the future one single compact nation." If France were to regain Louisiana the future of the United States was clear. And if France was acting toward the Federalist government not out of revenge but out of a cold-blooded plan of exploitation, then both the agonizing of Republicans over betrayal of the alliance and their aspirations for a French counterweight against British power were species of illusions, some of them dangerous for the American future.

In the short run Jefferson saw his own plans for American foreign policy in ruins: the benevolent neutrality toward France converted into hostility, a centralization of political and economic power in the hands of men of a monarchical bent, the development of ties with Great Britain which strengthened that country's war effort. In the long run Jefferson the president did not disown the major achievements of Federalist foreign policy and ultimately adopted a stand on Washington's Farewell Address that was not too distant from Washington's—or even from Hamilton's.

In the first eight years of Federalist rule American statecraft had grown and prospered, putting to good use some of the devices of colonial experience, such as the special mission. The principles of the Plan of 1776, always in the background of American thinking, were thrust forward whenever possible, as Jay did in seeking binational commissions to replace military solutions for disputes and as Hamilton did in underscoring America's interest in remaining aloof from the troubles of Europe. Hamilton's great success was in understanding the nature of America's link to the Old World and seeking to bend it to the service of the New. In 1796 this meant a detachment from France's embrace and the fashioning of new ties to England, based less on affection than on the national interest. Within the next few years Hamilton was to lose both his detachment and his keen sense of the national interest in ways that rendered suspect, perhaps unfairly, the soundness of his guidance to Washington.

CHAPTER IX

The Quasi-War

☆ 1797-1800 ☆

IT WAS FITTING in so many ways that John Adams should have succeeded George Washington in the presidency. His long service to the nation from the Revolution in Massachusetts to the peace commission in Paris to the ministry in London had elevated him to the vice presidency in 1788. No man was more worthy of the honor. As Jefferson delicately phrased it after his defeat in 1796: "He has always been my senior, from the commencement of our public life, and the expression of the public being equal, this circumstance ought to give him the preference." Only the former secretary of state himself, now vice president, possessed credentials comparable to those of Adams that laid a claim upon the highest office of the land.

The major problems confronting the president at the end of the century were precisely of an order that the diplomatist of the Revolution and the author of the Plan of 1776 should be able to deal with successfully. Wary of close ties with any European power, jealous of America's *amour propre* in dealings with foreigners, uncommitted to any faction, John Adams was above all his own man following his own conception of America's interests amid partisan passions that could push him to the side of France or of Great Britain. His independence was repeatedly challenged in the next four years, as he waged an undeclared war against one of the European belligerents and considered a joint campaign with the other. Yet he ended his single term in office by detaching the nation from Europe's embraces much in the fashion he would have advocated a generation before. The Convention of Mortefontaine in 1800, which formally terminated the entanglement with France, was a personal triumph that never received appropriate recognition.

Adams looked upon himself as a failure, and so did a large part of America at the time. Many of his troubles came from deficiencies in his virtues. His penchant for misanthropy which inspired reasonable doubts about the values of aristocrats and democrats alike was joined by an unduly exaggerated vanity and an almost paranoid sensitivity to slights that invited the rebukes he always expected—and frequently received. His skepticism about the future of the Latin American revolutions destroyed Hamilton's plans for a dangerous adventure in liberation, but his behavior was as much a function of his unseemly jealousy of the influential New York lawyer as it was the result of rational analysis. Even as a young man he was nostalgic for an earlier and purer era where rewards went to men of virtue. Edward Handler strikes an appropriate note when he identified Adams as an "archaic survivor of a past age,"[1] whatever that age was. Although the president recognized that his old collaborator, Jefferson, shared most of his values, he yielded in the crisis of 1798 to a conviction that Jeffersonian malevolence conspired with the French enemy against himself and the nation. Adams was a difficult man to work with, and he was a fortunate man to have a wife and family that supported him and his foibles throughout his long life.

What is especially noteworthy about Adams' misanthropy was the justice of his claim that he was frequently persecuted, unfairly reviled, and victimized by accusations of a partisanship he did not share. He was a genuine nationalist, not an Anglophile or a Francophile, who was a casualty of an Age of Passion, a label Marshall Smelser has properly tagged on the so-called classic decade of Federalism.[2] On the one side were the Jeffer-

[1] Edward Handler, *America and Europe in the Political Thought of John Adams* (Cambridge, 1964), p. 197.

[2] Marshall Smelser, "The Federalist Period as an Age of Passion," *American Quarterly*, X (Winter, 1958): 391–419.

sonians either confusing Adams with the Hamiltonian enemy or, at best, treating him as a weakling whose vanity and naïveté could be played upon to detach him from the Hamiltonians. On the other side were Federalists of the Hamiltonian persuasion whose machinations in aid of Thomas Pinckney during the presidential campaign of 1796 eloquently testified to their distrust of the New Englander. Such details as the new president may have lacked concerning his intrigue were promptly supplied to him by Jeffersonians. Adams had every reason to feel isolated in office; his perception was not a matter of mental derangement.

The president had no help from his official family. The vice president, that old friend and associate in Europe, was not only a recent rival but also the leader of the faction which Adams had identified with France and with Jacobin democracy. The president's consequent grudging and hesitant steps toward rapprochement were met with the rejection he had anticipated all along. His cabinet was no better. Its members were appointees of Washington and were High Federalists, almost to a man, in 1797. Their collective loyalty was to Hamilton. They were prepared to pursue policies independent of the president if the presidential advice conflicted with their own perceptions of the national interest.

The most difficult of his associates was Secretary of State Timothy Pickering. This proud fellow countryman from Massachusetts was jealous of the president, doubtful of his abilities, and above all resentful of his unwillingness to wage full war with France. Pickering had no intention of following the presidential leadership unless it coincided with his own direction. Adams' tottering path between France and England was made more tortuous by the hostility he encountered from his secretary of state.

More than Pickering's bristly disposition accounted for this conflict. The cabinet offices had all blossomed under Washington as independent entities. If there were few outbursts before 1797 it was largely because Washington had respected the autonomy of the secretary's office, and the secretary in turn subscribed to most of the president's policies. The result of this experience was the nurturing of an almost proprietary sense of officeholding with a minimal sense of obligation to the man who by Constitutional designation was empowered to appoint a minister and presumably remove him at will. Pickering did not conceive of himself serving at the president's pleasure. Nor did he regard opposition of cabinet members to the president as insubordination. On the contrary, years later he could still assert: "I should think it was their duty to prevent as far as practicable the mischievous measures of a wrong headed President."

Given the president's own obstinacy, independence, and suspiciousness, it is remarkable that Pickering and other friends of Hamilton held their posts in 1797 and survived until the last year of the Adams administration. A sense of continuity with the recent past, combined with the difficulty of securing replacements, helps to explain their retention in the cabinet. Dismissal in the brief history of the Federal Union was connected with overt malfeasance in office, and such behavior was not evident to the president when he assumed office. Had he realized the extent of the disloyalty he would face he might have adopted a different position in 1797.

Adams' record reveals that he had surmounted his disabilities, internal and external, with conspicuous success for his country if not for himself. Despite all the provocations on both sides Franco-American relations did not descend to full-scale war. His persistence in the use of special diplomatic missions, even after the failure of Pinckney's, was justified in the treaty produced in 1800; his exploitation of unofficial and even illicit connections in Europe made the Ellsworth mission possible. Above all, his dogged ability to pursue his own course, in maintaining a balance between national pride and national security, triumphed in the end. The country may have repudiated him in the election of 1800, but it approved ultimately of his works.

The opening months of Adams' term were not as gloomy as his initial fears and later judgments would indicate. Not that he had underestimated the French threat. Having failed to win the presidency for their choice, the Directory had turned on America, rejecting the new minister, Charles Cotesworth Pinckney, and instituted new punitive decrees against American commerce which went beyond the presumptions of the British in violating American rights on the seas. The order to hang American seamen impressed by the British and subsequently captured by the French was an intolerable action of an ally—and intentionally so. What mitigated the president's situation in this crisis was the honeymoon spirit in Philadelphia which inspired caution in Hamiltonian councils and reconciliation among Jeffersonians. The former feared a war with France at this juncture, and the latter hoped to detach the president from the High Federalist position.

Adams saw immediately that his first act must be to repair the breach in the French relationship, and he could say with complete sincerity: "If I have looked with any accuracy into the hearts of my fellow citizens, the French will find, as the English have found, that feelings may be stirred which they had never expected to find there. . . ." Thomas Jefferson could be the conduit for the expression of these feelings by using his celebrated friendship for France to reduce French animosity toward America. The president may have had some questions about the quality of his vice president's judgment in light of his conduct in recent years, but he trusted "that his advancement and his situation in the Senate, an excellent school, will correct him. He will have too many friends about him to flatter him, but I have hope we can keep him steady."

The early meetings between Adams and Jefferson in Philadelphia after years of separation nourished this hope. The Virginian responded to the overtures eagerly, although there was continuing ambivalence about the emotional balance of the president. Genuinely admiring Adams' character, Jefferson still felt it was flawed by an "Anglomania" and a distrust for popular government. He was willing to suppress his reservations, however, if by doing so he might wean Adams away from the Hamiltonians. As often was the case, Jefferson's draft of a letter of cooperation was so effusive that Madison warned him against committing himself irrevocably to the Federalist administration in the event it returned to an anti-French policy. Jefferson, according to his friend, must keep his independence of the executive branch. That Jefferson was guided by this caution in the brief and edgy rapproachement with Adams was evident in his refusal to be a candidate for a new mission to France and in his coolness to Madison's possible nomination to that office.

By the time of the Pinckney mission the honeymoon between Jeffersonians and the president was over anyway. Adams was miffed at Jefferson's offhanded reception to the suggestion of Madison for commissioner, and by Madison's outright dismissal of the invitation. Adams' huffy rejoinder was that the cabinet would have rejected Madison anyway. The mistrust of the recent past was quickly revived in spite of a common foe in the Hamiltonians. After the exchange about the mission Adams never again consulted the vice president on policy; and after the president's bellicose reply to the French decrees of March, 1797, Jefferson was never tempted to take the initiative. The leaking of the Mazzei letter of 1796 in May of 1797, in which Jefferson had attacked Washington and his friends, confirmed Adams' worst suspicions about his former colleague.

The initial cordiality of the Hamiltonians to the president's conciliatory inaugural address and to the proposal of a new peace mission lasted a longer time than did the abortive reunion with the Jeffersonians. Hamilton was well disposed toward the president's French policy. The former secretary of the treasury had no wish for war with France in the spring of 1797, and made this sentiment clear to his friends. First, there was no profit in it: "Trade she has none, and as to territory, if we could make acquisitions they are not desirable." More important was his fear of dividing a nation that had just praised the virtues of abstention from Europe's wars at a time when the United States could be left to stand alone against a French Europe. Should Great Britain sue for peace, an American war with France would be a disaster. Hamilton's temporary loss of faith in Britain permitted him to see virtues in the president's program that might not have been evident otherwise.

Pickering, Secretary of War James McHenry, and Secretary of the Treasury Oliver Wolcott, Jr., were less inclined to share their mentor's reasoning on this point. As ideologues who found the virus of Jacobinism spreading everywhere in America, they welcomed the chance to strike at its vital center in France whenever the opportunity arose. The abrupt and humiliating French rejection of Pinckney in Paris seemed to be a perfect excuse for hostility. So it was with some reluctance that they swallowed Hamilton's point that a peace mission was necessary to hold the nation together. If such a mission had succeeded in England a few years before, it was important for Federalists to demonstrate that they were at least as eager to mend ties with France as they had been with France's enemy. More likely the cynical note in Hamilton's advice was more persuasive than any specific argument: "the idea is a plausible one, that as we sent an Envoy Extraordinary to Britain, so we ought to send one to France. And plausible ideas are always enough for the multitude."[3]

In yielding to the imperatives of a diplomatic mission to France, the cabinet, and even Pickering, displayed a flickering confidence in Adams. The breakdown of collaboration between the president and the vice president accounted for part of this fleeting benevolence; and the virility of Adams' excoriation of France's action in expelling Pinckney and his vigor in insisting upon showing the world that "we are not a degraded people, humiliated under a colonial spirit of fear and sense of inferiority" lulled their customary suspicions. The president's determination to dictate the terms of a reconciliation with France by means of a show of strength—arming the merchantmen and increasing the militia—rendered acceptable for the moment the three-man peace commission that would go to Paris.

But the actual dispatch of the commission left no faction satisfied. The Jeffersonians listened only to the bellicosity of the president's defiance of France and concluded from its tenor that the commission would be a prelude to war with France. Jefferson was convinced that the cabinet had pushed him over to the camp of the High Federalists. The Hamiltonians were unhappy about the appointment of Elbridge Gerry to the team of Pinckney and John Marshall. Their disappointment was all the keener because for a time it seemed that Adams had acceded to their wishes by adding Chief Justice Francis Dana to the com-

[3] Bowman, "Struggle for Neutrality," p. 273, sees a cynical and ruthless Hamilton anticipating the failure of the mission to produce war. Hence his reason for suggesting Madison and Jefferson for membership. Had he expected success one of them would have received enormous credit for a diplomatic victory.

mission after the attempt to enlist Madison had aborted. But when Dana declined and Adams went back to his earlier choice of Gerry, a Massachusetts man of Jeffersonian sympathies, he antagonized his cabinet without appeasing the Republicans. Gerry went to France over the explicit objections of the secretary of state.[4]

Whether or not the president was in error in sending a figure out of harmony with much of Federalism is moot. Adams knew Gerry as a friend whose record was ambiguous enough to claim Jefferson as well as himself in friendship. Essentially he was not a party man, and not even the critical view of historian Samuel Eliot Morison, in which Gerry emerges as a "strange combination of obstinacy and vacillation," faulted his integrity or sense of duty as he saw it.[5] On the other hand, the president erred in failing to arrange some integration of Gerry's views with his colleagues'; he might have had him consult at least with Marshall in Philadelphia before their separate departures for France, the former from Boston and the latter from Philadelphia three days earlier.

The schism within the commission presaged the disaster which overtook it in Paris. While attention is usually focused upon the conflicts of personalities involved—Pickering and Talleyrand, Gerry and his colleagues, X, Y, and Z and Pinckney—there probably would have been no rapprochement even if the personal relationships had been more harmonious. For the moment each party was totally unable to grasp the other's perception of itself or to find means of bridging the gap.

France's sense of betrayal at American hands in Jay's Treaty was nourished by the acquiescence of Jeffersonians in her interpretation of the policy. The Republicans no less than the French government shared the belief that the treaty had given to Britain services to that country's war effort which were denied to America's ally. Not even the tactical error of French interference in the election of 1796 could shake this view. In

[4] Marvin R. Zahniser, *Charles Cotesworth Pinckney: Founding Father* (Chapel Hill, 1967), p. 159, notes, however, that Pinckney was pleased to have Gerry for a colleague.

[5] Samuel Eliot Morison, "Elbridge Gerry: Gentlemen-Democrat," in *By Land and By Sea: Essays and Addresses* (New York, 1953), p. 192.

fact, Jeffersonian anger over the outrage became the more fierce as their dependence upon a French victory in Europe became greater. With Adams a captive of the Hamiltonians the only salvation for the republic was the destruction of Hamilton's power base in London. This was not a new departure for Jefferson. Two years before he had dilated on the pleasures of dining with General Pichegru in London to "hail the dawn of liberty & republicanism in that island." In 1797 he could regard rumors of a French interest in Louisiana not as a justification for Federalist vigilance but as a warning to Americans against waging war with France lest outraged Frenchmen take over Spanish territory in America in revenge. The disgrace of Monroe showed Jeffersonians the fate that Gerry, man of good will that he was, would suffer in the company of the Pinckney mission.

Buoyed by these sentiments in America the French government was prepared to receive an American delegation if it came bearing apologies and restitution for the psychic and material damage done to the French cause, the cause of a fraternal ally. The instructions given to the Pinckney mission were utterly unresponsive to any such expectations. The three major directives to the commissioners emphasized above all else the need for compensation for losses suffered by American commerce from French decrees. Although this was not a *sine qua non* for further talks, it colored the American approach to rapprochement by minimizing the American offenses which presumably gave rise to French retaliation. The Americans not only made light of their general obligations but sought formal release from their specific obligation under the treaty to defend the West Indies from attack. And lastly the commissioners were expected to adjust the Franco-American commercial treaty to accord with the provisions of Jay's Treaty, a tacit confession that the latter had indeed violated the terms of the former. In exchange for these adjustments the United States promised nothing more than a vague benevolence to the French cause that was contradicted by the precise services presently offered to the British cause.

That there was genuine dismay among French military planners over the maritime implications of Jay's Treaty was obvious and reasonable. But their subsequent behavior had little to do with pique over America's ingratitude. France's policies in the Revolutionary War had always been a reflection of the national interest, and never the result of some disinterested altruism. Jay's Treaty, which widened the contraband list and admitted British prizes to American ports, represented a temporary frustration over a new obstacle in the prosecution of the war, not a profound disillusionment over the character of Americans. On the contrary, it offered certain compensatory features in that it permitted France the luxury of a moral posture while affording an opportunity to seize American ships and property. America's acceptance of a position in the British system did not really surprise French strategists. The country had not been taken seriously as an ally at any time. Such advantages that were extracted from the alliance had the character of gratuities. As for America's embarrassment over the Jay Treaty, it was an occasion for extra profits, and the French intended to make the most of it.

In their fearful suspicions about the objectives of the Directory's foreign policy, the High Federalists were much closer to the mark than their Jeffersonian opponents. France had plans for world conquest which included the United States as another weak pawn in their chessboard, rendered all the more vulnerable because of the fatuous Francophilism of the Republicans. The imagination of Harrison Gray Otis of Massachusetts who claimed that the French have "an eye upon a *Cis Appalachian* as well as upon a *Trans Appalachian* Republic—their mapmakers mark out their map of America—" was neither fanciful nor hysterical. The dynamic French Republic of 1797 did eye Louisiana and in its intention to secure that territory it looked upon the United States as it did Venice, a position and comparison that was unequivocally made by Z (Bellamy) of the XYZ notoriety. Repeatedly the imagery of France's interest in America invoked European models—bribes from Austria in the Treaty of Campo Formio and similar extortionary arrangements with other European countries in 1797. Talleyrand left no room for doubts about the course of his thinking when he noted that Federalist America "merited no more consideration than Genoa or Geneva." The experience which the Pinckney mission was to undergo, then, represented no deviation from French practice at the time: vassals were expected to pay tribute, privately and publicly, to the government of the Directory.

Where the Federalists strayed from their estimation of France's intentions was in a judgment that France was on the brink of war with the United States, to be accompanied by an invasion. The vulnerability of the French West Indian islands and the dangerous proximity of Louisiana to the United States inhibited such precipitate action, at least until Great Britain was defeated. The president was sharper in his diagnosis of the problem in seeing that war was not imminent from French initiative, no matter how passionate their denunciations of Jay's Treaty may have been.

The legacy of that treaty also plagued the Adams administration's relations with Spain. It provided its chief minister, Godoy, an occasion to renege on the pledges he had given in panic during the negotiations for the Pinckney Treaty in 1795. Then he had been worried about an Anglo-American assault upon Latin America. He had recovered his poise since that time as he observed American difficulties with both France and Britain, and was anxious to undo the concessions he had made with respect to the 31st parallel. Baron de Carondelet, governor of the Louisiana Territory, was secretly ordered to hold such posts as Natchez, north of the agreed boundary line, to see how far Spain might go in frustrating the Spanish-American treaty.

While Jay's Treaty was to be Godoy's major instrument in his contest with the United States, it was raised only after the Spanish had exhausted the issue of a British attack upon Louisiana as their excuse for not consummating the treaty. The fiery Pickering for once made relatively cool responses to these accusations and to the accompanying allegations of American complicity in his communications with Chevalier Casa de Yrujo, the Spanish minister in Philadelphia. In fact, he did not even inform the president of them at first, much to the latter's embarrassment when Yrujo confronted Adams personally with questions about British intentions in Spanish America. It was just as well that Pickering's voice was low on this matter, since Yrujo was able to uncover a genuine conspiracy against Louisiana involving British agents and Senator William Blount of Tennessee in the summer of 1797. Robert Liston, the British minister, was able to disavow his own and his government's responsibility, although he had more than a vague knowledge of the affair; and Pickering, whose short temper had been rising over Spanish charges against American collaboration with Britain, checked his natural inclination toward invective until he could accept British professions of innocence in the Blount conspiracy.

No such inhibitions softened the secretary's rhetoric on the matter of Jay's Treaty. Yrujo's exploitation of the treaty followed the line laid down by Spain's powerful neighbor, France, when he complained that Article XXVII of Jay's Treaty nullified the free ships, free goods provision of Pinckney's Treaty, and that the two treaties defined contraband in a fashion that discriminated against Spain. On both counts Yrujo considered Spain justified if she refused to honor Pinckney's Treaty until the questions were settled. More than a replication of France's complaints was involved; the Spanish wanted to avenge the gratuitous insult America committed by her guarantee in Jay's Treaty of the British right to navigate the Mississippi River.

The intemperate tone of Pickering's retorts was stimulated by his conviction that Spain was merely echoing the views of the French master, and that Yrujo's posture was a part of the unacceptable behavior France had been exhibiting toward the United States ever since the European war had begun. To the secretary of state the Spanish minister was playing the opportunist, leaning on the weight of France to push Spanish objectives, and doing so without the explicit approval of his government in Madrid. Pickering was outraged over the minister's wish to use an anticipated Franco-American war as a cover for Spanish obstinacy over the southern and western boundaries. The secretary of state was mistaken in dismissing Yrujo's sharp attacks and his newspaper campaign—in the manner of Adet the previous year—as unsanctioned by Godoy's government. Godoy gave full backing to Yrujo, and what passed for personal recklessness was in truth Spanish policy. Pickering's misjudgment of the meaning of Yrujo's behavior could have had serious consequences for the United States, including a war with Spain that was not a part of President Adams' thinking.[6]

[6] Gerard H. Clarfield, *Timothy Pickering and American Diplomacy, 1795–1800* (Columbia, 1969), pp. 138–139.

Ultimately it was Godoy who crumpled before the personal invective exchanged between his envoy in Philadelphia and the secretary of state. The very extravagance of Pickering's language, in which Yrujo was accused of dishonoring the king, opened familiar doubts about America's intentions and abilities. French support notwithstanding, Godoy in a crisis—real or apparent—succumbed to his fears in 1797 as he had in 1795. Yrujo, under instructions from Madrid in the spring of 1798, notified Pickering that the provisions of the Pinckney Treaty would be respected. The secretary of state had won a notable victory by his bluster. Perhaps it was an unwitting success, but it is questionable if he would have acted any less firmly or less obnoxiously had he known that Carondelet and Yrujo were speaking for Spain as well as for themselves.

If the treaty could have had happy consequences anywhere in this period, it should have been in Anglo-American relations. In a measure it did. The "first rapprochement," as Bradford Perkins has called the decade of 1795 to 1805, was the fruit of the detente.[7] Boundary problems, financial claims on both sides, and the troublesome questions about the direction of Anglo-American economic relationships were all accounted for in Jay's Treaty.

The exchange of ministers—Robert Liston and Rufus King—in 1796 was a particularly happy augury for the future. King, an Anglican since his Harvard days and an Anglophile in the 1790s, was *persona grata* from the moment of his arrival in England. He was also a friend of Hamilton and a doughty champion of Jay's Treaty. The Jeffersonian label of "an Englishman at heart" was helpful in breaking down the reserve and winning the friendship of the cold Grenville. Robert Liston flattered Americans in turn by stepping down from a more prestigious embassy to Turkey to come to America with his new wife. Philadelphia was not customarily considered on a plane with Constantinople. Moreover, the mild and pleasant-mannered Liston made a striking contrast to the flintier personality of George Hammond, who had grated on Jeffersonian nerves so regularly during his ministry to the United States. The new minister's

[7] Perkins, *First Rapprochement*, p. 47.

equable personality helped to calm passions raised by maritime matters on which the British were intractable.

Despite the improved climate, storms continued to break over the Anglo-American connection. The continuing capture of American merchant vessels in 1796 pushed the normally complaisant Pickering into vigorous protest. British reaction had to weigh dangers in Federalist vulnerability to Jeffersonian charges of indifference to the fate of American victims of impressment against the dependence of the island empire upon its navy in the mortal combat with France. Was it worth antagonizing a friendly government which supplied so many vital parts of the war machine in order to safeguard the navy from attrition through desertion? Impressment was not a matter of caprice for the hard-pressed British worried about the superior attractions of the American maritime service. Although Grenville made no public pronouncement renouncing the right of impressment, the steady decline of press-gang activity in 1797 suggests that Great Britain attempted to placate American opinion on impressment at least for the time being. Seamen who could prove their American nationality were released, even though West Indian authorities never formally accepted the presence of the American agent, Silas Talbot, whose mission was to look after the interests of those sailors illegally forced into the British navy.

Great Britain by these actions had signaled her continuing need for amicable relations with the United States. She was willing to pay for assistance to a government which restricted French privileges in American harbors. Other concessions followed. The Northwest posts were evacuated with dispatch, the machinery of the arbitral boards on boundaries was established, and American ships were permitted to move freely into the East and the West Indies.

India, where Americans had operated freely but surreptitiously for a decade, became a legitimate area for penetration after the ratification of Jay's Treaty, although the privileges conferred by the treaty were hedged by various barriers. Whatever strings may have been placed on the trade, they did not hamper American movement into the Indian Ocean in large numbers and with little opposition from the East India Company. By 1801 the United States may have controlled as much as 70 percent of India's foreign trade and probably carried as much cargo as the Company itself.

In the West Indies there was no pressing need for the American minister to demand removal of restrictions on the American trade. Despite Lord Hawkesbury's subscription to the British mercantilist views of the 1780s, Sheffield's handiwork was essentially undone. In practice it did not matter what the Jay Treaty had to say about admission of American ships to the West Indies. As long as the islands required American supplies to prosper, American vessels would have unrestricted entry during the war. American trade with the French West Indies enjoyed parallel prosperity. A loose interpretation was made of French properties bound for Europe as long as the ships stopped first at any American port and reshipped the goods as American. The *Polly* decision of 1800, accepting this principle of broken voyage—even when the transfer of ownership was spurious—merely gave juridical rationalization to a French trade with the West Indies through American shippers that had been in existence throughout the war.

When it is reckoned that in the Anglo-American trade alone in the last years of the century American ships outnumbered British by ten to one, American criticisms of British maritime policies loom as monuments of ingratitude. Impressment, contraband, boundaries, and spoliation continued to flare up periodically but the sting had gone from most of the complaints. The importance of such widespread benefits to the United States from Anglo-American commerce provides an underpinning in 1797 for a harsh line toward a more recalcitrant France.

There were few happy auguries for the success of the Pinckney mission which finally rendezvoused in Paris in early October, 1797. Its instructions were rigid and unrealistic; its members were divided over the appropriate tone to take in dealing with the Directory; and the team impressed French officials either as hopelessly closed to compromise or fully open to intimidation in the manner accorded a Holland or a Switzerland. At least these were the impressions of Charles Maurice de Talleyrand-Périgord, minister of foreign affairs, who fancied himself an expert on American habits on the basis of his two years of involuntary exile in Philadelphia earlier in the decade.

Consequently, the indirect approaches of Hottinguer, Bellamy, and Hauteval, the agents of the foreign minister later identified as X, Y, and Z in the diplomatic dispatches, represented a simple and familiar way of dealing with minor diplomats. If the Americans expected to receive sympathetic consideration for their problems, they would have to provide a *douceur* for Talleyrand and a handsome loan for the French government. Should they object to these arrangements, their fears would be played upon, or they would be replaced by more malleable envoys. The country that made Jay's Treaty deserved nothing better.

In light of the subsequent furor over bribery and extortion it is worth noting that the commissioners' shock seemed to have been well under control during the early part of their stay in Paris. They did not pale at the insult, and considered sending one of their number home for new instructions if the French would suspend their attacks on American shipping while negotiations were underway. This idea fell through when Talleyrand made it clear he had no more intention of suspending the discriminatory decrees than he had of granting American spoliation claims. Even the *douceur* was not beyond the bounds of propriety initially, for, as Marshall observed, "we might not so much regard a little money as he [Hauteval] stated to be usual altho' we should hazard ourselves by giving it."

The Directors and Talleyrand rebuffed the Americans' terms. The Directory had no intention of suspending the discriminatory decrees during negotiations, and had no objections to an indefinite impasse developing over the matters of loans and bribes. He was ready to keep the commission in isolation and in suspense, refusing to accept their commissions. Not that any of them felt that the weeks of waiting were wholly wasted. Madame de Villette, adopted daughter of Voltaire and agent of Talleyrand, was the attractive young landlady of Marshall and Gerry, who diverted the Americans pleasantly even if her attentions gained no special favors for the Foreign Ministry. American impatience finally erupted in the form of a memorial written by Marshall in January, 1798, which all three signed, even the reluctant Gerry. It recounted the national grievances against France and the personal difficulties the commissioners had in presenting their case. There was no response on the part of the French; indeed, new and harsher decrees making liable to condemnation any ship with products of British origins aboard had been promulgated while the memorial was being written.

The result of these studied insults was a demand for passports by Pinckney and Marshall, with Gerry splitting from his colleagues on this issue. To the extent that the Directory backed off from a private gift as a *sine qua non* for negotiations and made the success of the mission dependent on a governmental loan, American stubbornness won a victory. But Marshall and Pinckney were correct in judging a loan as a symptom of the contempt France had for the United States and as punishment for an unruly satellite. By this time Talleyrand was no longer interested in keeping the commission intact, and concentrated instead in cultivating Gerry as the instrument of Franco-American reconciliation. Hence his reply to Marshall's statement merely reiterated the old French complaints against the United States, dismissed Marshall and Pinckney as British sympathizers, and pointed to Gerry as the only acceptable American representative.

The Pinckney mission finally broke up in April in bitterness and division. Gerry, agitated over Talleyrand's threat of war, remained behind to help preserve peace, to repair some of the damaged relationship, and if possible to bring home a new and better treaty with the French. Whether his behavior was soundly or foolishly motivated, his decision gave rise to French hopes of successfully intimidating the United States into an acceptance of a role in France's world scheme. Instead, it brought the two countries to the brink of war.

Talleyrand was quick to see the consequences of actions he himself had blithely set in motion. War with the United States would place in jeopardy France's plans in Louisiana as well as provide a gratuitous service to Britain's naval capabilities. But he failed to comprehend that the United States was wholly unable to extend a loan to France any more than it would permit a bribe, as long as either implied servitude to France's imperial program. The French demand was more than an insouciant offense to American innocence or an arrogant challenge to American pride. If "No, no; not a sixpence"—or "Millions for defense but not one cent for tribute," as it was translated into American folklore—articulated both sentiments accurately, they did not embody all the views of the commissioners. Their more immediate agitation was over the risk of war with Britain which accession to France's demands might produce. America's reliance upon British commerce and fear of British reprisal dictated a negative response to France's preconditions for negotiations.

Certainly the state of public opinion in America in the spring and summer of 1798 was ripe for war in reaction to the failure of the Pinckney mission. There was no question about the expectations of High Federalists who saw in the passions of the country an opportunity to make common cause with the British. What pulled both parties back from the brink were the combined wills of the administration and the French government. And, it should be added, the perceptiveness of the commissioners themselves. When Pinckney and Marshall, the two heroes of the day, returned to American shores, they did not bring with them a report that France had purposely provoked war. Marshall in particular disappointed the secretary of state by observing that both during his stay in France and on his arrival home the French were not seeking hostilities. As early as November, 1797, Marshall noted to Pickering that "this haughty, ambitious government is not willing to come to an absolute rupture with America during the present state of the war with England but will not condescend to act with justice or to treat us as a free & independent nation." He never changed his mind about France's wish to avoid a full break or about that country's belief in the efficacy of intimidation. On the strength of Marshall's advice, the president withheld a request for a declaration of war in June, 1798, and instead maintained an avenue open to further diplomacy.

Marshall's estrangement from Pickering over a French war distinguished the Adams Federalist from the Hamiltonian at this juncture. The rage of the Virginia Federalist against France and her American friends was no less severe than Pickering's. Despite reservations about some of the repressive legislation which followed in the Congress from revelations about the XYZ scandal, Marshall shared the spirit that produced the alien and sedition laws in 1798. But on the question of war, Marshall was adamant. He incurred the enmity of the secretary of state by refusing to seize the moment of his triumphant arrival in New York to pronounce inflammatory judgments on the imminence of war.

The division between Adams and the Hamiltonian Federalists was not especially visible in the spring of 1798, even to a man as sensitive as Pickering. The XYZ affair enveloped all Federalists. Nothing that the Jeffersonians tried at this point came out well. Convinced rightly that the president had presented only partial information on the problem of the commission in France, the opposition leaders in the Congress charged the Federalist with concealing dispatches which showed some progress toward mending the ties between the two countries. They demanded full disclosure. Actually, the only reason for the president's failure to set forth the complete record was the delay in deciphering dispatches. Adams in March, 1798, was angry enough with the contents of what he read to ask for war at that moment, and expected that the more information he would receive the more ammunition he would have. Only a recognition that the Jeffersonians might frustrate his call for war inhibited the president. By the time he had seen the full story of French intrigue he was as ready as any Hamiltonian to demand full-scale hostilities against the enemy. The Jeffersonians played into his hands by their insistence on publication of all the communications between the commissioners and the Department of State.

Formal war with France did not follow the XYZ crisis, but everything short of a declaration did. Alien and naturalization laws aimed at Frenchmen and other subversive foreigners, and a rigorous sedition law directed against the internal disloyalty of American Jacobins were measures of a society at war. The president, swept up in this mood of fear and belligerence, prepared the nation for conflict on the seas. A Department of the Navy was established, in part to remove the vital area of naval affairs from the province of the inept secretary of war, James McHenry. Congress authorized the building of twelve new ships which would facilitate the capture of French raiders molesting American commerce along the coast. An embargo against trade with France was authorized for the duration of the Congressional session unless the French government modified its behavior. Additionally all French ships would be prohibited from entering American ports under any conditions except extreme distress.

President Adams gave his full blessing to all preparations involving the navy. He was less enthusiastic over the legislative program expanding the power and size of the army, although this was the heart of the Federalist plan. The regular army was to be increased to 50,000 men; a "provisional army" was to be formed when war or national emergency was declared; and above all, the president was granted the authority to appoint commissioned officers for an "Additional Army" of 10,000 men which would serve for the duration of the quarrel with France. It was the strengthening of the military that created the most anxieties within the nation, not only among Jeffersonians who believed the measures were directed against themselves, but also among the president and his friends. This particular consequence of the XYZ affair widened the gulf between the president and the Hamiltonians.

The simplest and psychologically most satisfying explanation for Adams' distaste for military preparations was his jealousy of Hamilton, who sought command of the augmented military forces. Jealousy was certainly present in abundance. It required little of Adams' perfervid imagination to transform the arrogant New Yorker into a militarist ready to use the war with France to destroy the American republic. The vigor with which Hamilton's supporters in the Congress pushed the expansion of the armies confirmed his suspicions; their success was a reproach to his own failure to control defense policies.

When the question arose over the appointment of a commander, who would be second to General Washington, Adams stood in Hamilton's way as long as he could. The position of inspector-general was in effect that of commander-in-chief, since the retired president would serve only in an emergency. Unable to keep Hamilton's name off the list of candidates he tried to evade the appointment by pressing the case of Henry

Knox, former secretary of war and Hamilton's senior in experience, for first choice. Washington's insistence upon making his own preference a condition of his cooperation foiled this scheme. Had Hamilton not been appointed, his patron threatened to return his commission.

Frustrated in his attempts to block Hamilton's path to power and abnormally resentful of his rival's influence in the cabinet and the Congress, President Adams then turned to peace efforts which he might not have made otherwise. Lending an ear to his son, John Quincy, and then to John Marshall, and ultimately to such *bêtes noires* of Federalism as Elbridge Gerry, the discredited commissioner, and to George Logan, a Quaker political missionary, the president set in motion a new peace commission to thwart Hamilton's career. Hatred for his enemy had superseded the emotions of revenge and the need for retribution against the French. So goes a plausible explanation of Adams' behavior in the last months of 1798.

This picture of a jealous president and his power-mad rival is obviously too simplistic to be accepted without important qualifications. For Hamilton's supporters, particularly for Secretary of State Pickering, the return of Hamilton from private life would undo any damage that a weak and unreliable president might commit at a time of peril. Pickering and his friends had no doubts about the depth of the crisis. In the spring of 1798 France appeared to be on the verge of ultimate victory in Europe. Her armies had swept across the Continent, leaving the left bank of the Rhine in French hands, Rome under French occupation, and the new Helvetian Republic under French protection. An invasion of England, beset by rebellion in Ireland and by possible bankruptcy in London, loomed next. If it were successful, nothing would stand in the way of a French movement into the south from the West Indies where slaves would be encouraged to rebel against their masters and Jeffersonians would rise against their fellow citizens. Given an apocalyptic prognosis of this order, Federalists looked to an army both to repel the invader from without and suppress the enemy's collaborator from within.

Hyperbolic though their apprehensions were, they were genuine enough among High Federalists. They were also self-serving, since the effects of military action coming from a war with France upon the Jeffersonian opposition was never lost on Federalist leaders. But both the emotions and the reasoning suggested above were only partly shared by their chieftain. Hamilton wanted war. His tactical caveats of 1797 had disappeared, and although he did not express the urgency of his friends in demanding immediate Congressional declaration of war, he expected France to perform that service for him. If the French opened hostilities they would strengthen Federalist leadership in the ensuing conflict.

It is unlikely, however, that the notion of a French landing in America ever occupied him more than momentarily. By the summer of 1798 the French defeat at the Battle of the Nile and the fiasco of the Irish rebellion had made talk of an invasion of England nothing more than a feint at best, while the expanding slave rebellion in Santo Domingo, led by Toussaint L'Ouverture, made a French expedition against the United States a practical impossibility. Yet his ardor for war was greater at the end of the year than it had been at the beginning.

Conceivably the possibilities of a Jeffersonian uprising that would have the effect of turning over the keys of America to France obsessed him. In December, 1798, Hamilton wrote to Washington that the Republicans were ready to form "a perpetual alliance, *offensive* and defensive, and to give her a monopoly of our trade by *peculiar* and *exclusive* privileges. This would be in substance, whatever it might be in name, to make this country a province of France." But how much of this is credible in light of his knowledge of the condition of French offensive power and the status of the disorganized and discredited Jeffersonians in 1798? Perhaps, as Gilbert Lycan would have it, the time had come for him to recognize that "since peace was impossible, he would promote the national interest by direct action" after having "used his energy and his talents in counseling statesmen and the people in the ways of peace."[8] More likely, he was carried away by the prospect of achieving the kind of power in the shaping and control of a new army which he could not resist putting to use.

[8] Lycan, *Hamilton*, p. 354.

Speculation aside, the one overriding excitement on Hamilton's mind in 1798 and 1799 was the opportunity opened to him by the Venezuelan adventurer, Francisco de Miranda, of engaging in a military expedition in collaboration with Britain against Spain and France in America which would yield to the United States both Louisiana and Florida as prizes. Here was a program at last worthy of his ambitions that would unite Great Britain and the United States in a grand alliance to extirpate French power in America. Not least, it could make of him a George Washington of all the Americas. These were incentives enough for war with France.

France's plan for reconquest of the Louisiana territories was the goad which attracted other Federalists to Miranda's schemes. In London Rufus King listened eagerly to the Anglo-American feature of Miranda's thinking, while in retirement in Virginia Washington was receptive to a defensive pre-emptive intervention if necessary. And all Federalists could envisage the strength a French Louisiana would give to Jeffersonians in the future. Miranda therefore was able to play on a variety of emotions as he unfolded his master plan of liberation of Venezuela and the rest of Latin America to American and British friends. A veteran of the American Revolution, he talked with Hamilton before moving on to London in 1798, where it was arranged that Americans and Latin Americans would provide troops while British sea power would keep the Spanish and French at bay. Hamilton's own position in the operation was central. He wrote candidly to Miranda through his enthusiastic friend, King: "I wish it to be undertaken. . . . The command in this case . . . would naturally fall upon me, and I hope I shall disappoint no favorable anticipation."

It was Hamilton who was to be disappointed ultimately. He should have predicted the president's unfavorable reaction to Miranda's plans if only because of the personal benefits it would have brought to the commander in charge. Given the president's instinctive revulsion from romanticism under the best of conditions, chances are Miranda would have fared no better with any other patron. Officially Adams ignored the Venezuelan, for fear of "engaging myself and my country in most hazardous and expensive and bloody experiments" that would reproduce the horrors of the French Revolution. So he reported years later. Unofficially Miranda impressed him as a "knight errant, as delirious as his immortal countryman, the ancient hero of La Manche." He had undoubtedly weighed the costs of both an entangling British connection and a resulting dramatic upsurge in Hamilton's power, and found them too high a price to pay.

The combination of the Miranda venture and the quasi-war with France enhanced the importance of Anglo-American ties for each party. The possibility of an alliance would have been alive even if the Latin American issue had not been a contributing factor in 1798. The British too flirted with the idea. Pitt told Miranda that his country would be most interested in working jointly with the United States in the enterprise against Spain. In June of 1798 his foreign minister, William Windham, Lord Grenville, seemed to consider seriously a formal alliance that would involve an exchange of American control of the Floridas for British control of Santo Domingo. Both statesmen manipulated American worries over isolation should Britain and France make a peace that would leave the United States exposed to the revenge of the Directory.

What checked the consummation of an alliance was not just the interposition of a suspicious president who remembered the wiles of the British and feared the machinations of his enemies, although these were always elements in Adams' behavior. He claimed to be willing to accept a temporary alliance but felt that public opinion would be inclined to reject such an arrangement. Even Hamilton articulated some reservations about Britain's eagerness for a connection. He understood and applauded an ally's action out of self-interest, but he foresaw in the British importunities a future constriction of his own independence as leader of the invasion of Spanish America. British partnership could mean British domination. Actually the British cabinet had its own hesitations about aiding a new revolution; and Hamilton was very likely correct in suspecting that such members as William Windham and Henry Dundas "were willing to consider joining the Americans," as Bradford Perkins observed, "not so much to further their plans as to direct them into safer channels."[9]

The American cabinet was less discerning. Despite periodic disclaimers, Pickering and other High Federalists were enchanted by the vision of an alliance with Britain. British overtures delighted and flattered them. Among other benefits Pickering dwelled upon the commercial benefits that should flow from a formal connection. He was quick to perceive hints of sharing in some of their monopolies and to carry them to extremes that their authors may not have intended. Eagerly he reported to Washington in Februrary, 1799, that "Mr. Pitt has made to Mr. King a proposition which implies an opinion that in certain articles (sugar & coffee in particular) Great Britain & the States may regulate the commerce of Europe." As Joseph Charles points out, even a junior partnership was welcomed by the Pickerings of America. "Compared with John Adams, these men were colonials," who had no compunctions about increasing American dependence upon Britain for the nation's prosperity.[10]

Nevertheless, the steady improvement of Anglo-American relations was not entirely a matter of British conniving, Hamiltonian ambition, or High Federalist naïveté. Jay's Treaty had set the direction and the related disruption of Franco-American relations had accelerated it. The advantage in the long run was probably more American than British. Although Louisiana never fell to the United States as a result of the new relationship, neither did Santo Domingo become the exclusive preserve of Great Britain. Such informal collaboration over that island as did develop reflected the strength of America's hand, since the hard-pressed British conceded for the most part the demands made upon them by the Americans.

Similarly the tacit admission of American ships everywhere in the British Empire illustrated a British dependence upon United States commerce in wartime fully as great as Pickering

[9] Perkins, *First Rapprochement*, p. 112.

[10] Joseph Charles, "The Jay Treaty: The Origins of the American Party System," *William and Mary Quarterly*, Third Series, XII (October, 1955): 622.

had sensed, even if it was not accompanied by a grant of full membership in the Navigation System. The ultimate expression of British anxieties emerged from the *Polly* decision wherein the British admiralty court judge in 1800 freed an American ship captured on the high seas carrying sugar from Havana to Spain despite the fact that it had made only a *pro forma* stop in an American port. According to precedents the sugar should have been condemned as Spanish property or at least as carried in violation of the Rule of 1756 inasmuch as American trade between Cuba and Spain had been denied before the war. By accepting as genuine the spurious payment of duties in the United States the British gave a sanction to a bogus "broken voyage" which allowed enemy property to be labeled American. In effect Britain gave the color of legality to the commerce of enemy colonies with their mother country using American ships as carriers. Small wonder then that there should be a widespread feeling of benevolence toward England accompanying hostility toward France as the century came to a close. More than partisan Federalists could indulge in these feelings.

Given concessions, legal and illegal, British actions in support of American navigation during the quasi-war appeared to represent something other than just a lure to an entangling alliance. They were obeisance to the American weight in the world balance of power. It took many forms. Among them were loans of cannon for harbor defense, the sale of small arms and the convoying of American ships to any shores of Europe. These specific military services permitted the still small American navy to concentrate upon the patrol of the Caribbean, relying on the British navy to cover the Atlantic sea lanes. John Bartlett Brebner calls these British gifts of cannon, formerly lying idle in Halifax, the first "lend-lease."[11]

The mood was not always idyllic in these years. There were some issues over which the British would not negotiate and some policies they remained reluctant to modify to America's satisfaction. There were always admiralty judges quick to declare against American vessels even when the evidence was scanty. Contraband was never clearly defined and thus

[11] Quoted in Perkins, *First Rapprochement*, p. 95.

remained open for loose construction; and the Rule of 1756 was frequently the vehicle used prior to the *Polly* decision for seizure of ships carrying French colonial produce to Europe despite Whitehall's efforts to reduce friction in this period. But when abuses were weighed against profits, the risks of seizure of ships were tolerable. Impressment of men, on the other hand, was plainly an emotional question of the most sensitive kind involving as it did the deprivation of the liberty of American citizens and an insult to the sovereignty of the United States. The continued stoppage and seizure of sailors evoked the strongest protest from the Federalist administration. Impressment never ceased. Indeed, to the very end of the war with France, the British government equated an official disavowal of impressment with a death sentence to the British navy. Nothing less than the survival of England seemed to be at stake.

Hamilton was sensitive to the damage his own ambitions could suffer from animosities arising from British practices, and his letters to Pickering and King were filled with advice urging pressure against the British to the point of reprisals similar to those being applied against France. As Stephen Kurtz interprets Hamilton on this issue: He "was an Anglophile but he was not a sentimentalist and was willing to suppress his admiration for English ways when his own ambitions seemed jeopardized by them."[12]

The *Baltimore* incident in November, 1798, might have created the very conditions Hamilton was trying to avoid. Fifty-five men from the American naval vessel *Baltimore* were summarily removed under British guns. Even though most of that number were released, the Navy Department, smarting from shame, courtmartialed the ship's captain and ordered resistance in the future to British boarding parties unless the opposing force was overwhelming. British anxiety to avoid subsequent clashes with the American navy combined with the Federalist understanding of the difficulties in distinguishing between British subjects and American citizens contained this fiery problem throughout the period. Despite the flashes of anger and mutterings about retribution the Adams administra-

[12] Kurtz, *Presidency of John Adams*, p. 304.

tion did its part in defusing emotions. Although efforts to provide certificates of citizenship to sailors invited fraud, conciliation brought some reward; at least the British never asserted the right to impress or denied the right of expatriation even as they acted out those assumptions. A major act of pacification on the part of Americans was the president's behavior in the Nash-Robbins affair in 1799 when he surrendered to the British a mutineer and deserter from the Royal Navy who claimed to have been a Connecticut native wrongfully impressed into the British service.

If the highly sensitive area of impressment could be managed without causing a break between the two countries, everything else could and did fall into place, including the frequently nasty wrangling over American payment of pre-Revolutionary debts to British creditors. The complicated division of power and authority in Santo Domingo between the United States and Great Britain illustrated the leverage Americans retained in dealing with the British. Although an Anglo-American alliance and a joint military operation never materialized, the close cooperation of Britain and America in Santo Domingo bore some of the characteristics of both an alliance and a military coalition. Here was an arena in which the relationship was not simply that of benefactor and beneficiary as in the transfer of cannon and arms, or of the patron-client quality of British convoying of American ships. In that disturbed island where French dominance was under challenge from rebellious slaves, Americans and British met on terms of rough equality.

For the United States the Negro revolution under the dynamic leadership of Toussaint was a mixed blessing. The black leader may have been an enemy of France but the effect of his rebellion against white masters could dangerously incite American slaves to emulate his achievement. But the logic of aid to Toussaint prevailed over misgivings, since that island above all others would have been the base of any future French invasion of the United States. Moreover, participation in the revolution there could yield substantive advantages for the sugar trade inasmuch as Santo Domingo represented a cheaper source of sugar than the British islands could provide. France's difficulties therefore opened too many opportunities for America's advantage to permit the slave problem to inhibit action.

But it was Britain's initiative, begun with an abortive invasion in 1793, that led the United States into a limited but not unequal partnership. Whitehall's decision to negotiate with Toussaint for commercial and military concessions induced Pickering to seek a role for the United States in the proceedings on the grounds that an independent regime, black or white, would fit into America's trading pattern more readily than Britain's. Minister King underscored this point by observing to the foreign secretary that if the United States were not included in any commercial arrangements Britain might make with Toussaint's forces, British ships would not be permitted to carry American goods to Santo Domingo, since the law forbade trade with French dominions. The introduction of this particular legalism strikes a piquant note by implying that a nation at war can trade legally with the enemy while a nation at quasi-war cannot. But the Americans were not indulging in casuistry; they were seeking to make an impression, and this unsubtle method worked.

Eventually the British not only effected a consortium for the exploitation of the island's trade but encouraged Edward Stevens, the United States consul general, to speak for both countries in negotiations with Santo Domingo. Residual suspicion of British imperial motives made American diplomats more acceptable to the revolutionary general at this juncture. Under an informal agreement known as "Heads of Regulations," Toussaint would be insulated from the outside world, French power in the Caribbean would be diminished, and American commercial privileges in Santo Domingo would be equal to Great Britain's.

The informal but genuine collaboration between the two countries was as close to an alliance as was possible and closer than some British and American diplomatists considered wise for the respective national interests. Robert Liston in Philadelphia expressed pleasure over the linking of the United States and Great Britain in a common enterprise, but his mood was not shared universally. Lieutenant Colonel Thomas Maitland, who had initiated unilateral proceedings with Toussaint as commander of British forces on the island, was less pleased with the American presence there. Rather than serving as a step in the United States route to war against France, the joint action would merely whet American appetite for more concessions at British expense.

Maitland went too far in his suspicions of America's ambitions. Hamilton and Pickering and King never wavered in their hopes for a British victory over France; and it is unlikely if they would have taken measures against Britain that would jeopardize the war effort. But they saw no inconsistency in extracting such economic and political advantages as they could manage from Britain's needs at this moment. Their steadfast Anglophilism never fully submerged a lively nationalism that, in Hamilton's case, manifested itself in a concern for the American military establishment which would render the United States independent of the kind of assistance Great Britain offered in the quasi-war with France. Rufus King, perhaps the warmest Federalist admirer of England, made an aggressive presentation of America's case in Santo Domingo. When Grenville's successor, Lord Hawkesbury, went a step further in 1801 and talked of a preventive joint occupation of Florida, the American minister made it perfectly clear that the United States had no wish to see the Floridas alienated from Spain in this manner. England no more than France was welcome in a territory which the United States had staked out for herself.

The Santo Domingo operation dampened rather than kindled the war spirit between the United States and France. It was another frightening portent which could have repercussions for future American plans of the French Republic, and another reminder of the need to repair relations with the United States. Had President Adams not taken an active part in reducing tensions it is obvious that France would have persisted in her search for channels to bring the informal conflict between the two countries to a close.

Actually, Adams' own search for peace was purposefully deliberate. When he acted it was on ground far more solid than mere jealousy of Hamilton. He had never been convinced that there was a French army intent on invading America which would justify the raising of new armies. His preoccupation was with a naval war; ground forces would be a diversion from the main problem as well as a temptation to put forth a military dictator. Should invasion be seriously contemplated a strong navy would protect American shores while the American navy loose in the Caribbean would cripple French trade and force France to the peace table. Naval power, in the words of Stephen Kurtz, was "the key stone of Adams' *Realpolitik*.[13]

The president's leisurely management of the peace negotiations with France was closely related to the lead time involved in constructing three squadrons for use in the West Indies. Only when they were completed did his diplomacy assume a vigorous cast. Adams' unhappy memories of the consequences of naval weakness, symbolized by a craven treaty with the Bey of Tunis which he had to sign in his first year of office, stimulated a predisposition toward naval preparedness that informed his entire foreign policy.

France spared no efforts to convince the president that she regretted the behavior which had sent two of the commissioners rushing home in anger. The unexpected publication of the XYZ correspondence was particularly compromising to Talleyrand, and his anxiety to keep Gerry in Paris in the summer of 1798 was a measure of his concern for his own personal security as well as a sign of the Directory's unwillingness to break fully with the United States. Gerry played Talleyrand's game when the foreign minister asked him for the names of the men who had improperly demanded bribes in his name. If Talleyrand could not keep Gerry in Paris beyond that summer, at least he could see him leave as a friend of France using his influence to help de-escalate the war and perhaps to save the job of the newly solicitous foreign minister.

Back in America by October, Gerry visited Adams at Quincy to tell the president personally of France's desire for peace. It was a visit which Adams was later to claim "saved the peace of the nation." Whether this critical meeting really effected this result is open to question. The president was not dependent

[13] Stephen Kurtz, "The French Mission of 1799–1800: Concluding Chapter in the Statecraft of John Adams," *Political Science Quarterly*, LXXX (December, 1965): 555.

exclusively upon his old friend to make his mind up. News of the destruction of the French fleet at Aboukir helped to provide reasons for France's renewed interest in peace. Moreover, letters from William Vans Murray, the American minister in The Hague, relating Talleyrand's confidential attempts to renew negotiations, arrived while the president was meeting with Gerry. Conceivably his special commendation of Gerry was a retrospective act of defiance against Pickering, who was voluble in his condemnation of Gerry as a dupe or cohort of the French.

The secretary of state had prepared a blistering rebuke to Gerry for ignoring his instructions to leave France. The former commissioner's response that he was unable to receive his passport until July and that he had used the time between May and July to modify French reactions to the publication of the XYZ dispatches was unacceptable to him. When the secretary of state denounced him publicly Gerry demanded the right of a published rebuttal which the president would have granted had he not wanted to quiet the internal tensions until he could assimilate fully the information Gerry had brought to him. Adams in essence took up Gerry's case in December, 1798, when he reopened possibilities of normal relations with France if that country would display "a sincere disposition . . . to desist from hostility, to make reparation for the injuries heretofore inflicted on our commerce, and to do justice in the future." Only after appropriate assurances had been made would an American minister be dispatched to France. Until that time there would be no relaxation of the quasi-war.

Pickering and his colleagues in the cabinet regarded this speech before Congress as an opening wedge in French and Jeffersonian intrigues against the war. The will of the cabinet, molded by Hamilton, had been expressed earlier at a caucus in Trenton where Wolcott had asked for an enlargement, not a contraction, of the war, and an assurance that no minister be sent until France had acted first with her own messenger bearing proof of contrition. Adams' speech had modified this demand to an extent the cabinet considered suspect.

But it was not Gerry or any specific informant with Republican sympathies that moved the president. Gerry's news fitted a pattern. All through the fall of 1798 information continued to come forth from Europe confirming Gerry's conclusions, and from sources as varied as his son John Quincy Adams, the minister in Berlin, and George Logan conducting his own private survey in Paris. The latter's mission may have been ill-advised and deserving of the Congressional rebuke it received, but the president felt Logan was an honest man whose reports, if not judgments, could be respected. When Murray's October dispatches reached Philadelphia in February, 1799, with news of Talleyrand's agreement to accept an American envoy on honorable terms, Adams was ready to act. He could offer the country such tangible earnests of France's intentions as the Directory's revocation of privateers' commissions in the West Indies and the lifting of an embargo on American ships in French ports. He also had the aid of George Washington in the form of his favorable commentary on a letter from Joel Barlow, an American Republican expatriate in Paris, who had urged the former president to accept France's interest in peace as genuine.

Sensing national encouragement but knowing cabinet opposition, the president acted swiftly without official consultation. On February 18, 1799, he nominated Murray to be minister with the provision that he not depart for France until given formal assurances of an appropriate French response. In making the nomination he discarded the public humiliation desired by the cabinet as a prerequisite of negotiations. He did not even wait for the direct assurances he had asked for in the presidential message two months earlier. It was a bold move, but not really a rash one; the combination of public opinion led by Washington himself and a growing band of personal supporters in the cabinet and the country, such as Secretary of the Navy Benjamin Stoddert and Governor John Jay, provided an impressive base. Indeed, Washington's name was a host in itself in his contest with the Hamiltonians.

Nevertheless the nomination came as a shock to most men of affairs, not excluding the Jeffersonians. The vice president himself, who was further removed from a knowledge of the internal workings of the Federalist administration in 1799 than he had been as a farmer at Monticello in 1796, made an inaccurate and unfair judgment of the president's actions. Since Adams could not conceal France's overtures, he merely pretended to accept them on the assumption that a Federalist Senate would reject Murray's nomination. When this failed he dawdled in sending the minister, added two men to the mission, and in general expected it to suffer the same fate that overtook the Pinckney mission in 1798. The fact that he signed the Logan Act and continued to have aliens arrested appeared to be proof to the Jeffersonians of Adams' determination to pursue the conflict with France. The vice president's clouded vision at this time was made visible in his clumsy attempt to wheedle Gerry into making public his rebuttal to Pickering's charges insinuating that Adams and Pickering belonged to the same camp.[14]

Had Jefferson understood the state of disarray among the Federalists his reactions would have been far more relaxed. Pickering could scarcely contain his outrage, even though Adams' action was precisely what he would have expected from him. The appointment should not have been a surprise. The president had given many signs of his disloyalty to the Federalist conception of America, and most specifically had anticipated the move by emasculating the damning exposé the secretary of state had prepared on Gerry's performance in Paris. The most that Pickering was able to salvage on the eve of the president's action was a censored statement which noted France's efforts to manipulate the gullible Gerry in order to divide the commission and the American people. His colorful elaborations on this theme, repudiated by Adams as the "most violent false and calumnious philippic against Gerry," were expunged from the published text.

But Pickering proved to be both resilient and indefatigable. Once the blow was struck, he and his colleagues looked for ways to defeat the president's purposes. After all, the appointment of a minister plenipotentiary was not the equivalent of a formal detente with France. Memories of the Pinckney mission were of some comfort, as was the knowledge that a Federalist Senate could reverse the products of negotiations. In writing to friends of his own ignorance and disapproval of the president's act, Pickering could assure them and himself that "no right

[14] Dumas Malone, *Jefferson and His Time*, vol. III: *Jefferson and the Ordeal of Liberty* (Boston, 1962), p. 434, admits that Jefferson "was not at his best when trying to be ingratiating."

thinking men" would ever back Adams for the presidency again. In deference to the apparent popularity of the mission, however, the Hamiltonians settled for the withdrawal of Murray as minister plenipotentiary and his inclusion in a new three-man commission joined by Governor William R. Davie of North Carolina and Oliver Ellsworth of Connecticut, then chief justice of the United States.

The Federalist senators who had forced this compromise on the president had every reason for confidence in their tactic. Adams looked thoroughly discomforted during his interview with the five senators. Even his threat to resign and leave the presidency to Thomas Jefferson failed to daunt his audience. While the senators caucused he surrendered to the logic of Chief Justice Oliver Ellsworth's arguments that three commissioners would "embrace more of the confidence of the country," providing of course that Hamilton was not one of the three. Unlike the preceding mission, all three men were Federalists, and Ellsworth himself was a High Federalist beyond suspicion of even a Pickering. This factor added to new and more stringent peace terms that required France to pay for spoliations, to admit American ships without the *rôle d'équipage*, and to remove American guarantees for the defense of French America, should have doomed the negotiations. Ellsworth's instructions were stricter than Pinckney's; the latter did not have to make payment of claims a *sine qua non* of further negotiations.

So if the High Federalists had failed to contrive a full-scale war between France and the United States, they could reasonably expect to undermine the major peace efforts initiated by the president. And Adams' meekness in yielding to Hamiltonian demands on instructions and on personnel seemed to confirm their perceptions. In practice his subsequent long absence from the capital in 1799 left the management of foreign affairs in the hands of the secretary of state, which in turn made the original appointment of Murray into a pathetic gesture of defiance against the real controllers of government.

The Hamiltonian plan was clear enough. Delay in sending the mission would permit the volatile condition of Europe to offer excuses for ending its existence before it ever left American soil. The coup of the 30th of Prairial in June, 1799, which resulted in the replacement of Talleyrand with Charles Reinhard in the Foreign Ministry and the rise of a new coalition in Europe, provided an occasion to justify postponement of sailing until conditions in France were more settled. If monarchy should be restored it would be sensible to wait for a new and more acceptable regime to make a settlement with the United States.

Pickering should have been content with the drift of affairs while the president was away in Quincy by the bedside of his sick wife. Yet the secretary of state could always scent danger and pluck misfortune out of the most promising of situations. This one was no exception. Gloomily he predicted that no matter what treaty might be made, even one entirely dictated by himself, it would be perverted and abused by the French. Moreover, the very establishment of a mission had turned the British against the United States, he feared, and gave a sinister meaning to the *Baltimore* affair. When Britain finally won the war, she would exact retribution from America for her dallying with France. No matter which way he might turn, the prognosis seemed to be disaster.

For reasons other than those he advanced, the secretary's brooding about the future was justified. The president had not been bludgeoned into apathy or withdrawal by the intensity of Federalist protest. If he had allowed an enlargment of the mission and a stiffening of instructions, it was not weakness that explained these apparent concessions. Adams saw an opportunity to press the French by exploiting the discontent of the cabinet. He was not convinced that France would mend her errors without further prodding. Since the French were unlikely to renew the belligerence of the previous year and had lost their power to hurt in the West Indies, he could tolerate delay. And he was confident that his extended stay in Massachusetts would make no difference to his peacemaking. He could administer the affairs of state from Quincy by mail. An excess of confidence rather than a loss of nerve characterized his behavior during the long months when Pickering was making his own decisions.

The secretary of state brought upon himself the fulfillment of his pessimistic prophecies by taking the initiative once too often with respect to the Ellsworth mission. Upon hearing rumors of a second coup in the summer of 1799 he anticipated the final overthrow of the Directory, and so urged the president to cancel the mission entirely. He went so far as to falsify the views of the cabinet when he wrote the president that the cabinet had recommended suspension. At this point the two members of the cabinet free from Hamilton's influence, Secretary of the Navy Benjamin Stoddert and Attorney General Charles Lee, communicated to the president that if he did not return to take personal charge of the administration, a "ministerial government" which had already abused his instructions would destroy his remaining authority.

The fact that Adams found Hamilton in Trenton, the temporary capital, when he finally arrived undoubtedly accelerated the pace of diplomacy. The New Yorker's presence in Trenton was technically a violation of his military duties; he should have been in Newark with his troops. That Hamilton thought he could sway the president against dispatching the mission by a personal appeal was as quixotic as any of his activities in his romantic career. The commissioners were ordered to leave by November 1, less than three weeks after the president had returned.

Adams triumphed, and the High Federalists were foiled in their conspiracy. But it was not a victory for the president, and no one understood this more clearly than he did himself. He foresaw his career in ashes and with considerable justice blamed both Jeffersonians and Hamiltonians for his personal tribulations. The Hamiltonians had their revenge. By his steadfast if tortuous road to reconciliation with France he had cost his party a war which it had felt was necessary to preserve American society from destruction. He had undercut the positions of power and glory that Hamilton had coveted and would have received from a military command in wartime. As a consequence of his actions the Federalists indulged themselves freely in their propensity for self-destruction. After achieving remarkable popularity for defending honor against France, for promoting commerce with Great Britain, and for securing territorial concessions from Spain, all of which were reflected in the election results of 1799, the Federalists then proceeded to tear themselves apart in the presidential election of 1800. Adams completed the debacle by ousting McHenry and Pickering from their offices in the spring of 1800 in formal recognition of the irreparable breach in the party.[15] John Marshall served as Secretary of State for the remainder of the Adams' administration. The Federalist split permitted Thomas Jefferson to move into the new White House in 1801.

The Jeffersonians, out of a combination of party prejudice and ignorance of the nuances of their opposition's discord, displayed no appreciation of Adams' pursuit of peace, although they ultimately took full advantage of it. Their suspiciousness confirmed Adams in his misanthropy, but at the same time bolstered his self-image of martyrdom. He lost the election but never wavered in his claim that the sending of the Ellsworth mission to France was "the most disinterested, the most determined and the most successful [action] of my whole life."

The defensive tone in his apologia suggested that his unpopular decisions ruined his chances for re-election but saved the country despite itself. The realities were otherwise. The president did indeed extricate the country from a needless and dangerous conflict, and in doing so followed a popular course. Adams in defeat won a stronger following in 1800 than he had in victory in 1796. Adams' Federalism was not a failure; it was destroyed by the willfulness and ideological blindness of the Hamiltonians. Jefferson was the beneficiary of both the internal conflict of Federalism and of the service Adams had given to the nation. Adams' old friend and rival inherited not only the presidency but also the Convention of 1800 which ended the quasi-war and the embarrassing Alliance of 1778 with France.

[15] Page Smith, *John Adams* (2 vols., Garden City, 1962), II: 1029–1031, believes that Adams' action was an emotional act which may have cost him a second term in office. Kurtz, *The Presidency of John Adams*, pp. 393–394, on the other hand, sees it as a calculated political move which enhanced his chances for re-election.

CHAPTER X

The Meaning of Mortefontaine

☆ 1800-1801 ☆

THE CONVENTION OF Mortefontaine, signed on September 30, 1800, encapsulated in its origins, in its negotiations, and in its significance the special qualities of American statecraft which had been evident since colonial times. In this peace treaty that tacitly detached the United States from the alliance with France at the price of claims for damages committed against American shipping since 1793, the gulf between the American path of foreign policy and Europe's was manifest. Above all, it dramatized American recognition that political alliances of any kind with Europe imposed intolerable burdens upon the young republic. The unhappy experiences with the French alliance confirmed the wisdom of John Adams in the Plan of 1776, of Thomas Paine in his *Common Sense*, and of Benjamin Franklin in his periodic reminders about the perils of a European connection. Mortefontaine released the United States from the penalties of alliance, at least for the time being.

The sense of realism in crisis that usually pervaded American action as opposed to theory was also present. The negotiating team in Paris realized it could not observe the rigid instructions set down by Pickering, and discarded them. While freedom of the seas remained an ideal for American foreign policy and was represented in the text of the treaty, the commissioners did not forget the vital importance of the practical collaboration with Great Britain. It was not jeopardized at Mortefontaine. In fact, the Jay Treaty was accepted de facto, including the British views on international law. At the same time, Adams' second secretary of state, John Marshall, did not bow before British displeasure over the convention, and maintained a firm stand on American claims upon Great Britain. Reconciliation with France did not lead to conflict with Britain. And the Treaty of Amiens which resulted in a temporary peace in Europe a year and a half later underscored the wisdom of the American policy of independence.

In terminating the alliance the workings of American diplomacy uncovered a pattern of thought and action that differed significantly from the Old World's. European foreign policy was customarily made secretly by a foreign minister or his agents, who were largely independent of any constituency outside the royal sovereign. In the United States both the fashioning and the administering of policies were a shared process in which the secretary of state was frequently just head of an executive bureau rather than chief policymaker in foreign affairs. For examples, Jefferson had to counter the influence of Hamilton from the beginnings of the Washington administration, and Randolph had to deal with John Jay, whose public line of communications ran directly to the president and whose private link was with Hamilton. In the Mortefontaine negotiations Secretary of State Pickering found himself outflanked by a largely independent Ellsworth mission which responded to national rather than to party pressures. The special agents themselves had deep roots in the colonial past, serving a variety of colonial masters from governor to council to Assembly, providing an invaluable body of diplomatic experience for the new nation. The transition from colonial agent serving a local constituency to a presidential agent serving a national authority was natural and well accepted.

That the realm of diplomacy was not the exclusive preserve of the executive branch of government was given constitutional sanction in the powers granted to the Senate and House of Representatives over foreign affairs. Senate approval of diplomats and treaties, and House control over finances were inheritances from the colonial period when diplomatists were agents of the lower houses of the legislatures as frequently as they were the governors' men. Mortefontaine itself was an occasion for the display of senatorial prerogative. Its dissatisfaction with the initial results of the commission's labors required a reconsideration of the convention. The differences proved to be minor and the terms of the convention in their final form were not substantially different from those originally presented. The importance lay in the fact that the Senate as well as the executive had spoken.

Not that the workings of the peace commission were beyond criticism. Actually there was no marked superiority in the conduct of negotiations over that of Jay in London in 1794 or the Pinckney mission in Paris three years later. The very extravagance of American terms of itself could have doomed the mission. France could not accept the kind of commercial treaty the commissioners proposed, which would not only deny France the right to bring enemy prizes into American ports but also deny specifically the liberal maritime practices which had characterized the agreement of 1778.

But the new Consulate was as anxious for peace as the Directory had been, for reasons which were as urgent as the latter's. Compared to the Directory, the leader of the Consulate, General Napoleon Bonaparte, was far shrewder in appealing to and manipulating American emotions. He was able to apotheosize Washington upon his death and apostrophize the virtues of freedom of the seas at the very moment that he bluntly rejected American demands. Without sending them home in a huff, Bonaparte made it clear that if the treaties of 1778 were to be ended they would have to surrender their claims payment on damages suffered by American ships during the quasi-war; claims could be considered only if the treaties were still in force. The first consul was perfectly content to allow the Americans time to assimilate the implications of his response. He had no real choice. Most of his time in the spring and summer of 1800 was devoted to the military crisis in Europe, and not until he had defeated the Austrians at Marengo did he have leisure to continue negotiations with the American commissioners.

The Americans had the apparent opportunity to renew the old treaties, including special privileges for France, and thereby open the way to securing indemnities. Or they might write a new treaty that would permit escape from the old obligations, but at the sacrifice of all hope of indemnification. Of the three commissioners brooding over this dilemma, Murray was the quickest to see that the best the United States could manage was withdrawal from the alliance irrespective of the effect upon claims. Ellsworth and Davie disagreed with their colleague. Bonaparte broke the impasse with a proposition at the end of August that bewildered the commission. He suggested reaffirming the validity of the treaties of 1778, and then creating a new commission to assess the damages done by each party to the other over the past half-dozen years. Additionally the United States would be given seven years to fulfill its obligations under Jay's Treaty admitting British privateers and prizes into American ports, after which this practice would cease. Should the Americans fail to liquidate this problem in Jay's Treaty, France would then be free from any commitment to repay Americans for her depredations. In contemplating the meaning of this proposition it dawned on the American commissioners that France had no intention of paying without exacting an intolerable price from the United States in the form of a break with Great Britain.

The Ellsworth commission faced realities when it departed from its instructions in order to gain freedom from both French entanglement and British retaliation. It determined to defer both the questions of indemnities and of treaties. Tacitly, then, both issues could be discreetly set aside. The major announced accomplishment was the abandonment of the quasi-war by mutual restoration of captured naval vessels and the discarding on the part of France of the burden of special papers for American ships in French ports.

Conceivably a more astute team of negotiators might have done better, and exploited Bonaparte's evident desire to arrive at an accommodation. The first consul's anxiety for an expression of concern for neutral rights, corresponding to those of Czar Paul I's declaration of August 27, was more than a frank invitation for America to lend her weight to Russia's revived Armed Neutrality. It should have been an invitation to press for new concessions. Instead Bonaparte seemed to outwit the Americans on every count. The latter had to give up indemnity to get out of the alliance. The French evaded indemnity without surrendering the advantage of the American alliance. The resourceful French leader was able to insinuate to the Russians without full realization on the part of Americans that the United States was in sympathy with or even prepared to join the European neutrals in an anti-British coalition. The alliance may have been dead, but its ghost was useful to the French.

A case, therefore, may be made for the argument that Mortefontaine was the first of many Napoleonic diplomatic victories over the United States in which American gullibility was exploited for France's advantage. Pickering damned Adams and his treaty, claiming that "he received the law from France. He even gave up the trophies of our victories, stipulating to restore to France her national vessels captured by ours. He *purchased peace* at the expense of twenty millions of dollars (for that was the estimated amount of French spoliations) relinquished to France without any equivalent." Pickering's hyperbole notwithstanding, the charge had some merit. Bonaparte extracted benefits from the convention. He escaped the financial consequences of France's depredations against American commerce, as Pickering had observed.

More important, he managed to manipulate the language of the accord with the Americans in such a fashion that the new League of Armed Neutrals he was attempting to create in 1800 could look to the United States for moral support if not for actual membership. The festive dinner at the Mortefontaine home of Joseph Bonaparte celebrating the conclusion of the convention was designed to honor the American signatories. It included toasts from all three consuls of the French Republic, most notably one offered by Third Consul Lebrun: "To the Union of America with the powers of the north, for the protection of the freedom of the seas." Here was a blend of a familiar American attitude on maritime rights with France's special concern for a new combination against Great Britain. For much the same devious purpose Bonaparte requested and secured a change in title from "provisional treaty" to "convention." The latter sounded more permanent and hence possibly more effective in assuring the northern powers of America's sympathies for their prospective league.

The first consul's purposes in signing an accord with the United States went beyond debts and maritime organizations. Mortefontaine as a symbol of reconciliation should lull Americans into quiescence while he continued his plans for the reconquest of Santo Domingo and retaking Louisiana. One day after the convention was signed at Mortefontaine the Spanish government at the royal court in San Ildefonso agreed to the cession of Louisiana to France in exchange for territorial gains in Italy. As neither arrangement could be consummated until the war in Europe had ended, harmony with the United States was essential until the time came for French troops to occupy the Louisiana posts.

Although neither the administration nor its critics recognized the dimensions of the first consul's guile in 1800, Federalists and Republicans alike sensed some of the dangers which could emerge from dealings with the new French government. Jefferson expressed his distaste for the "dictatorial consulate" which he identified with Hamilton, "our Buonaparte," who he felt was capable of destroying American republicanism with the same kind of coup the French general delivered. Suspicious from the start, the president-elect called the convention a "bungling negotiation," but did nothing to prevent it from becoming the law of the land, even after Bonaparte had made his own interpretation of its meaning. Moreover such criticism as Jefferson had of the convention itself was not for ending the alliance or for limiting the possibilities of financial compensations from France but, rather, for the difficulties the convention might produce in America's relations with Great Britain! Here was a reluctant tribute to Adams' service. Neither his former Francophilism, which should have pushed toward the renewal of the alliance, nor his present dislike of the new French leadership affected Jefferson's acceptance of the convention. The nation needed disentanglement from France, and it needed continuity in its commercial ties with Great Britain. President Jefferson understood these realities.

Hamilton was not behind Jefferson in recognizing the importance of the convention. Unlike most American statesmen in 1800, he saw through Bonaparte's game with the freedom of the seas, noting that the convention "plays into the hands of France by the precedent of those principles of navigation which she is at this moment desirous of making the basis of a league of the northern powers against England." But when the question arose over the acceptance or rejection of the arrangement, Hamilton concluded that the solution at Mortefontaine was the least harmful of all the potential threats inherent in the Franco-American relationship. Once his own ambitions had been crushed, Hamilton was able to bring to bear all his great powers to serve the national rather than a personal interest. He no longer had a stake in war or hope for a military command.

Adams himself shared most of these reservations about the convention, but like Hamilton and Jefferson found no acceptable alternative. As his son put it, "For although it did not secure us what we ought by good right to have obtained, I am afraid we shall never get anything better, and that the longer settlement is delayed, the greater our damage will be." Since the only alternative in sight was war, there was no challenge to the verdict of Murray who claimed he could "find no instance of a nation's doing better, except in the case of humiliation by great superiority of military force." What the United States really wanted from an accommodation with France was not monies but disengagement from the entanglement with France without the loss of the benefits which Jay's Treaty had brought with England. Both were achieved. British reactions were mild as they themselves moved toward peace with France.

In their own way the men at Paris in 1800 had served the nation as well as their predecessors had in 1783. The latter were more spectacular in every way: their personalities sparkled and took on distinctive patterns which were lacking in the Ellsworth mission; the diplomatic legerdemain of Franklin or Jay could not be matched in Murray or Davie; and the tangible acquisition of territorial prizes had no counterpart in the negative separation of France and the United States. But with all their achievements the legacy of 1783 did not include freedom from

European interference or security from reconquest; the two giants of Europe still stood astride the destiny of the United States. They continued to do so after Mortefontaine but the more sober diplomatists who made that treaty learned from experience and took steps, small as they may have seemed at that time, in advancing American independence. Among the lessons acquired over the past generation was the importance of limiting political obligations to any European power, of maintaining economic links with as many of them as possible, and of disowning ideological affiliations with all of them.

The reception of the treaty in the Senate demonstrated a grudging but genuine understanding of international realities. True, the cries of dismay from every side helped to stop ratification of the convention when it was first presented. But once these emotions were expended the Senate agreed to take a second look at the document, and reversed itself in early February, 1801. Perhaps the lure of peace implied in the convention, or the pressures of merchants pursuing their own interests, made the major difference. At any event, the senators could foresee no better treaty forthcoming, any more than Hamilton and Jefferson could, and revealed this sense of the situation by striking out Article 2 which had called for further negotiations over both the treaties of 1778 and the indemnities. They also limited the duration of the convention to eight years. The treaty then went back to France where it encountered no objections to the removal of the indemnities or to the eight-year limit in exchange for ending possibilities of reviving the alliance. With a Napoleonic twist the French interpreted the expunging of Article 2 to mean renunciation in the future of all claims for indemnities. William Vans Murray, still in Paris in 1801, accepted these terms, and so did President Jefferson in a terse communication to the Senate.

Whatever exaggerations may have crept into Adams' recollections of his presidency, his dramatic evaluation of his position on negotiations with France has stood the test of time: "I desire no other inscription over my gravestone than: 'Here lies John Adams, who took upon himself the responsibility of the peace with France in the year 1800.'" It is reasonable to add that when the partisanship of the moment subsided, all factions subscribed to the wisdom of the president's actions, although not every statesman of the time gave him the thanks he felt was due.[1] But then, given his personality, he never expected such appreciation, and probably would not have recognized it if it had come to him.

Mortefontaine by itself was scarcely the answer to America's problems with the Old World. The implications of France's regaining of Louisiana were yet to be realized; and the effects of the later Napoleonic Wars were to prove more difficult to bear than were the wars of the French Revolution. But the passions of Anglophilia and Francophilia were now gone from most parts and most groups in America, and the dangers of European ties were accepted by almost everyone. Jefferson captured the national mood in his First Inaugural Address when he contemplated the trials the United States had recently undergone in coping with a hostile world: "During the throes and convulsions of the ancient world, during the agonizing spasms of infuriated man, seeking through blood and slaughter his long-lost liberty, it was not wonderful that the agitation of the billows should reach even this distant and peaceful shore." In the past Jefferson may have had a hand in roiling the waters himself, but as president he would use his power to exorcise the winds and storms and spirits that blew across the Atlantic from the Old World.

In retrospect Jefferson did not succeed in fully controlling European influence, just as he did not succeed in paying appropriate homage to the work of his predecessors. But his triumphs and troubles in foreign affairs come after 1801. As he opened his administration he could look back upon a record of diplomacy in the colonial experience which had brought forth a new nation, first into being, and then through a stormy infancy. The errors of the diplomatists seem diminished in the presence of achievements: independence had been won and preserved; border territories had been secured and expanded; and the republic had revealed an energy and intelligence to conduct a foreign policy that added the perceptions of the New World to the

[1] Alexander DeConde, *The Quasi-War: the Politics and Diplomacy of the Undeclared War with France, 1797–1801* (New York, 1966), p. 339, confirms Adams' claim although DeConde would have Adams share credit for peace with Talleyrand.

conventional wisdom of the Old. The United States survived to face a new century with the help of remarkably sophisticated diplomatists—amateur and professional, private and public, Federalist and Republican, executive and legislative.

Further Reading

General Works

WHILE THE PERIOD under review in this volume comprises a coherent unit in American history, the division between colonial and national status raises obvious problems for its diplomatic aspects. Two useful introductions which unite the period are Arthur B. Darling, *Our Rising Empire* (New Haven, 1940) and Esmond Wright, *Fabric of Freedom, 1763–1800* (New York, 1961). A. L. Burt, *The United States, Great Britain, and British North America from the Revolution to the Establishment of Peace after the War of 1812* (New Haven, 1940); Felix Gilbert, *To the Farewell Address: Ideas of Early American Foreign Policy* (Princeton, 1961); and Paul Varg, *Foreign Policies of the Founding Fathers* (East Lansing, 1963), offer important insights into the thinking of diplomatists. The foundations supporting American experience in statecraft may be found in Max Savelle, *The Origins of American Diplomacy: The International History of Angloamerica, 1492–1763* (New York, 1967), the product of a lifetime's labors in the study of early American diplomacy.

Textbooks in diplomatic history usually devote considerable space to the problems of the founding fathers, although the colonial experiences inevitably receive less attention than the post-Revolutionary. The most authoritative of all texts remains Samuel Flagg Bemis, *A Diplomatic History of the United States*

(5th edition, New York, 1965). Robert H. Ferrell, *American Diplomacy* (2nd edition, New York, 1969), is a well-written account from the vantage point of the generation after Bemis. William A. Williams, *The Contours of American History* (Cleveland, 1961), and especially his "The Age of Mercantilism: An Interpretation of the American Political Economy, 1763–1828," *William and Mary Quarterly*, Third Series, XV (October, 1958): 419-437, speaks eloquently to those who see the primacy of economic factors in American diplomacy. Thomas A. Bailey, *A Diplomatic History of the American People* (8th edition, New York, 1969); Julius W. Pratt, *A History of United States Foreign Policy* (2nd edition, Englewood Cliffs, N.J., 1965); and Alexander DeConde, *A History of American Foreign Policy* (New York, 1963), are all important contributions to the field. The latter is particularly impressive for its unobtrusive exposure of citations.

For monographs, Samuel Flagg Bemis and Grace Gardner Griffin, *Guide to the Diplomatic History of the United States, 1775–1921* (Washington, 1935), is still valuable for the quantity and quality of contributions from scholars long departed from the academic scene which are too often overlooked by contemporary students. Oscar Handlin *et al.* (eds.), *Harvard Guide to American History* (Cambridge, 1954), brings the bibliographical record up to the early 1950s. For recent contributions of diplomatic historians, see Alexander DeConde, *New Interpretations in American Foreign Policy* [pamphlet, Service Center for Teachers of History] (2nd edition, Washington, D.C., 1961).

Samuel Flagg Bemis (ed.), *The American Secretaries of State and Their Diplomacy* (10 vols., New York, 1927–1929), has useful brief sketches of the careers of the secretaries. Volume I serves the period to 1801. Beckles Willson, *American Ambassadors to France, 1777–1927: A Narrative of Franco-American Diplomatic Relations* (London, 1928) and *American Ambassadors to England: A Narrative of Anglo-American Relations* (New York, 1929), have capsule accounts of the ministers to the two most important countries involved with the United States in the formative years.

There are a number of readily available and well-edited documentary collections in diplomatic history. Among them are

Ruhl J. Bartlett (ed.), *The Record of American Diplomacy: Documents and Readings in the History of American Foreign Relations* (4th edition, New York, 1964); Norman A. Graebner (ed.), *Ideas and Diplomacy: Readings in the Intellectual Tradition of American Foreign Policy* (New York, 1964); and Armin Rappaport, *Sources in American Diplomacy* (New York, 1966). For the reader who wishes to go beyond the above editions, Francis Wharton (ed.), *Revolutionary Diplomatic Correspondence of the United States* (6 vols., Washington, D.C., 1889); W. C. Ford *et al.* (eds.), *Journals of the Continental Congress, 1774–1789* (34 vols., Washington, 1904–1937); W. Lowrie and M. Clark (eds.), *American State Papers: Foreign Relations* (6 vols., Washington, D.C., 1832–1859); and B. F. Stevens, *Facsimiles of Manuscripts in European Archives Relating to America, 1773–1783* (24 vols. London, 1889–1895) publish much of the substance of diplomacy in this period. Frederick Jackson Turner, "Correspondence of the French Ministers to the United States, 1791–1812," American Historical Association, *Annual Report*, 1936 (Washington, D.C., 1941), point up French and British policies toward the United States in the early national period. Additionally, the papers of the founding fathers, notably Julian P. Boyd *et al.* (eds.), *The Papers of Thomas Jefferson* (Princeton, 1950—); Leonard W. Labaree *et al.* (eds.), *The Papers of Benjamin Franklin* (New Haven, 1959—); and Lyman Butterfield *et al.* (eds.), *The Adams Papers* (Cambridge, 1963—), expose the reader to the ideas of the leading diplomatists of the time. These magnificent projects, begun in the years after the Second World War and encouraged by the National Historical Publications Commission, eventually will extend to the works of all the major figures connected with policymaking in the early republic.

Even though these publications are still in their early stages, they have already stimulated the writing of monographs on the diplomacy of the founding fathers. Louis M. Sears, *George Washington and the French Revolution* (Detroit, 1960), and Lawrence S. Kaplan, *Jefferson and France: An Essay on Politics and Political Ideas* (New Haven, 1967), are examples of recent work. Particularly noteworthy are the studies of Gerald Stourzh, *Benjamin Franklin and American Foreign Policy* (Chicago,

1954) and *Alexander Hamilton and the Idea of Representative Government* (Stanford, 1970). Leading biographies of diplomatists include Carl Van Doren, *Benjamin Franklin* (New York, 1938); George Dangerfield, *Chancellor Robert R. Livingston of New York, 1746–1813* (New York, 1960); Samuel Flagg Bemis, *John Quincy Adams and the Foundations of American Foreign Policy* (New York, 1949); Frank Monaghan, *John Jay* (New York, 1935); Page Smith, *John Adams* (2 vols., New York, 1962); and Dumas Malone's monumental but still incomplete *Jefferson and His Time* (New York, 1948—). The most recent and most satisfactory biography of Monroe is Harry Ammon, *James Monroe: The Quest for National Identity* (New York, 1971).

The Colonial Years, 1763–1775

Given the colonial status of America the definition of monographs and essays on diplomacy and foreign policy requires a loose construction. There are few scholars who have addressed themselves specifically to the problem of an embryonic diplomatic establishment. A major exception to this generalization is Max Savelle, "Colonial Origins of American Diplomatic Principles," *Pacific Historical Review*, III (September, 1934): 334-350 and "The Appearance of an American Attitude toward External Affairs, 1750–1775," *American Historical Review*, LII (July, 1947): 655-666, which should be a point of departure for investigation in this area.

The development of colonies into nation, particularly the timing of the transition, has been a matter of interest among students of nationalism. Hans Kohn, *American Nationalism: An Interpretive Essay* (New York, 1957) and Richard L. Merritt, *Symbols of American Community, 1735–1775* (New Haven, 1966), approach the question from different angles, impressionistic as opposed to quantitative. Paul A. Varg, "The Advent of Nationalism, 1758–1776," *American Quarterly*, XVI (Summer, 1964): 169-181, suggests that nationalism was the product of an external stimulus, wilting after the Revolution. Judith A. Wilson, "My Country Is My Colony: A Study in Anglo-American Patriotism," *The Historian* XXXX (May, 1968: 333-349, emphasizes colonial patriotism as the dominant factor on the eve of the Revolution. Max Savelle, "Nationalism and Other Loyalties in the American Revolution," *American Historical Review*, LXVII (July, 1962): 901-923, observes that the image of a genuine American nation had its gestation in the war years, and "toward the end of the war, its birth."

Any broad picture of Angloamerican relations in the period after the French and Indian War encompasses the beginnings of American foreign policy. John C. Miller, *Origins of the American Revolution* (Boston, 1943) and Lawrence H. Gipson, *The Coming of The Revolution, 1763–1775* (New York, 1954), a volume in the "New American Nation Series," are good introductions to the development of the institutions of sovereignty. The most detailed one-volume study is Merrill Jensen, *The Founding of a Nation, 1763–1776* (New York, 1968). A shorter volume, but more directly pointed to Angloamerican relations, is Ian R. Christie, *Crisis of Empire: Great Britain and the American Colonies, 1754–1783* (New York, 1967). The traditional Whig view of the west dividing the empire is in Clarence W. Alvord, *The Mississippi Valley in British Politics: A Study of the Trade, Land Speculation, and Experiments in Imperialism Culminating in the American Revolution* (2 vols., Cleveland, 1917). Jack M. Sosin, *Whitehall and Wilderness: The Middle West in British Colonial Policy, 1760–1775* (Lincoln, Neb., 1961), is more sympathetic to Britain's problems. The most magisterial of all studies in British imperial diplomacy is Lawrence H. Gipson's series, *The British Empire before the American Revolution* (14 vols., New York, 1958–1969).

British attempts to deal with American opposition to new imperial policies are well treated in R. A. Humphries, "Lord Shelburne and British Colonial Policy, 1766–1768," *English Historical Review*, L (April, 1935): 257-277; Margaret Spector, *The American Department of the British Government, 1768–1782* (New York, 1940); David S. Lovejoy, "Rights Imply Equality: the Case against Admiralty Jurisdiction in America, 1764–1776," *William and Mary Quarterly*, Third Series, XVI (October, 1959): 459-484; Carl Ubbelohde, *The Vice-Admiralty Courts and the American Revolution* (Chapel Hill, 1960); John Shy, *Toward Lexington: The Role of the British Army in the*

Coming of the Revolution (Princeton, 1965); and Francis B. Wickwire, *British Subministers and Colonial America, 1763–1783* (Princeton, 1966).

Jack P. Greene, *The Quest for Power: the Lower Houses of Assembly in the Southern Royal Colonies, 1776–1789* (Chapel Hill, 1963), uncovers the growth of colonial sophistication in statecraft. Studies of northern and middle colonies suggest similarities in the pattern of relations with the mother country, as shown in Oscar Zeichner, *Connecticut's Years of Controversy, 1750–1776* (Chapel Hill, 1950) and David S. Lovejoy, *Rhode Island Politics and the American Revolution, 1760–1776* (Providence, 1958).

The role of the colonial agent as a proto-diplomat has long attracted scholars. The literature from the beginnings of this century is extensive. Among the more prominent of the older contributions are Edwin P. Tanner, "Colonial Agencies in England during the Eighteenth Century," *Political Science Quarterly*, XVI March, 1901): 24-29; Beverley W. Bond, "The Colonial Agent as a Popular Representative," *Political Science Quarterly*, XXXV (September, 1920): 372-92; James J. Burns, *Colonial Agents of New England* (Washington, D.C., 1935); and Ella Lonn, *The Colonial Agents of the Southern Colonies* (Chapel Hill, 1945). L. H. Gipson, *Jared Ingersoll: A Study of American Loyalism in Relation to British Colonial Government* (New Haven, 1920); Marguerite Appleton, "Richard Partridge: Colonial Agent," *New England Quarterly*, V (April, 1932): 293-309; Ross S. J. Hoffman, *Edmund Burke, New York Agent . . . 1761–1776* (Philadelphia, 1956); and Nicholas Varga, "Robert Charles: New York, 1748–1770," *William and Mary Quarterly*, XVIII (April, 1961): 211-235, treat the careers of individual agents. In the last few years Jack W. Sosin, *Agents and Merchants: British Colonial Policy and the Origins of the American Revolution* (Lincoln, Neb., 1965) and particularly Michael G. Kammen, *A Rope of Sand: The Colonial Agents, British Politics, and the American Revolution* (Ithaca, N.Y., 1968) and *Empire and Interest: The American Colonies and the Politics of Mercantilism* (Philadelphia, 1970), have given new importance to the functions of agents as diplomatists in the making and breaking of the British Empire.

The movement of Angloamerican relations from crisis to crisis after 1763 had its effects upon the development of organs of diplomacy, implicitly if not always explicitly. They appear in the following monographs: Max Savelle, *The Diplomatic History of the Canadian Boundary Dispute, 1749–1763* (New Haven, 1940); R. A. Humphries, "Lord Shelburne and the Proclamation of 1763," *English Historical Review*, XLIX (April, 1934): 241-264; Allen S. Johnson, "The Passage of the Sugar Act," *William and Mary Quarterly*, Third Series, XVI (October, 1959): 507-514; Edmund S. and Helen M. Morgan, *The Stamp Act Crisis: Prologue to Revolution* (Chapel Hill, 1953); Arthur M. Schlesinger, *The Colonial Merchants and the American Revolution, 1763–1776* (New York, 1918); Jack P. Greene and Richard M. Jellison, "The Currency Act of 1764 in Imperial-Colonial Relations, 1764–1776," *William and Mary Quarterly*, Third Series, XVIII (October, 1961): 485-518; Richard Walsh, *Charleston's Sons of Liberty: A Study of Artisans, 1763–1789* (Columbia, S.C., 1959); Roger Champagne, "Family Politics versus Constitutional Principles: The New York Assembly Elections of 1768 and 1769," *William and Mary Quarterly*, Third Series, XX (January, 1963: 57-80; and Edward D. Collins, "Committee of Correspondence of the American Revolution," American Historical Association, *Annual Report* (1901), I: 245-271.

Biographies also have their place in the development of American statecraft. For Samuel Adams, Stewart Beach, *Samuel Adams: The Fateful Years, 1764–1776* (New York, 1965), is a good introduction to the activities of that politician. Among the many studies of Benjamin Franklin, his work as a colonial agent in England is summed up, though often pejoratively, in William S. Hanna, *Benjamin Franklin and Pennslyvania Politics* (Stanford, 1964) and Cecil B. Currey, *Road to Revolution: Benjamin Franklin in England, 1765–1775* (New York, 1968). For lesser figures two collections of essays—Richard B. Morris (ed.), *The Era of the American Revolution* (New York, 1939) and Alison Gilbert Olson and Richard Maxwell Brown, *Anglo-American Political Relations, 1675–1775* (New Brunswick, N.J., 1970)—have contributions. In the former, see Louise B. Dunbar, "The Royal Governors in the Middle and Southern Colonies on the Eve of the Revolution: A Study in Imperial Personnel" and Max Savelle, "The American Balance of Power and European Diplomacy, 1713–1778"; in the latter, John Shy, "Thomas Pownall, Henry Ellis, and the Spectrum of Possibilities, 1763–1775." Other British figures in the Angloamerican relationship are treated in P. D. G. Thomas, "Charles Townshend and American Taxation," *English Historical Review*, LXXXIII (January, 1968): 33-51, and Alan Valentine, *The Life and Times of Lord North* (2 vols., Norman, Okla., 1967).

The Revolution and Confederation

Since diplomatic activity was as intense as military on the eve of revolution the breakdown of Anglo-colonial ties has received considerable attention from historians. Major studies include Charles R. Ritcheson, *British Politics and the American Revolution* (Norman, Okla., 1954), an approach from the Whitehall view of America, with some influence from Namier. Bernard Donoghue, *British Politics and the American Revolution: The Path to War, 1773–75* (New York, 1964), examines intensively the war years and the options open to the North ministry. B. D. Barger, *Lord Dartmouth and the American Revolution* (Columbia, S.C., 1965), is a sympathetic assessment of Dartmouth's role as American secretary. Gerald S. Brown, *The American Secretary: The Colonial Policy of Lord George Germain, 1775–1778* (Ann Arbor, 1963), provides understanding if not rehabilitation for Dartmouth's successor in the Colonial Office. Ian R. Christie, *The End of North's Ministry, 1780–82* (London, 1958), presents the collapse of Britain's American policy. Weldon A. Brown, *Empire or Independence: A Study in the Failure of Reconciliation, 1774–83* (Port Washington, N.Y., 1941), found opportunities open to both sides for changing direction until 1775. Alan S. Brown, "The British Peace Offer of 1778," *Papers* of the Michigan Academy of Science, Arts and Letters, XL (1955), explains the problems of the Carlisle Commission.

The French role in the supply of spirit and material was appreciated early among students of American diplomacy.

Edward S. Corwin, *French Policy and the American Alliance of 1778* (Princeton, 1916), was a milestone in the scholarship of the period. Claude H. Van Tyne, "French Aid before the Alliance of 1778," *American Historical Review*, XXXI (October, 1925): 20-40, fills in some of the lacunae. Bernard Fay, *The Revolutionary Spirit in France and America: A Study of Moral and Intellectual Relations between France and the United States at the End of the Eighteenth Century*, trans. R. Guthrie (New York, 1927), reflects the Franco-American spirit of the First World War as much as it does the Revolution. More acceptable is the work of Durand Echeverria, *Mirage in the West: A History of the French Image of American Society to 1815* (Princeton, 1957).

The diplomacy of the Revolution continues to attract scholars. The classic study is Samuel Flagg Bemis, *The Diplomacy of the American Revolution* (New York, 1935). Three major works in the last decade supplement it, each with a special emphasis. Richard W. Van Alstyne, *Empire and Independence: The International History of the American Revolution* (New York, 1965), plays on the theme of American diplomacy against the background of a world in war; Richard B. Morris, *The Peacemakers: The Great Powers and American Independence* (New York, 1965), is an able presentation of the stagecraft of the Peace of Paris, with particular emphasis on Jay's contributions; and William C. Stinchcombe, *The American Revolution and the French Alliance* (Syracuse, 1969), focuses attention on Congressional involvement in foreign policy. Richard B. Morris, "The Diplomats and the Mythmakers" in *The American Revolution Reconsidered* (New York, 1968) deplores myths which obscure the accomplishments of American diplomatists in the Revolution.

The spadework for peace done by formal and informal American missions abroad has often been treated as parts of larger problems. For example, John Adams' successes in Holland are well presented in Robert R. Palmer, *The Age of the Democratic Revolution: A Political History of Europe and America, 1760–1800, Vol. I: The Challenge* (Princeton, 1959). Julian P. Boyd, "Silas Deane: Death by a Kindly Teacher of Treason," 3 Parts, *William and Mary Quarterly*, Third Series, XVI (April, July,

October 1, 1959): 165-187; 319-342; 515-530, relates the complicated tale of diplomacy and espionage surrounding Deane, Franklin, and their secretary, Dr. Edward Bancroft. Orville T. Murphy, "Charles Gravier de Vergennes: Profile of an Old Regime Diplomat," *Political Science Quarterly*, LXXXIII (September, 1968): 400-418, explains some of the actions of France's foreign minister in this period. American attempts to win Russian support are examined in Frank A. Golder, "Catherine II and the American Revolution," *American Historical Review* (January, 1915), 92-96. David M. Griffiths, "American Commercial Diplomacy, 1780–1783," *William and Mary Quarterly*, Third Series, XXVII (July, 1970): 379-410, identifies Russian fears of American competition as a factor in inhibiting Russian recognition of the United States.

Problems of diplomacy were among the many confronting the Articles of Confederation during its stormy decade as the basic law of the new nation, and they are treated in all the major accounts of the Confederation period, such as John Fiske, *The Critical Period of American History, 1783–1789* (Boston and New York, 1888); E. C. Burnett, *The Continental Congress* (New York, 1941); and Merrill Jensen, *The New Nation: A History of the United States during the Confederation, 1781–1789* (New York, 1950). Unlike the others, Jensen sees problems of foreign policy as soluble under the Confederation.

Given the overwhelming problems of the economy at this time the work of Robert Morris as superintendent of finance figures importantly in the conduct of foreign affairs, as presented in Clarence L. VerSteeg, *Robert Morris: Revolutionary Financier* (Philadelphia, 1954) and in E. James Ferguson, *The Power of the Purse: A History of American Public Finance, 1776–1790* (Chapel Hill, 1961). Dangerfield, *Chancellor Robert R. Livingston* and Monaghan, *John Jay*, along with M. L. Bonham, "Robert R. Livingston" and S. F. Bemis, "John Jay," in Bemis, *American Secretaries of State and Their Diplomacy*, present the problems of the two secretaries of foreign affairs under the Confederation.

Indian affairs as a pawn in the west in American relations with Britain and Spain are considered in Francis Prucha, *American Indian Policy in the Formative Years: The Indian Trade and Intercourse Acts, 1790–1834* (Cambridge, 1964). The introductory chapter sharply defines the shortcomings of the Confederation's Committee on Indian Affairs. Both Samuel Flagg Bemis, *Pinckney's Treaty: America's Advantage from Europe's Distress, 1783–1800* (Baltimore, 1926) and Arthur P. Whitaker, *The Spanish-American Frontier, 1783–1795: The Westward Movement and the Spanish Retreat in the Mississippi Valley* (Boston and New York, 1927), devote considerable space to the tangled Spanish intrigues in the west during the Confederation. Anglo-American commerce as well as the Anglo-American frontier are treated in the early chapters of Samuel Flagg Bemis, *Jay's Treaty: A Study in Commerce and Diplomacy* (New York, 1923) and in P. Smith, *John Adams*, (2 vols., New York, 1962). Charles R. Ritcheson, *Aftermath of Revolution: British Policy toward the United States, 1783–1795* (Dallas, 1969), gives an appreciative account of Britain's side of Anglo-American relations. Dumas Malone, *Jefferson and His Time*, Vol. II: *Jefferson and the Rights of Man* (Boston, 1951), is a thorough analysis of Jefferson's accomplishments as minister to France. Merrill D. Peterson, "Thomas Jefferson and Commercial Policy, 1783–1793," *William and Mary Quarterly*, Third Series, XXII (October, 1965): 584-611, shows the unfolding of Jefferson's plans for France's role as a counterweight to Great Britain's economic control of America.

The Federalist Era, 1789–1801

Given the dominance of the French revolutionary wars in American domestic affairs John C. Miller, *The Federalist Era, 1789–1801* (New York, 1960), is a useful summary. He is sympathetic to Hamilton's contributions to the period. More Jeffersonian are the lively comprehensive volumes of Alexander DeConde on the politics and diplomacy of Federalism in *Entangling Alliance: Politics and Diplomacy under George Washington* (Durham, N.C., 1958) and *The Quasi-War: The Politics and Diplomacy of the Undeclared War with France, 1797–1801* (New York, 1966). Dumas Malone, *Jefferson and His Time*, Vol. II: *Jefferson and the Rights of Man*, continues to the end of the first Washington administration, while Vol.

III: *Jefferson and the Ordeal of Liberty* (New York, 1962), brings Jefferson's side of the story to the election of 1800. His major antagonist, Hamilton, has been the subject of much recent study to accompany John C. Miller's perceptive *Alexander Hamilton: Portrait in Paradox* (New York, 1959). Gilbert L. Lycan, *Alexander Hamilton and American Foreign Policy: A Design for Greatness* (Norman, Okla., 1969), follows the direction of its subtitle. Gerald Stourzh offers an insightful examination of Hamilton's motives in *Alexander Hamilton and the Idea of Republican Government*, previously cited. For John Adams see John R. Howe, *The Changing Political Thought of John Adams* (Princeton, 1966) and Edward Handler, *America and Europe in the Political Thought of John Adams* (Cambridge, 1964) both of which are admirable essays on the ideas behind John Adams' foreign policy.

Hamilton's early interference in the Nootka Sound crisis is viewed pejoratively in Julian P. Boyd, *Number 7: Alexander Hamilton's Secret Attempts to Control Foreign Policy* (Princeton, 1964). Louis M. Sears, *George Washington and the French Revolution* (Detroit, 1960), shows the influence, year by year, of the Revolution upon Washington's attitudes toward France. Beatrix C. Davenport (ed.), *A Diary of the French Revolution* (New York, 1939), presents the views of the Federalist minister to France, Gouverneur Morris, from 1792–1794. The major impact of the French Revolution on American foreign policy appears in the works of Bemis, *Jay's Treaty* and *Pinckney's Treaty*, and in Whitaker, *Spanish-American Frontier*. But the specific issues of confrontation are thoroughly treated by historians. Charles M. Thomas, *American Neutrality in 1793: A Study in Cabinet Government* (New York, 1931), exposes the cabinet decisions facing Washington. Albert H. Bowman, "Jefferson, Hamilton, and American Foreign Policy," *Political Science Quarterly*, LXXI, (March, 1956): 18-41, points out the burdens Hamilton's role imposed on Jefferson's conduct of policy as secretary of state. Merrill Peterson, "Thomas Jefferson and Commercial Policy," identifies Jefferson's rationalizations for the support of France against England in 1793. Irving Brant, "Edmund Randolph, Not Guilty!" *William and Mary Quarterly*, Third Series, VII (April, 1950): 179-198, vindicates Jefferson's successor of the charges brought against him by Federalist enemies. Bemis, *Jay's Treaty*, remains the major study against which all others are measured. Josiah T. Newcomb, "New Light on Jay's Treaty," *American Journal of International Law*, XXVIII (October, 1934): 685-692, focuses on the meaning of the British Orders in Council of 1793. Jerald A. Combs, *The Jay Treaty: Political Battleground of the Founding Fathers* (Berkeley, 1970), explains the argument over the treaty in terms of each party's conception of the national interest, and minimizes the roles of personalities in the conflict. Thomas Pinckney's labors in London are treated critically in Samuel Flagg Bemis, "The London Mission of Thomas Pinckney, 1792–1796," *American Historical Review*, XXVIII (January, 1922): 228-247, and with more enthusiasm in Jack L. Cross, *London Mission: The First Critical Years* (East Lansing, 1968). Beverley W. Bond, "The Monroe Mission to France, 1794–1796," *Johns Hopkins University Studies in Historical and Political Science*, XXV (Baltimore, 1907), presents Monroe's case for his indiscretions as minister.

The most authoritative discussions of Washington's Farewell Address are in Samuel Flagg Bemis, "Washington's Farewell Address: A Foreign Policy of Independence," *American Historical Review*, XXXIX (January, 1934): 250-268, which emphasizes the Address' rebuke to France; Alexander DeConde, "Washington's Farewell Address, the French Alliance, and the Election of 1796," *Mississippi Valley Historical Review*, XLIII (March, 1957): 641-658, which stresses the partisan nature of the document; and Felix Gilbert, *To the Farewell Address: Ideas of Early American Foreign Policy*, who finds in Hamilton's contributions to the Address an objective guide to America's future ascendancy in the Western Hemisphere. Burton I. Kaufman (comp.) *Washington's Farewell Address: The View from the 20th Century* (Chicago, 1969) and Arthur A. Markovitz, "Washington's Farewell Address and the Historians; A Critical Review," *Pennslyvania Magazine of History and Biography*, XLIV (April, 1970): 173-191, sum up the varieties of recent interpretations.

Relations with France and Great Britain dominate and ultimately consume Adams' administration to the exclusion of almost every other issue. Bradford Perkins, *The First Rap-*

prochement: England and the United States, 1795–1805 (Philadelphia, 1955), explains the conjunction of events and ideas that brought the two countries together at the end of the century. Albert H. Bowman's forthcoming "The Struggle for Neutrality: Franco-American Diplomacy during the Federalist Era," will be the major contribution to the complicated Franco-American relationship in the Federalist era. Diplomacy of Adams' administration and the undeclared war with France is thoroughly considered in DeConde, *The Quasi-War* and in Stephen G. Kurtz, *The Presidency of John Adams: the Collapse of Federalism, 1795–1800* (Philadelphia, 1957).

The missions to France, official and unofficial, have an extensive literature of their own. Elbridge Gerry's role in the Pinckney mission of 1797 is treated in Samuel Eliot Morison, "Elbridge Gerry, Gentleman-Democrat," *New England Quarterly*, II (January, 1929): 6-33 and in Eugene Kramer, "John Adams, Elbridge Gerry, and the Origins of the XYZ Affair," *Essex Institute Historical Collections*, XCIV (January, 1958): 57-68. Marvin R. Zahniser, *Charles Cotesworth Pinckney: Founding Father* (Chapel Hill, 1967), provides a masterly biography of a major actor in this period. Gerard H. Clarfield, *Timothy Pickering and American Diplomacy, 1795–1800* (Columbia, Mo., 1969), presents the most recent account of Adams' secretary of state. His assessment does not change Pickering's unattractive image. Frederick B. Tolles, "Unofficial Ambassador: George Logan's Mission to France, 1798," *William and Mary Quarterly*, Third Series, VII (January, 1950): 10-20, interprets the sources of Logan's conduct in 1798. The Ellsworth mission of 1799 is the subject of Alexander DeConde, "William Vans Murray and the Diplomacy of Peace: 1797–1800," *Maryland Historical Magazine*, XLVIII (March, 1953): 8-9; Peter P. Hill, *William Vans Murray, Federalist Diplomat: The Shaping of Peace with France, 1797–1801* (Syracuse, 1971); and Stephen G. Kurtz, "The French Mission of 1799–1800: Concluding Chapter in the Statecraft of John Adams," *Political Science Quarterly*, LXXX (December, 1965): 543–557. Jacob E. Cooke, "Country Above Party: John Adams and the 1799 Mission to France," in Edmund P. Willis (ed.), *Fame and the Founding Fathers* (Bethlehem, Pa., 1967), 53-77, offers a minority view, contending that Adams himself was largely responsible for the disastrous impact of the mission upon the fortunes of the Federalist Party. Hamilton's failure to win his own objectives are well illustrated in Marshall Smelser, "George Washington Declines the Part of El Liberator," *William and Mary Quarterly*, Third Series, XI (January, 1954): 42-51, and in Robert Ernst, *Rufus King: American Federalist* (Chapel Hill, 1968). Hamilton's relations with King, the minister to Great Britain, are developed in Henry Cabot Lodge (ed.), *The Works* of Alexander Hamilton (12 vols., New York, 1904) and in Charles R. King (ed.), *The Life and Correspondence of Rufus King* (5 vols., New York, 1894–1900). George Gibbs (ed.), *Memoirs of the Administrations of Washington and John Adams* (2 vols., New York, 1846), presents selections from the papers of Oliver Wolcott, Adams' secretary of the treasury, and reveals the extent of High Federalist hostility to Adams' foreign policy.

The intricate Spanish-French-American tangle reflected in the Convention of 1800 has been viewed from a number of angles. The Spanish aspect is particularly evident in Arthur P. Whitaker, *The Mississippi Question 1795–1803: A Study in Trade, Politics, and Diplomacy* (New York, 1934) and in "The Retrocession of Louisiana in Spanish Policy," *American Historical Review*, XXXIX (April, 1934): 454-476. E. Wilson Lyon, *Louisiana in French Policy, 1795–1804* (Norman, Okla., 1934), treats the same issue from the French perspective. Mildred Stahl Fletcher, "Louisiana as a Factor in French Diplomacy from 1763–1800," *Mississippi Valley Historical Review*, XVII (December, 1930): 367-377, sees all of France's policies after 1796 directed toward the repossession of Louisiana. The standard account of the contention itself is E. Wilson Lyon, "The Franco-American Convention of 1800," *Journal of Modern History*, XII (September, 1940): 305-334. Arthur A. Richmond, "Napoleon and the Armed Neutrality of 1800: A Diplomatic Challenge to British Sea Power," *Royal Service Institution Journal*, CIV (May 1959): 1-9, examines the role Bonaparte would have the United States play in the projected League of Armed Neutrals. Jefferson, the president of a united nation in 1801, is the subject of Dumas Malone's most recent volume in *Jefferson and His Time*, Vol. IV: *Jefferson the President: First Term, 1801–1805* (New York, 1970).

Index